Bully

A.M. McCoy

COPYRIGHT

Copyright © 2025 by A.M. McCoy

All rights reserved.

No part of this book may be reproduced in any form or by any electronic or mechanical means, including information storage and retrieval systems, without written permission from the author, except for the use of brief quotations in a book review.

This is a work of fiction. The names, characters, incidents, and places are products of the author's imagination and are not to be construed as real except where noted and authorized. Any resemblance to persons, living or dead, or actual events are entirely coincidental. Any trademarks, service marks, product names, or names featured are assumed to be the property of their respective owners and are used only for reference. There is no implied endorsement if any of these terms are used.

The author acknowledges the trademarked status and trademark owners of various products referenced in this work, which have been used without permission. The publication/use of these trademarks is not authorized, associated with, or sponsored by the trademark owners.

This book is intended for mature audiences.

Contents

Author's Note	VII
Dedication	VIII
1. Chapter 1 – Tamen	1
2. Chapter 2 – Tamen	11
3. Chapter 3 – Sloane	21
4. Chapter 4 – Tamen	29
5. Chapter 5 – Tamen	35
6. Chapter 6 – Sloane	45
7. Chapter 7 – Tamen	53
8. Chapter 8 – Sloane	59
9. Chapter 9 – Tamen	71
10. Chapter 10 – Sloane	75
11. Chapter 11 – Tamen	83
12. Chapter 12 – Sloane	93

13.	Chapter 13 – Tamen	99
14.	Chapter 14 – Sloane	107
15.	Chapter 15 – Tamen	119
16.	Chapter 16 – Sloane	125
17.	Chapter 17 – Tamen	135
18.	Chapter 18 – Sloane	143
19.	Chapter 19 – Tamen	155
20.	Chapter 20 – Sloane	163
21.	Chapter 21 – Tamen	175
22.	Chapter 22 – Sloane	187
23.	Chapter 23 – Tamen	193
24.	Chapter 24 – Sloane	205
25.	Chapter 25 – Sloane	213
26.	Chapter 26 – Tamen	225
27.	Chapter 27 – Tamen	237
28.	Chapter 28 – Sloane	247
29.	Chapter 29 – Tamen	257
30.	Chapter 30 – Sloane	267
31.	Chapter 31 – Sloane	271
32.	Chapter 32 – Tamen	281
33.	Chapter 33 – Sloane	291
34.	Chapter 34 – Tamen	303
35.	Chapter 35 – Sloane	305
36.	Chapter 36 – Tamen	311

Epilogue – Sloane	315
Audiobooks	319
Other Books	320
Stalk Me!	322

Author's Note

THE LINE WALKERS

Let's be real for a second, this story is about sex, not reality.
So when we're talking about brothels and sex clubs, don't go running to Google hoping to find a legal one. Because we know that shit won't happen unless you're partying around Vegas. (If you are, you'd better invite me.)
But that's why I'm here to create a fictional world for you to dive into without worrying about the cops showing up and ruining your big O moment.
Enjoy.

To the baddies that like to argue and fight to get the blood pumping before they take it.

The angst makes it so much hotter when the man you're sparring with uses his words to pretend he hates you, but uses his dick to prove he doesn't.

Stay wild, just like The Feral Post Office Lady.

Chapter 1 - Tamen

THE LINE WALKERS

"Good evening, Mr. Duke." The front desk attendant greeted me with a smooth, practiced purr as I walked through the doors, the scent of polished wood and expensive perfume filling the air. Her name was Cherry, or Strawberry, maybe even one of the other berries. Christ, the place needed an upgrade, starting with the girls' names.

She was a damn wonderful hostess; I should have known her name for as many times as I visited The Vixen's Den the last few weeks. Even so, I was drawing blanks.

"Evening." I replied, glancing around the open lounge to see how busy it was for a Thursday night. Impressively, the lounge was busy, but a better incentive could have drawn far more customers.

Something I would change right away as the new owner.

The best part about my frequent visits to the establishment was nobody had a bloody clue who I was. Everyone believed I was just a rich prick who showed up multiple times a week to get his jollies off. Even women I had hired through the Velvet Cage before it burned to the ground with Damon Kirst's messy death didn't catch me as they mingled with customers at their new place of employment.

Damon had it coming. Really, I was a little upset that I wasn't the one to kill him though. He was a fucking pig who deserved everything he got, and if the situation had been different, I might have even begged Maddox to make it last longer or let me in on the fun. Regardless, his death had a significant impact on the business due to the void it created in the sex market that I planned to capitalize on.

Enter the private sale of Boston's only exclusive sex club, turning it from The Vixen's Den to—literally anything else. That name was dreadful. The potential inside of Vixen's was outstanding, but poor management and even worse ownership left it subpar, and desperately in need of a change.

And I was just the man to get the job done and make the club incredibly profitable. It would keep me in the states longer than I had ever desired to be, but there were other things around to keep me happy here once work slowed down.

"Which desires are you hoping to fulfill tonight, Mr. Duke?" Apricot asked.

Maybe her name was Apple?

"A massage." I replied, noting the way the next customer entered behind me, lurking and waiting for his turn to order his girl for the night like we were at a fast-food counter. It was a low-class procedure, and in desperate need of a change.

"Ooh, fantastic choice." Peach cheered excitedly, like she gave a damn about how I emptied my balls tonight. It was almost believable, though, which made her perfect for the job. The name Peach wasn't right though, for the perky little blonde, maybe Plum? "On the screen is the list of available dates for the evening." She nodded to the tablet screen facing me and I scrolled through, contemplating who I was going to fuck for the night like I was choosing a meal, and settled on a blue-eyed blonde with tits bigger than my face. Those would be fun to play with for the night. "Perfect," Dragon fruit smiled brightly, "You've been assigned to room forty." She leaned forward and stage whispered, "It's our most requested room." Before leaning back behind the counter, "Valentina will join you in a few minutes. Enjoy your evening Mr. Duke."

"I plan to." I nodded and moved away so the next chap could order his meal. As I stepped further into the bar area, I overhead the man behind me greet the hostess.

"Good evening, Honey." He said, and I rolled my eyes.

Damn, I was *way* off.

Leaving the sweet treat hostess behind and moving through the lounge, I watched men and women interacting across the floor. Most of the customers were men, but I recognized a few women as buyers as they mingled and flirted with various available girls. Mingling in the lounge was one of the most common ways for customers to book girls in any club, but the Den lacked something vital.

Order takers.

The working girls were in charge of attracting customers in the lounge if they weren't already booked for a private session, but then they needed to take care of the business side of the deal themselves at the front desk.

Pushing pause on the event to pay and take care of paperwork killed the vibe. It took the high out of the hunt for the customer.

Making it another item on the short list to change when I took over.

When The Vixen's Den re-opened in a few weeks under its new owner, there would be hostesses walking around the floor with tablets in hand, ready to swipe a card or apply a charge to an account so the girls could take their customers back to handle the only business they had any interest in for the night without disruption.

Hardly any of the current customers, laughing and chatting over drinks this evening, would likely be present for the reopening. They wouldn't be able to afford the membership, let alone the booking fees.

The only clients I was interested in hosting had deep pockets and strong connections across many platforms.

Random Johns off the street could hire a girl from the corner if they so pleased, but my club would be too elite for the same transactions occurring tonight. This would be the last night that The Vixen's Den would be operating, as it had been for the last decade.

The next time the open sign was switched on, the women would make triple what they did before.

As would I.

THE LINE WALKERS

Room number forty was underwhelming, to be honest. But compared to the other rooms I had rented; I could see why it was highly requested.

Champagne colored fabric covered the walls, and the lights were low and warm, creating the ambiance of elegance. In the center of the room lay a massage table, fit with matching champagne-colored sheets and an array of lotions and oils on a rolling stand.

My shoulders nearly screamed, just eyeing up the paraphernalia as I pulled my tie loose. I really hoped Valentina would be as good with her hands as she looked, because I had some tension to break through in my back before I released it into her body.

I tossed my jacket on the chair and stripped out of my shirt mindlessly as I stared at the fixtures and features of the room, when something caught my eye. The fabric on one wall was thicker and hung differently, drawing me into it as I pulled my belt free.

I slid my fingers through the thick drapery and pulled it aside where it split down the center, revealing a giant mirrored window behind it. The window looked out over a large open stage below, I'd been a guest on it multiple times before during my visits to The Den. Mirrors surrounded the room on the second floor, my guess was all the rooms that circled above, had a pretty view of the show below.

News to me.

Not that I cared a bit knowing that an unknown number of people had potentially watched me fuck prostitutes on the stage below.

It was an exhibition stage, after all. That's what it was for.

At the time, I just didn't know that there were more eyes watching than just the spectators seated around the raised platform below. What was more interesting, though, was the scene playing out on the stage. My earlier assessment of how busy Vixen's Den was this evening had been wrong.

A vast majority of clients had been hidden in the shadows of the private room when I arrived.

And I could see why.

On stage was a woman wearing a teal blue harness outfit and a pair of sky-high stilettos. With her rainbow-dyed hair cascading in soft waves down her curved back, she gracefully walked the stage, instructing couples locked in passionate embraces.

A sex teacher?

I'd seen instruction occurring before in various clubs, but never here at the den. The old owner, Tony, didn't like the attention the shows took away from paid girls. He was old school and didn't see the potential draw that classes and exhibitions could hold for a club like his.

Or so I had thought.

I tracked the kaleidoscope of colors on the woman's head as she moved around the stage, altering positions and adjusting angles of the six couples around her. She moved with a grace I'd never seen.

Her legs moved like they were dancing on stage at a pristine ballet—instead of a stage in a seedy sex club. Muscles flexed and rippled up the back of her calves and thighs as she turned on her toes and stood with that same graceful swoop to her spine right above her lush ass.

God, her ass was incredible. Over two handfuls and tight enough to know it was real, while supple enough to distract a man's thoughts from anything else of importance as it rippled with each step.

Bloody hell.

My dick stirred in my slacks as I stood at the window and watched.

She was standing with her back to me, and I scanned my eyes over her exposed skin around the blue leather harness lingerie, wishing there wasn't a stitch of fabric between us. When was the last time I physically ached to see a woman's nudity?

I had no clue.

That was one downfall to being surrounded by sex and nakedness as often as I was, sometimes. The allure and the effect it had on me had diminished over the years, so much so that I usually didn't even get hard until my dick was deep inside of something wet.

But standing against the glass, simply observing the vixen on the stage below, I was rock solid and aching.

The door opened quietly behind me, and the sharp click of heels on the polished wood floor preceded a smooth, calming feminine voice. "Hello, Mr. Duke."

I glanced away from the woman on the stage over to my purchase for the evening, already regretting the money spent on her. Not because there was anything wrong with the sweet blonde standing behind me in a baby pink nightgown and white heels with her massive fake tits plumped up over the top of her barely there lace bra. There wasn't anything wrong with her at all.

She just wasn't the rainbow below.

The blonde was normal.

Expected.

Predictable.

However, the rainbow; mercy me. The temptress's hands were on a man's hips, and she was slowing down his thrusts, using her own body to roll against his, adjusting his thrusts until the woman beneath him started moaning and coming on his dick.

That man didn't understand how lucky he was as she helped him make his date orgasm for everyone to watch.

I had never wanted to be someone else so badly before.

The blonde I hired, Valentina, interrupted my thoughts again, "Would you like to get undressed the rest of the way for your massage, Mr. Duke?"

I didn't look back at her, unable to tear my eyes away from the scene below as I replied, "Who is that woman?" Valentina joined me at the window, pressing her body against my side as she peered down onto the stage. "The rainbow."

"Mmh," Valentina purred, as she smirked, rubbing her hands up my bare arm and back. "That's Ember." The woman touching me was a professional, and she knew what she was doing as she caught on to my body's desires. "She's fascinating, isn't she?"

Ember. Her bright eyes glowed in the lights shining down on her from beneath the row of windows, and they looked like liquid gold fanned out by thick black lashes.

"Why have I never seen her here before?" I asked, glancing at my date out of the corner of my eye as she slid her hands over my bare abs from behind. "I've never seen her on the booking list."

Valentina pressed her lips against my back, moving to look around the other side of my body as her hands dipped down to the waistband of my slacks. I had never hired the blonde before, but I was going to request her exclusively if she was always going to be so damn good at getting down to business, even as I stared at another.

"She's booked out months in advance." Valentina replied, pulling the button of my slacks free and then dragged my zipper down against my erection like a teasing edge of pain on the most sensitive part of my body. "Ember only takes on our most exclusive clients here. And she rarely lets them fuck her. She's the owner's pet."

"How much?" I asked as she slid her hand down into my pants and dragged her nails over my shaft.

"She only books by the night."

"How much?" I repeated it firmly.

"I believe for a private client; she charges seven thousand."

Seven grand for a private evening with the rainbow. And you didn't even get a guaranteed fuck out of her.

She was worth twenty grand.

Even more.

"Change of plans, Valentina." I pulled her wrist until she circled around the front of my body and crowded her in against the glass. "No massage. Get on your knees."

She bit her plump lip and slowly sank to her knees like a goddess, instantly fisting my dick for me and stroking me before twirling her tongue around the head.

"You're going to suck me off while I watch her." I instructed as she opened her plump lips and sucked the head of my dick straight into her waiting mouth, already aware of my plans. But I wasn't going to be disrespectful about it. "I've booked you for two hours. And I'm going to come down your throat multiple times in that span. When those two hours are done, I'm going to tip you very," I groaned when she deep-throated me, and then continued, "*very* fucking well in cash for your efforts and I'll double your nightly profits if you introduce me to her when we're done."

She hummed and stroked my sack as she twisted her lips and fist around my shaft. "It would be my pleasure."

I chuckled sinisterly as she gagged when I pushed all the way down her throat as the Rainbow enchanted me below. "No darling, it will be all mine." Laying one fist against the glass as I tightened the other in her blonde hair, I watched Ember below.

There was a man tied down on a bed like the woman had been, but his date was riding his dick as he laid there helplessly, being used like a toy for her pleasure. His date looked frazzled as perspiration beaded on her forehead as she hopped up and down on his dick like a bad porno.

Ember's rainbow hair flowed like a waterfall of melted metal as she gracefully climbed onto the bed and straddled the man's chest, facing the woman riding him. Ember's ass was right below the man's chin and my balls tightened as she took the cowgirl's hands, laid them flat on his abs and started rocking her own body against his chest, showing what she wanted the wild rider to do.

His date stopped her manic movement and clumsily started rolling her hips, mirroring Ember, changing the way she was taking his dick. I knew for a fact that her pleasure was the main focus with the new motions and, for some reason, knowing that Ember flipped the script to please the woman instead of the man, made me even harder.

"Is Ember a lesbian?" I asked Valentina, pulling her head back as she gasped for her breath even as she continued to stroke my shaft in her mouth's absence.

"We're all a little lesbian for the right amount of money, baby."

I grinned at her eager to please response and pushed back into her mouth.

"That woman is different," I mused out loud, though I didn't care if she agreed or not. "She does nothing she doesn't want to, strictly for someone else's pleasure. It shows."

As if the rainbow below could hear my assessment of her character, her liquid gold eyes flicked up away from the woman she was teaching and glanced from window to window until they landed on the piece of mirrored glass I was staring through. I knew she couldn't see me.

She didn't know which room had clients and which didn't, but it didn't bloody matter.

It was all I needed.

Ember's lips curled up in a satisfied grin as the woman in front of her started orgasming with her head tipped back and I followed suit, filling Valentina's throat with come as I stared at the only pair of eyes to ever captivate me before.

"Ember." I growled, orgasming as she finally blinked away, releasing me from the trance I was stuck in on my side of the glass. "My pretty little Rainbow."

Chapter 2 - Tamen

THE LINE WALKERS

"I've got everyone that worked tonight assembled." Tony, the old crotchety owner of the Vixen's Den, said as we walked down the long corridor from his office. "Some that were off came in, but the ones that didn't will hear everything second hand within the hour, I'm sure."

The man was one foot on a private island in the Bahamas thanks to my purchase money and the other was barely still touching his toes to the club. He was done, and I was more than ready to dive in headfirst.

It was after four in the morning, but I was on a high like no other. *She* would be at the meeting, just a few doors away at this point.

My pretty little Rainbow.

Ember. Even though I knew that wasn't her real name, it fucking fit her perfectly. As soon as she left the stage earlier, I abandoned the room I booked a half hour early and went straight to the private office of the man who owned the club and pulled every bit of information I could find about her from his files. It wasn't much, but I studied every morsel I could on her like my newest obsession. In a way, she was, and I couldn't figure out why I was so hung up on her from simply watching her do something I watched people do all the time.

It was something else about her that ensnared me and I couldn't get my brain to let it go until I understood it.

Her name was Sloane Archer, and I was her new boss. She was mine.

Tony opened one last door, and we walked out of a hidden panel in the wall straight into the exhibition stage room. The same room I just spent the last few hours watching Ember from above as she performed for guests.

The girls were all assembled, sitting around in the chairs and couches, flanked by the other various employees that worked for Tony, including three bouncers and various bartenders, both male and female. Overall, there were over a hundred employees I was now responsible for.

A hush fell on the people as Tony walked through the crowd, with me following him up to the center stage.

"Uh-oh." A startled voice caught my attention, and I glanced to my side, where Valentina sank into her chair, staring at me with wide eyes.

The girl no doubt thought she was in trouble, given that she had just spent the evening with me and now I was standing in an employee meeting with her boss after I left her before my allotted time was up. Poor chit.

I winked at her and slid my hand into my slacks pocket as Tony started it off.

"Thank you all for joining me, you all know I hate these types of things, so I'll keep it short and sweet and get right to the point." He announced, "A few hours ago, at midnight, I sold The Vixen's Den to this fine man beside me, and he will immediately assume all operations."

A collective gasp rang out through the room and one sharp voice snapped, "Excuse me?"

All heads turned to the voice, and I smirked when I locked on eyes with its source at the back of the crowd.

Ember.

My Rainbow.

She sat in a chair with a black sweatshirt on and her rainbow hair tied up in a twist on top of her head. She still wore full stage makeup, and her frumpy clothes did nothing to diminish her lethal appearance as she angrily glared from me to Tony and back, then snapped. "What do you mean?"

I spoke up, holding her stare powerfully and taking my new role as owner, "He means that he's running off to the tropics with a couple million dollars more in his pocket and couldn't give a rat's ass about you or this place anymore."

She stood up in a flurry, gripping the back of the chair ahead of her, and tilted her head angrily at me. "I wasn't talking to you."

"Well, that's a shame." I tsked at her, staring her down, and announced, "Three hours ago, you were promoted to head manager of this place. Which means you'll need to be speaking to me a lot, as your new direct boss." She shut her mouth with an audible clack of her teeth, surprised by my statement. Good, that made two of us. I turned to Tony and waved him off toward the exit he had been eyeing for days now, "You can go."

"Wait," An older woman stood up and glared at me before flicking her glance over at Ember dismissively. "I'm the manager here. I have been for six years."

The house mother, if you will. God, she looked awful. There was no place for someone that looked that miserable with life in a sex club. "You're fired." I waved. "You can leave with Tony."

The man didn't even hesitate, throwing a half-assed wave over his shoulder as he grabbed his jacket and left.

I knew he was a shit owner, but that was almost painful to watch.

Almost. The middle-aged woman who looked like she had been ridden hard and put away wet by life huffed angrily, I made no move to recant my statement; she grabbed her purse and marched through the crowd toward the exit.

As she passed by Ember, she glared at her and snapped, "You won't last two weeks answering to a man like that. You don't have what it takes."

Luckily for her, she didn't dare make any other comments on her way out, so I continued with my show.

"Now that they're gone," I rubbed my hands together and then raised one eyebrow at Ember, who still stood, frozen in indignation and shock. It was almost comical to watch her try to decide if she wanted to be angry or surprised more. "If you don't mind, I'd like to continue with the meeting so these good people can go home for the night." I tilted my head slightly at her in a way that unnerved most people I interacted with. It was something my father did that always made my skin crawl when I was a kid. As an adult, I loved turning the tables on everyone else doing it myself. "Is that okay with you, Rainbow?"

Her thick lips tightened together as anger bloomed in the absence of her abandoned shock, but she slowly sank back down into her chair.

"Good." I turned my attention away from her to the rest of the crowd, some I'd slept with, but I had no idea what their names were. There was an array of unique looks on the faces of the employees staring at me. Lots of anger and confusion, sure, but there were a lot of employees looking excited and happy too. Which was all I needed to keep going with the big bombs of info I was about to drop on the poor people. "The Den is no more. And tonight was the last night that it will be open. This building will undergo massive remodeling starting in two hours, which means that this business is closed for the next four weeks."

That turned the cheerful part of the crowd sour to join their coworkers as angry jeers sounded from the lips of nearly every person in the room. People worked because they needed the money, and I just told them they weren't working for a month.

Holding my hands up, I silenced the crowd so they could hear me over their disapproving comments. "I'm an entrepreneur, and I understand money better than literally anything else in this world, so chill out. I'm not taking away your pay. Your employment and current wage will continue throughout the four weeks. There will be mandatory classes and training that will occur while the business is closed."

"Training?" One girl argued, "We're all trained! We work every fucking night."

"Wrong." I silenced her dismissively. "You worked at a low-class establishment that barely scraped up enough money every night to keep the lights on, and your skills and talents show it. Like I said at the start, The Den is no more. When those front doors open in four weeks, nothing here will look or run the same as it has up until this point. The talent I employ will be luxurious, the venue will be classy, and the clients will be rich." I lowered my gaze to the employees. "Does anyone want to take a guess at what will happen when those three things change?"

No one moved, though I half expected Ember to shout out some smart mouthed answer. Slowly, Valentina raised one hand, eyeing me cautiously.

"Valentina?" I called on her by name to annoy the other women.

"The clients will pay more."

I snapped my fingers and gave her a smile that melted the fear on her shoulders. "Correct." I looked back at everyone. "The clients that come through the front door will expect class and they will pay very well for it."

"So, you'll make more." Ember's warm whiskey voice cut through the crowd, once again drawing my attention back to her. As if I needed the help.

"Yes." I replied firmly and her eyes squinted fractionally in anger. "And so will you. All of you."

"And the clients we have now?" Someone piped up, forcing me to look away from my Rainbow. "Some of them have been coming here for a decade."

"Feel free to entertain the same blue collar saggy balls you've been rubbing for a decade if you'd like." I shrugged nonchalantly, "I believe I saw a Motel 6 by the highway. I'm sure their nightly rates will accommodate your new income."

Huffs echoed again.

"I will not stand up here and answer every single little question you have all night long. That will be the job for your new manager, and she'll be happy to answer every one of them in three days' time when you're all expected to report back for your first day of re-training. But I will tell you this before I dismiss you for the evening." I put my hands back in my pockets and schooled my features so everyone in the room would understand the dominance of what I was about to tell them. "This club will focus on luxury and class, and if you don't have it, you won't work here. So, I suggest you get on board with retraining your mind to learn the new skills I'm going to teach you. No one will be upset if you get fired but you. There will be a line down the street of women willing to take your place to make ten grand a night sucking millionaire dick in Chanel dresses and Louis heels. I don't have to be the monster in this story, I'm your fairy fucking godfather here to finally help you shift the power in this game in your favor. Because with money comes power, and you're all welcome to an extensive amount of it, if you work for it. That's all for tonight. Come back Sunday evening at eight for your first night of training. Goodnight."

I didn't leave it up for discussion. I also didn't leave room for them to stick around and gossip about the entire ordeal because if they gossiped and shit talked about me and the changes, negativity would take root.

Slowly, they all started moving toward the exit.

"Valentina." I called out, drawing the attention of the blonde as I signaled for her to come to me, but my Rainbow also watched. So focused on the back of the blonde's head, Ember missed the way I watched her as Valentina eagerly joined me onstage. Was the fiery little Rainbow jealous? "Ember, you too."

Her golden eyes snapped to mine as people moved around her to the exit, gazing at the three of us remaining as they left.

I didn't wait to see if she'd follow my direction, a part of me hoped she would defy me and leave. Instead, I turned my attention to Valentina and pulled my money clip from my pocket as she fought the urge to watch me count bills out. "I won't be needing that introduction after all," I grinned at her, and she bit her bottom lip. "But a deal is a deal."

As Ember climbed the steps eyeing the money, I folded a couple thousand dollars and offered it to my date for the night with a wink. "I don't feel like I've earned this." Valentina said coyly with a seductive smile on her plump lips that were still a little swollen from my dick.

"You pleased me very well tonight, Valentina," I smirked, looking over at Ember as I replied. "Take your pay and go home."

"Yes, Sir." She purred and beamed at Ember as she left the stage, joining the last of the stragglers as they left.

Leaving me alone with the first woman to hold my attention for more than a moment in time in as long as I could remember. On the other side of the stage, she stood with crossed arms and a hip jutting out, looking bored with me.

My dick twitched at her bratty attitude. I hated brats. But Ember—damn, I'd make an exception for her.

"You took Tony's announcement personally." I started cutting to the chase. "Why?"

She tightened her lips into a line, and she looked away from me, "Because I was going to buy this place."

I raised my brows in surprise, "Seven grand a night is impressive, especially for this clientele." I replied and her lips parted in surprise, "But it would have taken you another lifetime to save up enough to buy it, surely you knew that."

That was the wrong thing to say to her, apparently. Because her golden eyes burned with indignation, and she uncrossed her arms. "Did you keep me back to insult me? That seems like a shitty way to start a professional relationship." I opened my mouth to reply, but she cut in, "Though judging by the way you've got Val acting like a simp at your feet for your attention, it seems you've already started building those *relationships* with your employees."

Ooh, my Rainbow had some lightning in her clouds.

"Jealous?" I cocked my head to the side.

"Of you?" She countered, trying to throw me off. "Val's a splendid girl, but she's not my type."

I smirked, giving in to the verbal sparring and the way I bloody enjoyed it. "Lesbian. Got it." I stated it, and she remained silent, although I was unconvinced that her sexuality was so simply categorized. "That should make working together even easier." I took a couple of steps toward her. "Because we'll be working together, Ember. Closely over the next month and beyond. At the end of the day you can hate that I bought this place out from under you all you want, but you seem like a highly intelligent woman and at some point, you'll have to admit that more money coming in these doors benefits far more than just me. All the changes coming, including the money can benefit everyone here including you. You just have to allow it instead of fighting it." I stopped a foot away from her. "Don't fight it, Rainbow. Help me, help you and everyone else."

I firmly threw down the innuendo between us, and I loved the way she stared at me. She worked in the sex industry, but she wasn't allowing her instincts to convince her one way or another about me.

Interesting.

"We have our first management meeting later today at three." I stated, cutting through the tension and rocking her again with my change in direction. "Meet me at this address," I pulled a card from my pocket and wrote my penthouse address on the back of it.

She hesitantly took my card and read the address, but said nothing else before turning away from me and walking toward the exit.

Would she show up for the meeting? Who knew?

I was an excellent judge of character, having spent years being tortured while I examined case studies on people for my dad's enjoyment, but my guess was that Ember would show up as instructed.

If for no other reason than to spar with me some more. She was far too feisty to let me have the last word.

"What are you naming it?" She asked as she got to the door, proving my point and keeping it going. "The club. What are you changing the name to?"

She didn't know it, but I hadn't nailed down a new name for it yet.

At least I hadn't until tonight.

"Prism." I replied, watching her face closely as the single word worked through her big brain. "I'll offer the world an entire luxurious kaleidoscope of pleasures to choose from." Her eyes squinted like it offended her, and I winked mockingly. "Don't be late for the meeting. Tardiness won't be tolerated."

The slamming of the door was her only response, and I grinned like a maniac as I finally admitted to myself why Ember sparked an interest inside of me.

Because I couldn't have her.

At least that's what she wanted me to think.

Chapter 3 - Sloane

My phone dinged annoyingly as I brushed my teeth. I eyed it, laying on the counter next to me and battled whether to open the group chat. I wasn't sure I had the strength to read what everyone was saying.

Anger still burned in my gut, and I felt like I was going to erupt with it if I gave in and read the messages other girls from The Den were sending.

Last night had been *incredible*. Finally, I had convinced Tony to let me run some sort of instruction class in the exhibition room and it had sold out almost immediately. And being on stage, *God*, it was the biggest rush.

How did my night go from the biggest high in memory to the ultimate low within just a few hours?

Oh yeah, Tony fucking Richards selling The Vixen's Den after we had been making plans for years for me to buy it. Fucking asshole.

And the new owner? What a prick!

A deliciously sexy, melt your panties and leave your legs shaking prick.

I knew nothing about him, aside from his name on his business card.

Tamen Bryce.

Even his name made my body tingle. But I hated him on principle alone. He was enemy number one as the new owner of the club.

He was also my boss and for some reason, he promoted me to manager last night in front of everyone. Even going as far as firing Mel, though to be honest, she needed to go. She was a miserable old hag who didn't look out for anyone but herself.

But still.

I recounted every word he spoke in the brief meeting and our private one after, trying to figure out as much as possible about the mystery man so I could get my brain and my hormones on the same page before I left for our meeting in an hour.

Of course, he stayed at the fanciest hotel in all of Boston.

Rich fuck.

I hated guys like him; they were all the same. They thought their fat wallet added five inches to their dicks and a full head of hair to their heads; as if the money meant something. I mean, it did to girls like me literally working for it, but the presumption behind it always just aggravated me.

Don't get me wrong, I wasn't in the business of trading my body for money simply because I needed the cash, but it was a nice perk. There wasn't some tragic backstory to my life that led me down the path of prostitution like so many other girls I worked with. It wasn't even because of some overbearing addiction to sex or attention, like some others, either.

I just enjoyed the life. As a call girl and entertainer, I reveled in the power it afforded me. I enjoyed the freedom of it all.

Obviously the money was nice, if I was going to sleep with a client for cash, I might as well get as much out of their pockets as I could before I took their pants off. It just wasn't the whole reason behind my profession. Which was why Tamen Bryce stepping in and throwing around words like class, luxury, and talents, like we were already beneath him, pissed me off.

Picking my phone up and walking out to my kitchen, I tried to focus on my daily routine as best as I could so I could ignore the feeling of impending doom weighing me down. My schedule was completely thrown off; I was supposed to meet my new boss at his hotel in an hour, a time that clashed horribly with my usual late start. The feeling of panic tightened in my chest.

"Ugh," I groaned, the frustration a thick, suffocating weight in my chest as I let the enormity of his actions sink in. I thrived on my routine. And he was fucking it up.

My phone dinged again, and I eyed the screen.

Forty-seven new messages to the chat.

And that was after I cleared them when I woke up without reading any.

Fuck it.

The screen of my phone blazed as I swiped it open, a chaotic array of texts from a dozen different girls. I didn't even have most of them saved in my contacts, but a few had names attached.

> *Who does he think he is? This ain't a monarchy! He can't just control everything like a king! -Unknown 1*

> *He's the owner babe, that's literally the perk of his position. – Unknown 2*

> *We're not all some back-alley hookers, though! How dare he call us classless! -Unknown 3*

> *Well, some of you are. – Unknown 2*

> *Fuck you. – Unknown 1*

> *Right back at you! – Unknown 2*

> *Hey, I'm actually excited to update the place. Think of all the new clients that will come in. Wouldn't you rather make more money with a little more luxury around? -Trixie*

Trixie was young. I remember the first night she came in for work; God, her eyes had been as wide as saucers as she walked into the locker room. At least they were until she got done with her first client of the night.

Because after that, they were screwed shut tight with tears.

She worked at The Den because she got kicked out at seventeen by her dead-beat parents and was just trying to survive. For three years now, she had worked almost every single night to make enough money to survive, and she was still just a kid in a lot of ways.

When I distanced myself enough from my anger, I could understand why a girl like her would be excited about the changes. She deserved a damn break.

> *Bitch, spreading your legs is spreading your legs. We're all still whores regardless of how much money we make for it. -Unknown 1*

> *Girls! Enough! Arguing amongst ourselves is not helping! – Val*

I paused, noting Valentina's name attached to one message. She slept with Tamen last night before the meeting and then he made a show about paying her extra in cash right in front of me like it would mean something.

Duh, we fuck for cash. No shocker there.

But even as I looked away from the messages to stare out my window, my body warmed as something like jealousy tried to burn in my gut. There was no way I was jealous of him fucking Val and then being nice to her. And yet, I couldn't quite place my finger on why I was bristling from the interaction at all.

Maybe it was because I hated him and wanted everyone else to as well. She obviously didn't.

It felt like there was a traitor in the group.

Scrolling through the rest of the messages, I saw some girls chiming in about knowing him from the past. Those girls had worked privately outside of The Den before, and while there wasn't much talk about what happened through The Velvet Cage, I was smart enough to realize it wasn't good.

But the girls from the Cage didn't have anything bad to say.

> *We called him the Duke at The Cage. He was actually fantastic to the girls. – Lola*

Lola and I were friendly with each other, both with pretty similar back stories. We liked the job, and that kept us coming back night after night. So obviously, I hated that she approved of him.

> *Girls loved getting booked by The Duke. We spent a week at a time in a luxury penthouse, having whatever food and drinks we could*

> *dream of. Going out on the town on his arm, wearing designer clothes he had delivered for us. Never mind that the man can fuck like a pro. He wants to run The Den? I say go for it. He makes money multiply for a living. He can take me home any night he wants as well. I'm here for it. – Raven*

Raven was a harder girl to get to know. She was one of those that counted every single dollar she made every day and then left without worrying about making friends in the locker room. Sure, she never made any enemies, she just wasn't overly friendly.

Scrolling through more praises of the man I hated; I passed one that caught my eye, so I went back. It caught my eye because my name was in it.

> *All I'm saying is our new manager may have more power in our favor than we could have hoped for. I think The Duke has a thing for Sloane. – Val*

My heart raced as I scrolled down farther, looking for an explanation for her claim, and finally found it dozens of messages later. I didn't even bother to bristle at the replies from the other girls that said things like *Go figure. Why am I not surprised?* And *Everyone has a thing for Sloane. I'm not even a lesbian and I'd bang her.*

I read Val's reply four times before I set my phone down to contemplate it all.

> *He booked me for a two-hour session in the champagne massage room last night. But when I got to him, he was watching the stage below. He hardly paid any attention to me as he watched Sloane run the show below. Like he couldn't look away. Then he said he'd tip me well and pay me double my nightly*

> rate in cash if I introduced him to her when we were done. I'm thinking if she holds that much sway over his man brain, it can be used to protect us all. What do you say, girl? - Val

Before I could reply though, Trixie asked what I had been wondering all night since meeting the man and seeing him interact with Val after the meeting.

> So, wait, he slept with you, but you think he's obsessed with her? He sounds like a typical man to me. - Trixie

> No, see that's why I think there's something worth using there. He didn't fuck me. He told me to get on my knees and then the man came in my mouth three times while he stared down at her. THE ENTIRE TIME! He kept calling her The Rainbow, and looked at her like he had never seen color before in his life. As soon as she got offstage, he was done. He was almost... wild looking as he watched her. And he was respectful to me in his own weirdly dominant way. I can't put my finger on it, but I'd dare to call him almost gentlemanly during and after it all. - Val

> Damn. Maybe there's something to it after all. - Lola

> Sloane? Care to share your thoughts with the class? We can see that you're reading these. - Val

I hesitated to reply. It wasn't like I could decipher my own thoughts long enough to share them, because Val's account of what happened last night—left me shaken. So, I played it safe, while trying to reassure them as best I could. Because the fact was, I was the new manager, and if I could help the girls better their lives with that role, I was sure going to try.

> If I can improve the job for any of us, I'm going to. But I make no promises. I might end up punching him for the fun of it and getting fired. - Me

Val's reply came back instantly.

> You know what they say, girl. Sometimes hate sex is the best sex. - Val

I muted the message thread and closed it before I let her words give my wicked mind too many ideas.

He was my boss. And I hated him because of it.

I couldn't think about how the idea of him watching me as he orgasmed three different times last night made me want to see if the claims of him being good in bed were true or not. He was off limits to me.

Maybe I'd just let him star in my masturbation fantasies to take the edge off. There was no harm in using him for my own sexual satisfaction if he never knew about it.

Chapter 4 - Tamen

THE LINE WALKERS

"You've got an enormous set of balls; I'll give you that." Dane's annoying voice called out as he entered his office, cutting my study session short. Or at least what I was trying to make into a study session, but his firewall was ridiculously strong these days.

"I told you Peyton would let him do something stupid." His annoying best friend Maddox's voice followed behind my brother, and I rolled my eyes, already regretting my stupid plan in the first place. "She has a weird soft spot for T."

"It's hardly weird." I called out, trying once more to break through the impenetrable force field protecting Dane's computer from me. Once upon a time I had no problem getting into his shit, but it seemed my big brother had reinforced his electronics. I wondered why. "I'm a very likeable mate."

Dane snorted, "Get up." I tried another combination of code to break through, out of spite, and Dane cringed at the electronic alarm it set off like it pained him somehow to have his force field scratched by me. "God, for fuck's sake, stop messing my shit up."

I groaned and stood up, shoving his chair back as I raked my hands through my hair. "Since when is this locked to me?"

"Since you made your permanent residence in Boston." Dane chided, sitting down in his chair and glaring at me. "What are you doing here?"

"Trying to watch your MILF porn, duh." Maddox added unnecessarily and both Dane and I turned to glare at him, but he just smirked. "What? MILF's are hot."

"How is my Little Hacker?" I squinted at the ugly bear, and his face darkened at the mention of his wife. "Ooh, trouble in paradise." I tsked my teeth, "Can't say as I'm surprised."

"I'll take the trash out." Maddox rose to his feet from where he had just sat down on the couch, "Free of charge, Dane."

"Enough you two." Dane sighed, "Christ, you both make it physically painful to be in the same room as you when you get like this."

"Get like this?" I questioned, "We've never stopped or been anything other than this. Aren't you used to it by now?"

"Maybe when I was fifteen years younger." Dane gave one last glare at Maddox, who returned to his seat and then turned to me. "You have to stop creating enemies simply for the sake of having them. Isn't it exhausting hating everyone?"

Sloane's golden eyes flashed through my mind's eye, and I blinked it away. I couldn't quite explain it, but her hate and anger warmed my soul every time she threw it my way the other night.

It was a rush and left me counting down the seconds until I'd be in her presence again for that same high.

"No." I replied, to keep him from digging into my mind. "I prefer it that way."

"You know who else enjoyed hating everyone?" Maddox quipped and my blood ran cold before he uttered his answer. "Rupert."

"Knock it off." Dane snapped, triggered by the mention of our father's name as much as I was. "What were you trying to do before I caught you?"

"I wasn't trying to hide it." Scoffing, I pretended it was no big deal. "I was just trying to get some background on someone."

"And your normal avenues for information are—" Dane paused, "Inadequate?"

"Unsafe." I surmised, hating even mentioning it, but the fact of the matter remained. I wanted information, and I was desperate enough to not go back to my suite empty handed. "I can't mix the two."

"So, it's personal." Dane raised his eyebrows. "I'll help."

Maddox snorted, "Seriously? Since when do you get involved with Tamen's love life?"

Dane glared at his friend momentarily, "Because if he's interested enough to bother me and deal with *our* shit, then it's obviously something worth knowing about. Someone worth knowing about."

"To be fair, I didn't plan on the bear being involved." I droned, "Do you two hang out every day? Like bro dates? Do you guys cut your lawns together in your jean shorts and white tennis shoes?"

"Never mind." Dane shook his head. "I'm not interested."

"Of fuck off, you wanker." I snapped, annoyed by the whole thing. "You make it too easy."

"So do you." Dane sighed, turning to his computer and typing in a random set of hieroglyphics to get into it. "Who is it?"

"Sloane Archer." I stated, feeling the anxiety building in my gut from just saying her name in their presence. Lucky for them, they were both already happily leg shackled to two of the scariest women in history, so I didn't worry about them trying to steal Sloane.

It took no time at all before he had a dozen tabs pulled up with her information. I stood at his shoulder and was acutely aware of Maddox moving in to watch too as her beautiful face popped up on the screen. It looked like a DMV photo, but still her beauty was jaw dropping.

Even if she had brown hair in the picture.

Dane began reading some files he loaded. "Sloane Archer, age twenty-nine. She lives in the South End of Boston," He clicked through the tabs, "Credit score is eight hundred and ten and she has over—" he whistled animatedly, "four hundred thousand dollars in her savings account." Looking over his shoulder at me, he shrugged, "Well done."

"Focus."

"Yeah, yeah, yeah." Dane droned, flipping through some more information at a speed far too fast for my eyes to keep up with.

"There." Maddox stopped him, pointing to a spot on the screen. "Occupation."

"Dancer." Dane surmised and then leaned back in his chair to look at me again. "As in, perhaps a dancer at your new club?"

"You're sticking your nose in places it doesn't belong."

"God, you're really no fun anymore." Dane moved on, pulling up more stats on Sloane. "Raised in Brookline by her parents, Tom and Meredith Archer. Two older brothers, Steven and Skylar Archer." My brother shrugged nonchalantly. "Straight-A student in high school, spent four years at Massachusetts College of Art and Design. Graduated with dual degrees in art history, and interior design and then—" He hesitated, clicking a few more times.

"What?"

"She never used the degrees anywhere." He said, looking back over at me. "She started working in your industry right out of college."

"So." I snapped, angry that he was judging her before he even knew her.

"So," He scowled, "Seems like a waste of time to spend four years earning something you never use from the moment you leave the school. I wonder what happened to her."

"God!" I groaned, rubbing my hand over my face. "Nothing had to happen to her to make her want to work in the sex industry. Not all stories are bad ones."

Maddox grinned, unconvinced. "Let me guess, one of your girls said that."

"You two are really so stuck-up Stepford Wife Street you forget where you came from, don't you?" I barked, staring them down. "You came from the fucking sewer! We all did! We had the tragic life and fucked up childhood and fell into the sex, money, drugs, and death lifestyle because of it! But that doesn't mean that everyone else in that life is broken somehow. And even if they are, we're no better than them! It doesn't matter who we are today, we're still trash!"

Dane stood up and put his hands up in defeat, "You're right. I didn't mean that there was something wrong with her. I just figured something happened to her to change the direction she went in. That's all."

"We remember where we came from, Tamen." Maddox joined in, "Because we fight every day not to go back. I fight every day to keep my kids shielded from that life."

"Well, I don't." I snapped, "I didn't run away from it. I changed it to work in my favor, and there's nothing I'd do differently." From his chair's armrest, I retrieved my jacket and put it on. "Thanks for the help." I nodded to his computer. "Delete it all."

"I'll email it to you." Dane called as I walked out of his office. "I'm sorry!"

But I didn't stick around to hear anything else.

Nothing had changed since we were kids, Dane and Maddox were always reminding me I was the broken one while they were the victims of it.

I chose that life.

I chose the darkness.

I couldn't walk away from it even if I wanted to, because so long ago, the darkness chose me back.

Dane and Maddox were taken to Harlow House when they were kids by an evil man who saw how vulnerable they were and all the ways he could mold them into the perfect little monsters he craved. I, on the other hand, made the mistake of loving that evil man and his little monster son just enough that I willingly joined them. I walked into that Hell on my own because I thought being with someone, anyone, was better than the days of complete solitude all alone without another human being around.

God, I had been so wrong.

Chapter 5 - Tamen

THE LINE WALKERS

She was late.

I warned her about her tardiness, but she was fifteen minutes late, anyway.

The bones in my neck cracked like twigs as I paced the plush carpet of my penthouse seating area, each footfall echoing in the otherwise silent space, the darkness inside me growing more intense with every passing moment. I couldn't stand someone wasting my time, it felt like a physical brand with a hot iron to my skin.

But Sloane being tardy, burned somewhere else too. My dick twitched in my slacks as I prepared to have her in my space all alone. I knew she'd show up, eventually, but I also knew she was making me wait in a power play.

The woman was a Domme, in a lot of different ways. And she was proving it with each second of time spent making me wait.

As if my thoughts summoned her, the ding of the elevator in the foyer made me pause near the giant windows overlooking the city below.

Go time.

She was the only one on the approved list of guests to have free access to my suite, and as her heels clicked across the marble floor, bringing her closer to me, I schooled the monster in my chest aching to take over and regain the upper hand immediately.

When she cleared the wall and entered the open living space, she paused, looking around the expansive space before finally finding me against the windows. Somehow, she looked even sexier today than she did last night in lingerie and stilettos. I let my eyes travel up her body, starting at her feet wearing black motorcycle boots with gold buckles, up her long dancer legs in skintight black jeans. Then up to her torso covered in a dressy jacket, the color of blood that tied around her waist brushing her upper thighs. It left me wondering what she'd look like coming to my door in just that jacket and a pair of red bottom heels to match. Dammit, there came another one of those random erections she caused me. Her hair was down in soft waves that made it look like cotton candy around her flawless face and molten eyes as she eyed me cautiously.

"You're late." I greeted her.

She raised one eyebrow at me and laid her large purse down on a chair and undid her jacket, before sliding it off her shoulders. She wore a gold tank top that matched her eyes perfectly and hugged her lush tits and narrow waist like a second skin. "You'll have to adjust your expectations when you give me instructions less than twelve hours before a meeting."

"Interesting theory." I walked away from the window and picked up my cup of coffee off the table to drink it, motioning for her to join me around the large surface covered in paperwork. "This is a list of employees currently receiving a paycheck from me in exchange for nothing." I handed her a packet with everyone listed as I glanced at my watch. "Choose sixteen names off that list to fire, effective immediately."

Her eyes snapped up to mine as her brows knitted in fury, the packet falling to the tabletop from her fingers like it burned her. "For what?"

"For every minute that you were late." I walked back around the table and took a seat, sipping my coffee. "I told you that tardiness would not be tolerated, yet you chose to defy me. Face the consequences for it like an adult." I nodded to the paper again and then held her angry stare. "Choose, or I will."

"You're evil." She hissed. "I'm sorry for being late."

"No, you're not, you did it on purpose to challenge me." I replied evenly before leaning forward on my elbows to finish, "And yes, I am evil. Something you'd do well to remember."

"You're punishing them for my choice." She shook her head and swallowed, giving away how much stress the topic put on her. "That's terrible leadership. And an awful start to a fresh beginning."

Leaning back in my chair, I took another sip and set my cup down. "Then convince me to keep them and punish you instead. Should I fire you instead for your own transgression?"

She took a deep breath, making the fabric of her shimmering top hug her breasts even more, though I doubt that was her plan. "There isn't anyone else on that list that can do this job as well as I can, and I think you know that already. But if you need to fire me to prove to yourself that you're in charge, then that's what you're going to have to do. Because I won't be responsible for sixteen people being unable to feed their families."

I mulled that over, hating how quickly she offered to sacrifice herself for others. Didn't she realize that, more than likely, no one else in that place would have done the same for her? Was it all a bluff, in hopes that I'd fold before she did?

Leaning across the table, I picked up a blue folder and opened it before tossing it right in front of her. "Right or left?"

Sloane squinted those molten eyes once more before giving in and looking down at the drawings laid out in the blue folder. She glanced back up at me and then leaned forward, resting her hands on the table as she looked more closely at the front sign renderings I had made. I needed to choose a design by the end of the day, and I was stuck.

She must have realized that it was her out of having to choose others to fire, and took a deep breath before replying. "Right."

"Why?"

Shrugging, Sloane stood back up to her full height. "It's more feminine and classy. The other one looks like a game show logo from the seventies."

She wasn't wrong, but the drawing on the left was bolder and more eye-catching, whereas the one on the right was softer and didn't give away anything aside from the name.

The word "Prism," written on what looked like a piece of glass, hung like a sun catcher, casting pastel rainbows against the building.

It was perfect.

I stood up and rounded the table, taking the folder from her and setting it aside, without telling her if I liked her choice or not. I took the next folder of decisions I needed to make asap to build them on time and held it out to her; she responded by rolling her eyes, walking to my seat, sitting down, and extending her hand.

"How many decisions are you stuck on?"

I hesitated, with the folder in the air, as I felt the power she was trying to take back from me with that question. But in reality, design details overwhelmed me. I didn't care what color the walls were, as much as I did about the material laying on the floor everyone would see when they first walked in. My brain didn't work that way. But Sloane, on the other hand, had a degree in interior design. She was the perfect person to help.

I handed the folder across the space, "A lot."

"Color me surprised," She opened the folder and took a deep breath, eying up the swatches of fabrics laid out. "Start telling me what I'm looking at so I can help you."

"Room colors." I uttered. "Different colors for each room. Different design concepts."

She whistled and tilted her head to the side as she started running her fingertips over the fabric batches. "How many rooms are we talking about? There are forty-seven rooms currently, but some aren't used at all anymore. That doesn't include the larger spaces like the exhibition stage and the lounge." She finally looked up at me, "Wait, you aren't getting rid of the stage, are you?"

I pulled a chair out next to her and sat down in it, crossing one ankle over my knee. "Does it get used? Last night was the only time I've seen it busy."

"It will be used." She argued. "When you allow me to book the talent using it."

"But has it *been* used?" I clarified, challenging her. She held that stage in high regard, and I wondered what she was willing to do to keep it.

"Not by staff, but clients could rent it for their fun if they want." She held my stare and then pressed on, desperate to plead her case for that room. "There's a market for instruction exhibitions. You said it yourself; last night, it was full."

"How many other shows have you done?"

"None." She pursed her lips. "That was the first one I got approved."

"Hmm." I hummed, eyeing the folder a few down in the stack that I knew held the design plans I had for the exhibition stage. Because she was right, there was a market for that style of event, and I knew it. But as she looked away from me and went through the paint colors attached behind the fabrics, I wondered if she'd approve of what I had planned originally for her precious stage. Before last night, the plans had been made purely with an economic return in mind.

But now—now I was already seeing something different in my mind for that space. Something deserving of having such a jewel standing upon it. Something worthy of my Rainbow.

Ember's brain worked fast and efficiently as she started dissecting the details, pulling fabrics out with paint sample cards and pairing them up. "I don't think you should do rooms with monochromatic color schemes. I hate the way the color blocking melts together and gets flat." She kept moving stuff around, working with her hands and talking quickly as she pressed on, "Take the champagne massage room, for instance," She stated and I paused, watching her as she talked a mile a minute. "The fabric gets lost on the walls because it doesn't stick out against anything. The textures and colors should complement each other, not match."

Hearing her mention the room I was in last night, watching her while I used one of her coworkers for my sexual satisfaction, made the hair on the back of my neck stand up. How did she know I was there?

What did the blonde tell my Rainbow?

"Look." She pushed the folder over in front of me and tapped it like I could miss the new arrangement inside. "Imagine that room, with this color scheme." Looking up at me, her gold eyes found mine staring at her and she sat up straight, creating space between us she had eliminated in her excitement. "Ke-keep the champagne in the fabric of the beds, chairs, and one accent wall." She stammered, trying to refocus on the task, looking down at the folder and pointing again, "Then do a dark burgundy on the other walls and ceiling. Add in gold fixtures and a golden floor." She hesitated, glancing back up at my eyes, which were still staring directly at her instead of the folder. "It creates depth and sensation."

I was feeling sensations, alright.

Just not about the colors.

"Do it." I closed the folder and handed it to her, still holding her stare. "Re-design the rooms. We'll be adding thirteen private rooms on the second floor and eliminating the larger unused space opposite the champagne room on the other side of the stage. Design them in a varying way so that no room is exactly the same and bring it back tomorrow." I stood up and removed myself from her tempting personal space to empty my coffee out and pour scotch instead. "Do it well and you can keep those sixteen employees you're supposed to fire." Turning back to face her where she still sat at the table with a bewildered expression on her face, I continued. "Do it poorly and you'll fire twenty."

She scoffed, and her shoulders deflated in disappointment. "You're an ass, aren't you?"

"For the fun of it most days." I admitted with a slight shrug.

Sloane rose, picking up the folder of color choices, and put it in her purse with a huff. "Anything else?"

"Why are you a hooker and not an interior designer?" I asked, and her eyes widened before squinting in disbelief. "It seems silly to have not one, but two degrees and not use them. Especially considering what you do for a living."

"You're such an ass."

"I thought we already covered that. So tell me why."

"Why?" She snapped, "It's not like you'd understand a word of my story from your high and mighty, prim and proper royal tower. You wouldn't get it."

"Try me." I challenged, and she paused, staring at me. Even though I wanted to look away from the answers I was already seeing in her fiery gold eyes, I forced myself to hold her gaze.

"I didn't want the life I escaped."

"Brookline was so terrible?" I scoffed, annoyed at her avoidance.

"The family life." She shot back, standing taller in defiance as she ignored the fact that I knew specifics about her personal life that she didn't offer willingly. "I didn't want to wake up one day, married and shackled to a white picket fence, just to realize it was all an act the whole time."

"Sounds a lot like that golden American Dream you all talk about so much." I raised a brow at her, "What's wrong with it?"

"It's not for me." Sloane shook her head. "It's only skin deep and fake. Nothing is real behind the fake smiles and public image. No happiness. No love."

"Love." I chuckled, "And you find love at The Vixen's Den?"

She rolled her eyes and shook her head. "No. And that's the point. I don't want any of that. I don't want to be tricked by the illusion of it. So I went to the most unlikely place I'd find it." I opened my mouth to dig deeper into her mind but she cut me off, "Anything else?"

I held back the urge to continue and let her go. Something told me Sloane was a runner, avoiding the real shit life could offer her. Maybe there was some truth to her tale about growing up in a lie. Perhaps she was running from something, but it wasn't the tragic life I imagined. Maybe it was just bland. "Report to the building tomorrow at two with the designs."

"Yes, Sir." She snidely replied, pulling her jacket on and tying it around her waist aggressively.

I silently watched her grab her things and head toward the elevator bay when I gave in to my desire to have the last word. Walking to the foyer entrance, she glanced at me out of the corner of her eye while she waited for the elevator, which thankfully dinged with its arrival quickly.

And that was when I hooked her.

"Sloane." I called, and she paused inside of the elevator with the doors wide open. "I'm doubling the size of your stage room. Start planning talent for it." Her eyes widened and her lips parted with excitement; so of course I had to remind her who the boss was. "Show up late again and you'll lose the entire thing. I'll put a cigar room in the middle of the building just to piss you off."

The doors slid closed as anger brewed on her face, encapsulating her inside before she could reply fully, though I heard the whisper of her voice as they shut, "Cocksucker."

I tossed back the liquor in my glass and walked through the obnoxiously large penthouse to my room on the other side of it, grinning.

She was going to look so fucking good on that stage when I was done building it for her. Too bad I'd dangle it in front of her like a carrot until the grand opening just to spite her.

Chapter 6 - Sloane

In a way, I knew Vixen's Den would be changing, which was a good thing, because it was as outdated as Tony's favorite cologne. However, walking through the front door and finding all the walls ripped out and bare wooden studs left in their wake was a shock.

Everything was gone, reduced to a pile of splintered wood and scattered plaster, although the renovation had begun the previous day. Work done that fast had to be expensive, how rich was Tamen Bryce?

Jesus, how out of my league was I against the man? We were two different classes of human beings, him a probable millionaire, and me a hooker. I was a high-class hooker, but a hooker, nonetheless.

No wonder Tony had sold him the Den out from under me, I never would have been able to afford the changes he was making.

Suddenly the jeans and low-cut shirt I was wearing made me feel far, far beneath my new boss. Which didn't set right in my gut. I never let someone make me feel beneath them.

"You can't be in here." A gruff Boston accent called out, drawing my attention from where I stood in what used to be the lobby area, but there was now one giant open space connecting the lounge, kitchen, and first floor bathrooms. Everything was gone. The man walking toward me wore a polo shirt and dirty jeans, yet judging by the size of his pop-belly, he didn't actually make a habit out of working.

Supervisor.

"I'm here to see—" I started, adjusting my bag on my shoulder to face him when he snapped his fingers at me, as he neared me.

"Are you deaf?" He bit out, "You can't be here, this is a construction zone."

"I did hear you." I replied, taking a deep breath to keep from clapping back at the middle age sack of toxic masculinity as he sneered at me. "You didn't hear me. I'm here for a meeting with—"

"I don't care!" He roared, wrapping his clammy beefy hand around my arm and pulled me off balance as he started walking back toward the door, dragging me with him. "Get out!"

"Take your hands off of her, immediately." A brisk English voice cut through the noise of the building, making the slob manhandling me pause.

"She's not wearing the proper safety gear." Grease stain Stan argued, tightening his hand on my arm when I tried to get free.

I felt Tamen's presence behind me even without turning to see him getting closer, simply because everyone else stopped to stare up at the man, announcing his presence. "Let go of me." I demanded, pulling my arm again but only received a deeper bruise to my bicep in the process when Meatball Mike tightened it once again.

"You're fired." Tamen barked, stepping around me and with a flick of his wrist, Lazy Lyle bellowed out in pain as his own wrist made a cracking sound, and then my arm was free. "Get the fuck off my job site."

"You son of a bitch!" The red-faced supervisor yelled, cradling his arm to his chest as he sputtered and spit in anger. "You can't fire me! There are rules we have to follow. Fuck, my arm!"

"Are you an OSHA officer, Mike?" Tamen bit back coolly. "I'd wager that you're not, or your men wouldn't be walking around with their own stupid violations so plainly visible." He reached for the shaking man where he stood sputtering in indignation, obviously not used to being out-manned by someone so publicly before. "Because I can see no less than five different violations standing and staring at me currently amongst your crew of dropouts and degenerates. If you'd like, I'll start naming them off and you can take them home with you when you go." Tamen put his hands on his hips and turned to stare out over the frozen crew of men watching the scene unfold. "Who's next in charge under Mike?"

No one moved at first, but eventually a man raised his hand where he stood with a roll of blueprints under his arm. "Guess that's me."

"What's your name?" Tamen asked.

"Kyle."

"Kyle." Tamen nodded, "Congrats on your promotion to superintendent. Call the owner of your company and inform him of the changes. If he has a problem with it, tell him to call me. I don't have time for any interruptions like this again, understood?"

"Understood." Kyle nodded his head, looking at me briefly, "It's your building Sir, you're in charge of who comes and goes."

"Good." Tamen nodded and then looked over his shoulder at me. "Let's go. Try not to walk off a set of scaffolds or something and make me look like an idiot, would you?"

I gritted my teeth to keep from snapping back with something snarky and followed him. I walked through the loud and chaotic construction zone until we reached what used to be a client payment room; it had been cleared out, and a makeshift desk was set up in the center.

"You won't be using the front door anymore." Tamen said as soon as the door shut behind us. "Enter through the employee entrance and come straight to this office from now on. Understood?"

"Say please." I replied and then rolled my eyes when it looked like his would pop out of his head. "I understand."

He glared at me and then pulled a pack of cigarettes off his desk and popped one between his lips, but didn't light it. "Do you have the designs?"

Grabbing the folder from my bag, I laid it on his desk and then put my stuff down on the extra table against the wall covered with more of the same kind of folders, no doubt stuffed with more decisions he seemed incapable of making. Was it because he was a man and didn't care for details? Or was it because he didn't know the business well enough to decide?

"Have you ever owned a club before?" I asked, flipping open the front of a random envelope, finding a menu of different meals outlined and noted through with angry red pen marks. "Or any business, for that matter?"

"Why?" He asked, sitting down in his chair to stare at me with that dark, piercing stare. It was fucking wild how a man with bright blue eyes that nearly glowed in the low light could have such a dark penetrating stare. It made him look like an animal instead of a man.

I broke the magnetic pull his gaze had on me and shrugged, closing that folder and opening another one. "You seem," I paused, turning back to face him as I leaned back on the table and crossed my arms over my chest. "Stressed."

His brows rose a fraction of an inch before he looked away from me and down at the folder. "Come, explain your pairings." He laid the folder on his desk and leaned back in his chair, staring back at me as I made my way to him. The man oozed power and authority, and all I wanted to do was flip him out of his chair to take his seat from him.

I hated opposing power.

I hated authority.

I hated him.

Even if for a second, I considered sitting down right in his lap to explain my designs as he had instructed, just to throw him off his game rather than dumping him out of his chair altogether.

Instead, I stood at his side instead.

Had twenty other jobs not weighed in the balance, I may have chosen one of my first ideas.

"Obviously, you need a variety of styles to meet different desires and personalities with as many rooms as you plan for." I flipped through the pages and found one I particularly liked. "By keeping one element, you can style four or more different rooms to be similar but not identical. That would keep costs down on materials, as well as production times, as your crews would be able to move straight into the next room after the first." I took the black lace from the center of the page and laid it over first the dark red paint color and then moved it to the emerald green color next to it, covering it to match. "One element, used across multiple rooms."

Tamen leaned forward in his chair and nodded to the page. "And the satin?" He ran his fingertips over the swatch of silky fabric hanging next to the emerald green. It was the same inky black color as the lace, but it completely changed the vibe of the design when I laid it across the same four sample colors.

"Emerald green, burgundy red, warm cream, and royal purple can be the main colors of all the rooms. Changing the accent colors," I flipped the page and showcased the different laces and satins displayed, "can leave the rooms all different without major changes."

"Customers will get bored." He countered, leaning back in his chair and looking up at me with a tilt of his head. The man was so tall, he came up to my shoulder where I stood with my hip against the desk facing him. "There needs to be more variety. The name of the club is Prism, remember." His eyes flicked up to my hair that was clipped back, "A kaleidoscope of variety. That's our motto."

"Maybe if you want it to look like a rave." I argued. "If that's the look you're going for, you might as well add black lights to the ceiling that will highlight every single sperm stain and shooter tubes in between the breasts of your bottle girls in the lounge." I tsked my teeth and flicked the folder closed, "I thought you wanted class and luxury, not an early 2000s rager."

I picked up the folder and went to walk away, but he grabbed my wrist as I turned away and held me by it.

My skin burned from his touch, and the air literally crackled between us as he stared up at me with his glowing eyes. What the hell?

"They'll get bored."

"No, they won't." I shook my head, challenging him with my ideas. "It will spark familiarity and comfort. Think about it from a customer's standpoint." I leaned back on the desk, and he let go of my arm, "Say a customer comes here for the first time and books the emerald green room with black lace and has a fantastic time." His eyes squinted slightly, like he was already judging my plan, but I kept going. "And then the next time he comes, he books the royal purple room that has that same black lace undertone to the fabrics and the accents. His mind is going to instantly slide back into the place where he found pleasure last time. He's going to relax and enjoy himself, even if it's only his second time, because it will be familiar."

"And if he has a bad time the first night?" He argued, "What happens when he comes back to a familiar room and the memories that return to him aren't good ones."

I grinned defiantly at him. "Did you enjoy your night with Valentina?" His blue eyes darkened, and his lips played with that cigarette he still hadn't lit. "Did you enjoy your other nights with girls here? Have you ever left unsatisfied?"

I was trying to use sexual tension to frazzle him, but my own body temperature rose under his dark stare as I imagined him using Val while he watched me.

Fuck, this was going to backfire. I swallowed and went on, even though he never answered me. "We're good at what we do here. And with your new *training*," I said, letting the word hang between us because I still wasn't convinced we needed training for something most of us had done for years, "your customers will always leave highly satisfied. And when they come back for more, they'll feel right at home in the dark and seductive rooms I have designed." I slid my hand across the desk and lifted his metal flip lighter, flicking it against my thigh and lighting it before bringing it toward his face. "Let's face it. We both know the room colors aren't for the male customers." I touched the flame to the end of his cigarette, and he instantly took a drag, burning the cherry tip brightly before releasing a breath of smoke out around it. I snapped the lighter closed with a flick of my wrist and tossed it down on his desk. "The seductive energy in these rooms will arouse the women paid to perform inside of them. And we can probably both agree that a sexually aroused woman will perform far better than an uninterested one will."

Tamen closed his lips around the cigarette again, inhaling deeply, but still he didn't speak.

He didn't have to though, because as I slid off the edge of the desk and walked back over to the stack of folders on the sideboard, the proof of my attention was visible against the zipper of his slacks.

Game on, Tamen Bryce. Good luck winning in a game against a woman who created her entire career around her ability to stroke a man's ego and leave with his money.

Game fucking on.

Chapter 7 - Tamen

THE LINE WALKERS

"I won't lie to you; seniority means nothing anymore. From this point forward, you're all starting at zero." I announced, as I paced the stage, surrounded by the women of Prism.

The women who previously worked at The Den, anyway.

They surrounded me. Watching and listening to me as the boss they hated simply because I ruffled the feathers of normalcy. I shook things up.

"I've hired twenty-seven new girls to join the lineup here at Prism." I announced, pointing to the temporary sign hanging by the entrance to the stage room. The threat of competition sparked immediate whispers amongst the women; a hushed, urgent tide of rivalry. "They're hungry for their share of cash. And they're willing to do their part to earn it."

"And we're not?" A woman spoke up from the crowd, glaring at me defiantly. She had black hair and eyes just as dark to match her all-black outfit. "You act like we're not the ones who came in here night after night when things were shitty, working our asses off for pennies. Like somehow we're going to give up now that you're promising us more."

"Raven, right?" I paused, facing her head on where she sat below me. I had been studying the employee line up because, as the owner, it was my job to know what each of my staff had to offer the business. And not just of the sexual variety. I wanted to know what they were going to bring to the table to make Prism as successful as possible.

The woman's dark eyes squinted slightly like she didn't like me knowing who she was, but nodded once. Or maybe it was because she had spent time with me before, but I didn't remember her.

"Right," I continued. "I don't want any of you to give up, but it will happen." Stating factually, "By the time the doors open for the grand opening, twenty percent of you will be gone." I shrugged, sliding one hand into my pocket. "That's over twenty-five of you, gone. Look around this room and pay attention to the company around you. I bet not a single one of you would pass a lie detector test if I asked you if every person in this room deserved to stay. Or better yet, if you would keep them if you were the boss." Wide eyes slowly glanced around at each other, silently assessing their counterparts and admitting to themselves that I was right. "Some of you will quit. Some of you will be fired. Some of you will leave kicking and screaming at the injustice of it all. But the facts remain the same, not all of you will survive."

"And you think fresh blood can survive the actual *job*?" Raven countered and more than a few heads nodded in agreement. "More than half of the girls that try this job quit after the first night. Most after the first dick comes their way."

"I'm aware. Anyone that fails will be replaced." I acknowledged. "I have a list a hundred names deep of women willing to do anything for a chance." Turning away from her, I went back to address everyone. "My point is, if you were out shined by someone before, now is your chance to become the object in the way, not the shadow. With that, I'll leave you to the talent management team I've assembled to work with you all. With their help, you'll establish what exactly your strengths are, and how you can improve where you struggle."

"Are they going to teach us how to have sex?" A younger girl toward the back piped up and as soon as the words left her mouth, a blush covered her cheeks. "I'm sorry, I just don't see how a talent company can help us here."

"What if I told you I only want twenty-five percent of the job to be about actual intercourse?" I asked, and her eyes rounded even bigger, which I didn't think was possible. The talent team lurked at the edge of the stage, a group of five women who I hoped would earn the respect of my employees so they could actually open up their walls and learn from them. "I don't want any of you to bank all of your earnings on what's between your thighs. Believe me when I tell you that high end customers want far more than just penetration from you. They can get that at home from their wives."

"Then what do they want from us?" The same young girl shook her head in confusion.

I nodded to the talent team, and the owner, Connie, stepped up on stage, taking over. "Attention." She replied with a sleek smile as she looked at the women. "They want to feel craved for." With one more glance my way as I backed away, she grinned, "Men want to be coddled and treated like our entire world revolves around them. Which we all know is far from the truth, but we're going to create the illusion that for the time they're here, they're the most desirable men in the world. And in turn, most of them won't even request sexual satisfaction from the transaction."

I walked out of the room toward the smaller makeshift meeting space where Ember was working with the new girls.

Sloane.

No matter how many times I tried to use her stage name, as she preferred while we were at Prism, I continued to use her real name in my head.

Or even the nickname I'd given her; Rainbow.

They fit her so much better than Ember, for there was so much more to her than just the glow of her eyes.

Even her rainbow hair no longer felt like the cause of her nickname from me. Everything else about her was colorful and powerful, casting different shades of her personality on me, depending on how she felt at that moment.

I silently entered the meeting space upstairs, where a few of the client rooms had been opened to create larger rooms for hosting group activities.

"You mean we don't get to pick who we sleep with?" A voice asked from across the room as I hid in the shadows to watch where my Rainbow stood at the head of the group with her arms crossed over her chest.

I'd started relating her moods to the colors dyed in her hair as a distraction to gauge how to interact with her.

Right now, she was annoyed; purple.

"Does a doctor get to decide which patients to treat?" Sloane snapped back. "Does a waitress get to decide which customers to serve? No." She held her hand up, stopping whatever probably dumb retort the girl was opening her mouth to clap back with. "The answer to those questions and yours, is no. You do not have a choice. That's not to say there isn't some begging, borrowing, or pleading that you can do with your coworkers or your managers to trade here and there. But it's not about picking and choosing unless there is some legitimate reason to pass on a client."

"There is no picking." I called out, announcing my presence and walking into the room as every head turned to stare at me. I hadn't met most of these women before, and the black-haired Raven from the other room's words came back to me as I looked over the crowd.

And you think fresh blood can survive the actual job?

Dammit, the answer was no. Looking at most of the fresh youthful faces in the crowd, I knew we'd lose more of them than I had expected after the first night.

I gritted my teeth and joined Sloane at her spot at the head of the room. "The customer picks. They're the ones with the power to decide. If you don't do the job you were hired to do, you won't work here anymore." I turned to Sloane and caught her fiery eyes as she stared angrily at me. "Change of plans, I'm hosting a party in two weeks." Looking back out at the women, "Any of you left employed here by that time, will work the party. Ten of the seasoned vets will work it too. But make no mistake, they're the best of the best and their sole task of the night will be to get you fired. Whoever makes the most money that evening wins. If you lose, all of you are fired."

Gasps and sputters filled the air, including some from Slone at my side. "What's the point of that?"

I looked at her, soaking in the way her eyes rounded when I stared down at her and imagined how she'd look on her knees, but kept going before I got anymore distracted.

"The point is, the Vets don't think any of the fresh blood has what it takes, and I'm inclined to agree with them."

Sloane shook her head, and waved her arm out at the crowd of shocked onlookers. "You hired them!"

"I know. And pretty faces and nice bodies will not be enough to survive. You know that."

"So what?" She sputtered, putting her hands on her hips, "You plan to pit them all against each other?"

"No." I shook my head, "I plan to let you spend the next two weeks training them to be the picture perfect entertainers of Prism. And if you do it right, they'll win. There's twenty of them to the ten vets. And then they'll get to make something of themselves at the grand opening."

Sloane rolled her eyes and shook her head, cracking her neck in aggravation. "You're just starting drama between the two groups before they even meet. They're supposed to be coworkers and equals. That's what you said!"

"Yeah, well, Raven makes a convincing argument against that plan." I turned back to the crowd. "If you want this job, listen to Ember and learn as much as possible from her. She's the best in the game. And then go out there and fucking earn it." I glanced back one last time at Sloane as I walked back through the crowd. "Oh, and Rainbow," Her eyes squinted angrily, "We have an event to attend tonight. Your outfit will hang in my office after training is over. We leave at ten."

"Sure, whatever you say, boss." Sloane groaned back as I walked out. I smirked and walked through the construction site whistling a stupid fucking tune as I went back to the stage room to share the new plans with the Vets of Prism.

It was time to give the women someone else to hate beside me.

Chapter 8 - Sloane

THE LINE WALKERS

I huffed, sucking in every ounce of willpower I had as I zipped up my dress. Well, not *my* dress, the loaner dress that magically appeared in Tamen's office. You know, the one that looked as though someone had sculpted it, stitch by stitch, to fit my body and personality perfectly.

Yeah, that one.

The one I was standing in admiring in the also magically appearing floor-length mirror in his office as well. The dress was gold, because of fucking course it was the exact same shade as my peculiarly light hazel eyes. But it had an iridescent sheen to it that made it look like it was liquid as I moved, changing shades and flowing to move with my body, almost like I was wearing a waterfall.

Similar to the one between my thighs as I put it on. Why did the man have to feed into my sick obsession with getting gifts? I was a shallow person, everyone knew that; I liked shiny stuff.

And here was the shiniest, most beautiful gown I'd ever seen before. From the man I wanted to hate the most.

Did hate.

I *did* hate Tamen Bryce. Even if I wanted to put a bag over his head and ride him like a donkey all the way to Bethlehem. I was a sexually expressive female, after all. And he was as sexy as sexy could be, aside from his arrogant, snarky, cold, British personality.

I turned in the mirror and admired the way the back of the gown draped right above the start of my ass crack, billowing down the back of my legs but leaving the entirety of my back bare aside from the tie at the back of my neck.

The front fell between my breasts and stretched across my wide hips. God, it fit like a second skin. My body hummed with arousal from the way the fabric slid across my skin with each movement as I pinned my hair up off my neck in a fancy twirl.

Thank God a show girl went nowhere without a full kit of makeup on hand for unexpected events like this. I ran the tip of my finger over my bottom lip, crisping up the line and then blew my reflection a kiss. I was delectable.

Tamen didn't mention where we were going tonight, and originally I had contemplated leaving the building altogether with the other girls after training to test his patience with me for the fun of it. But one peek at the outfit he left for me, and I was hooked. I had to wear it.

Even if it was just for one night.

Shallow, remember.

The door clicked open, and I looked in the mirror as Tamen walked into the room, with his causal grace I envied and leaned his shoulder against the frame.

Fuck, that man could wear a suit.

Sure, I'd seen him in a dress shirt and slacks every day since he announced himself as the new owner, but tonight, the three-piece suit he wore felt more personal somehow.

Like it made him more human somehow.

His deep voice traveled across the room, "Does it fit?"

I raised one brow at him, still looking through the mirror at him as I fussed with my lip again, although it was already perfect.

Bending over at the waist would simply give him a better view of my best asset. "Borrow it off your girlfriend for me?"

He grinned almost hauntingly and tilted his head against the door frame. "Fishing for information, are we? I thought you had more skills than that."

I hummed like I was uninterested. "It fits." Turning to face him, I picked up the matching purse he provided and stood still while his eyes slowly roamed over my body. "Where are we going?"

"You'll find out when we get there." He leaned up and then walked back out of the room, without even a *follow me*.

I held my hands up, mimicking what it would look like to strangle the man from behind, and followed him. Did I want to strangle him more or fuck him more?

Sighing and forcing myself to take a deep breath to level out my rage at his infuriating self, I settled on the answer. I wanted to strangle him while I fucked him.

THE LINE WALKERS

"You have to be shitting me." I cursed, sliding from the back seat of his hired town car. Tamen, of course, didn't hold his hand out to help me, but was I even surprised?

Maybe. I thought the English were supposed to be proper.

"Just do as I say, and we'll be fine." Tamen adjusted his jacket and walked toward the bouncers at the door, who immediately moved the rope and let us in.

As we stepped inside the building, a loud thumping bass from the music caressed my body, reminding me of my early years in the business. "Oh yes," I hissed, ticking off the steps to his plan on my fingers in a hushed, angry whisper. "Step one, pretend we're together." I shuddered, "I'd rather throw up in my handbag and then eat it." He glared at me over his shoulder as he moved around a few people mingling at the entrance. "Step two," I continued, "Distract anyone who might take notice of you wheeling and dealing with the staff. I'm *not* going down for you." I grabbed his jacket to stop him as he kept going, "And the last step of the plan, do whatever it takes to close the deals you make. Fuck all the way off. This entire plan is as flawed as your style is."

He stopped and faced me, looking appalled at my diss toward his suit. My statement was a lie, his suit was immaculate. It was the man beneath the fabric that was flawed. "Don't fuck this up, Rainbow." Tamen went to walk deeper into the club, but I held firm on his jacket sleeve and pulled him back.

"I'm not helping you at all until you tell me the truth about why we're here." I demanded, "I deserve to know what's going on if you want my help."

He rolled his eyes and pulled free of my hold, "The new girls I hired won't make the cut." He admitted, holding my stare from above for the first time since we left Prism. The man hardly ever made actual eye contact with me unless it was to glare at me. But he was giving me his full attention finally as he explained himself. "I didn't realize how fresh they were until they showed up tonight. They will not make the cut, and if they do, we both know they won't make it the first week we're open. Which leaves me way understaffed and us both in a do or die situation. I have the opening planned, but not enough girls to supply the demand."

"And we're here," I glanced around the fancy strip club that sat just outside of the city but managed to gain popularity over the years. A lot of girls who worked at the Den started at a strip club just like this one. "To recruit?"

Tamen scoffed, "We're here to steal." He turned his body, caging me into the wall as a bouncer walked toward us, leaning his arm against the wall over my head and putting his hand on my hip. His lips hovered right at my temple as he spoke, while I tried like hell to pretend his proximity didn't affect me. "We're going to steal women from this club for ours. And we're going to do it without getting caught."

I put my hand on his chest to push him away, but he moved faster and grabbed me by the wrist, lifting my fingers to his lips as the bouncer lurked behind us. "Tam—"

"Not here." He cut me off, pressing a sensual kiss to each fingertip as I finally tilted my head back to stare up at him. "No real names here."

I caught the edge of the bouncer's shadow as he moved away from us, but Tamen didn't pull back. "Then what the fuck do you want me to call you?" A bitter hiss escaped my lips as I asked, the anger a burning coal in my chest, fueled by his deceit and my own gutless agreement to play along with it.

"I don't care, call me Daddy if it makes you happy. Just pick something and stick to it." He backed up, pulling his body away from mine, and I fought the urge to throw my knee up into his balls for the fun of it.

"You're more likely to call me Mommy than the other way around, toots." I stood up and flicked my hair over my shoulder in a power move. "Now, let's get to work."

He grinned like a cheshire cat and adjusted his jacket before turning away. "Let's go get some lap dances."

THE LINE WALKERS

Silently watching Tamen work was—entertaining to say the least. It gave me a better understanding of how the man so effortlessly exuded the confidence to run a high-end brothel. The man was smooth, drawing women to his lap repeatedly, regardless if I sat right next to him, pretending like we were a dysfunctional couple, out on the town for some fun.

Each time he had a new girl on his lap, he'd use the guise of chatting them up to invite them to Prism for a working interview. Most of them had heard the name by now, and even if they hadn't, I could tell by looking at the way they stared at him, they'd show up and check it out firsthand, anyway.

He currently had a pretty blonde in his lap, looking down at him while she played with the hair on his nape while he covertly told her about his new club. The bouncers didn't have a clue what he was up to, because he was paying the women well and kept them moving fast enough not to draw any attention to himself.

If anything, I was pretty sure I was drawing more attention to our private spot next to the stage than he was. I wasn't used to being left out of—anything. And being left out of picking women to invite to Prism to interview for the spots he was trying to fill wasn't sitting well with me. I was the manager after all, and I've done the job for years. I should know what kind of women to invite better than anyone else.

I also noticed a theme to the women he was extending invitations to. The women who sat on his lap all looked similar to each other. Leggy, thin, and all in varying shades of blonde.

With massive tits.

Tamen Bryce had a type. And no matter how hard I tried, I couldn't stop picking apart the differences between myself and them.

The longer I sat by, chatting when it was expected and playing the role he wanted me to play like a good little girl, the bigger the fire in my gut burned. I tried to keep my lips sealed, pulled up into a pleasing and approachable smile like he expected, but I couldn't play the role anymore.

"Can I get you another drink?" Our waitress leaned over my shoulder to get my attention, and I looked up at her as an idea struck me. She was probably in her late twenties, with light brown hair and tattoos up and down her body.

She was beautiful. But she was only working at the bar, though something about the way she watched the other girls on the floor made me think she wasn't happy serving just drinks. "What's your name?" I leaned back in my chair and crossed my legs, letting the slip of my dress fall over my knee as I laid my arms on the arms of the chair like a queen.

"Mya." She answered and glanced over at Tamen as the blonde of the moment tipped her head back and laughed like he was the funniest thing in the world.

"Mya." I purred back and felt Tamen's gaze turn away from the girl on his lap for the first time all night and move to me. "Are you *just* a server?"

She swallowed and leaned her hip against my chair, "For now, the roster of dancers is full right now."

"Hmm." I hummed, looking out over the crowd momentarily and then back up at her. "And what if a paying customer, someone lingering over an empty glass of wine, wanted something more from you than just a drink for twenty minutes?" I ran my fingertips across my collarbone and, as expected, her eyes followed it. Sexual seduction didn't know limitations, and even if she was straight, sexual tension flowed in the air all around us, drawing her in. "Would your boss let you switch roles?"

"I could ask." Her dark brown eyes flicked over my shoulder to Tamen, and she licked her lips. "Do you want me to ask for your—boyfriend?"

Smiling, I trailed my fingers across her black leather skirt, grazing my chair. "I'm the customer in question, sweetheart."

"I'll be right back." She turned and walked away toward the bar as I glanced back over at the suddenly attentive man at my side.

"What are you doing?" He asked with an interested look on his face.

"Diversifying your surplus of blonde barbies." I lifted my new glass of red wine and took a sip as I watched him. "I thought the whole motto was a kaleidoscope of variety. Yet, all the girls you've paid attention to tonight appear to be related."

"I should hope not." He scoffed, "One offered to have a threesome with two others so I could watch them in action."

I rolled my eyes and took another sip. "Did you know that seven out of ten times at the Den, a blonde was picked second behind a girl with some other characteristic?"

His eyes squinted slightly as he looked over toward the bar to where Mya was now in discussion with a manager. "Characteristics like tattoos?"

"Anything to make them stand out in a crowd, yes." I clarified as I waved a hand over my colorful hair, "One could say something to make them different from the rest."

"Is that why you choose to look like a sticky kid's treat? To stand out?"

I tightened my lips to keep from biting back at his dig and took another sip of wine as I caught Mya coming back. "It got me off the floor and into private bookings only," I challenged, "Didn't it?"

He didn't have time to reply before Mya kneeled next to my chair, "I've got the all clear to give you a dance." She smiled excitedly, "But it has to be in a private room, so the other girls don't get fussy about it."

"Mmh," I purred seductively as I uncrossed my legs and rose, "VIP treatments are my favorite." Glancing back at Tamen, I winked, "I'll be back."

But the man was already standing up from his chair, towering over me and Mya. "Like hell am I going to miss this." He said, in a voice thick with desire as Mya took my hand and started leading me toward the private wing of the club.

Fucker.

He wasn't going to ruin this for me.

When we got to the room, I sat down on the loveseat in the center as Mya selected a song on the console. "You have to sit over there." I instructed him, nodding to the chair in the corner. "You can't talk or touch."

Mya chuckled and looked over at him. "Yeah, this is all about *her* right now. You've had enough attention tonight."

"Fine by me." Tamen unbuttoned his jacket and sat down, spreading his legs wide like a dominant male did, and stared at me. "I'm going to enjoy this."

I scoffed and looked away from him to Mya, "Not as much as I will." Mya closed her eyes and started moving to the music in between Tamen and I, sliding her hands up her body and into her dark curly hair. "Have you done this before?" I asked her.

And she smiled as she turned around and glanced at me over her shoulder, "I'm from Vegas, I've done so much more than this." She giggled lightly, turning back to face me. "It almost seems more exciting to simply dance for someone again after so long."

"This club isn't the only one in Boston." I stated as she moved closer and slowly started touching my body with hers. First it was with her fingertips as she leaned over me. Then it was with her legs as she slid one between mine. And then it was with her torso against mine as she straddled me on the couch and got to the actual lap dance part. "You're a beautiful woman, you have options."

She rolled her eyes as she took my hands and ran them down the front of her body, under hers. "The competition is stiff. It's way crazier out here than in Sin City."

I leaned my head to the side when she grazed her cheek against mine so I could speak softly in her ear, "And what if I told you that you're showing the owner and the manager of Boston's most elite sex club exactly what you could bring to our roster without even knowing it?"

Mya pulled back and stopped moving as she stared down at me. I wasn't dumb enough to think there wasn't some sort of security device in the room, either a camera or a mic, so I tapped my fingers on her thigh and whispered, "Keep moving."

On autopilot, she resumed swaying, but stared directly at me, no longer merely trying to entertain me. "There's only one that I can think of to match that title, and they're not even open yet."

I grinned up at her, "We're recruiting tonight. And now's your chance to get on the roster above all the other girls you've been stuck behind in line here. That is, if you're interested in doing more than just dancing."

"I'm interested in making more money for my time." She replied quickly. "The rumors make it sound like that club is going to be bringing in the big whales."

I nodded to where Tamen sat as Mya brought my hands to her ass, to keep the illusion of a lap dance going. "He's the biggest whale out there. And the new club is going to be very profitable for girls like us."

"Sign me up." She thrust her hips and rolled them. "I'm so ready to get back in the game."

"Good girl." I purred and then glanced over at Tamen, regretting it instantly.

His blue eyes were on fire as he stared right at me. I recognized that look on a man's face without hardly even trying.

He wanted me so badly; he was nearly salivating over it.

And I licked my lips as I leaned back further into the chair, giving Mya all the access she needed to my body. Let him fucking watch and wish it were him instead.

Tamen Bryce could do with a little envy. Maybe it would humble him a bit and make him more human. More personable.

Nicer even.

Chapter 9 - Tamen

I entered my office and lit a cigarette to soothe the anxiety that had been building within me for hours. We were only a little over a week into the remodel, but already the pop-up problems were testing my nerves.

I wasn't used to being tested. Things that tried to fuck with my day usually ended up dead. But plumbing and drywall were hardly satisfying to sink my knife into. Which left me on edge.

And my favorite distraction was ignoring me.

Sloane.

My Pretty Little Rainbow.

She was playing with me, teasing me and building up a power struggle like she would with a paying client who wanted to be dominated one second and then pin her up against the wall the next.

I wasn't a client. By nature, I was not even a switch in the bedroom.

I was a motherfucking alpha man who couldn't understand why on earth I was allowing it.

Each time she played a card in our game, I contemplated firing her and ending the little experiment. But just as quickly, my body would tense and panic would slither its way up my throat at the mere idea of her being away from me.

So, I'd throw my own card down on the table, and most of the time, it trumped hers. But not last time.

Last time, I lost my hand.

And I reacted—poorly.

We were at Prism, overseeing the new training of staff, when it happened. We weren't even overseeing the same group, yet we ended up mixing. And if I had learned anything in the last week of working with Sloane daily, we were oil and water.

No, scratch that. We were petroleum and fire. One small spark away from igniting and burning the entire place to the ground.

Tell me why I was walking around with a match between my teeth, begging her to strike it?

Fuck all, who knew. But that was exactly what I was doing.

All day, every day, hard as a brick the entire time, I fucked with her for the fun of it.

And she would cut right back, throwing her own barbs and sass into the already smoldering fire, daring it to engulf us both.

I had put her in charge of the new girls I hired to pad the lineup of talent available to clients. Some were singers, some were actresses, some were dancers, but most of them were from the strip club we snuck into together the other night. They were... eager.

And willing to do just about anything to earn their place on Prism's new lineup. Word was spreading fast about the changes being made to the establishment, and already the amount of membership applications was overtaking my inbox.

Changing the privacy of the club from public to member only was one of many steps I was taking to ensure a higher earning for the girls. And the new girls wanted that cash.

Maybe even more than those who worked at the Den before I bought it. And I was rewarding them for their enthusiasm by prioritizing their positions above those who still doubted and fought me at every turn.

Which is what caused last night's blow up between Sloane and me. I couldn't be sure, it wasn't like she'd ever admit it to me, but Sloane gave off the vibes that she was jealous of the new girls.

And that sick part of my brain that always liked to ruin things preferred to think she was jealous of the attention I was giving to the new girls. Meaning, of course, I doubled down and made it worse.

Leading her to throw a glass at my head in the stage room, where she was teaching a class to all the girls on how to host a client with more than just their bodies.

With conversation.

I had volunteered to be the client of the night, and each girl role-played as if they were trying to convince me to buy their attention. And it had worked so fucking well. When Valentina slid onto my lap, breaking the script, and laying it on thick, I ate it up like catnip. Not because I was interested in Valentina's assets at all, even as they were almost in my mouth thanks to her perch on my thigh, but because I could see the smoke rolling out of Sloane's ears as she watched from afar.

She probably looked a hell of a lot like I had when I yanked her from the strip club the other night, after she let Mya rub her tattooed body all over hers for show. For my show. And my pleasure.

Fuck. To see those two together in my bed, whew.

Pretty sure I'd give my left nut to watch Sloane work a woman over sexually while I watched. I wouldn't even need to join in, I didn't even care to touch whoever she brought in with her. But I'd melt for the chance to watch Sloane fuck.

Given there was a real possibility, I'd never get to experience it myself. The girl was bad for my health.

Enjoying myself from afar might be my only option.

Because she sure as hell wasn't letting me get anywhere near her at the moment, and not at all since she stormed out after training. I should be the mad one, given that she threw a glass at my head.

Yet all I was, was hard.

And celibate. In a brothel. Surrounded by dozens of women that would willingly sleep with me if I asked. I knew that because most had offered in multiple different ways.

Bloody hell, I needed to find a way to get my head on straight so I could work alongside Sloane without wanting to slam her against the nearest wall to fuck her out of my system.

I needed... peace.

There was only one person on the entire planet that gave me that.

And I knew exactly where she'd be tonight. But there was something else I needed to do first to level the playing field between me and Sloane. To remind her who the biggest asshole was.

Chapter 10 - Sloane

THE LINE WALKERS

I was supposed to be on my couch, elbow deep in pizza sauce and wine, unwinding from the hellish week Tamen Bryce had put me through. Instead, I was in heels, red couture, and jewels that once again didn't belong to me, walking into a restaurant I'd never even dreamed of getting a table at before.

All because Tamen Bryce said to do it.

He had the pretty gifts delivered to my apartment with a handwritten note of what to do and where to go, according to his instructions.

I really needed to get a handle on the obsession I had with gifts, because it seemed Tamen was onto me and knew my weakness.

Well, my weaknesses—gifts and *The Winstonian*.

It didn't hurt that the name of the restaurant alone made my mouth water thanks to the classy reviews I'd been stalking online for months now. So of course, I jumped right up and played puppet to the master, starting with an everything shower that primped my body in ways I only did for paying customers.

In a way, that's exactly what Tamen Bryce was.

He paid me to be at his disposal, and maybe that was why I fell in line so quickly with him. Though as I primped for him, I wondered if he planned to have me served raw food to give me food poisoning for my outburst last night. It was something I would do to him for revenge.

In my defense, I hadn't meant to throw the glass at the man. Or even at Val, I would have felt awful if my frenzy had hurt her. I just couldn't help it, after spending over a week in the man's presence and fighting the highs and lows of my attraction and my hate for him, constantly in battle. I *snapped*.

There was an entire documentary named after the act, for Christ's sake, it made sense. I could see why so many women did it now, too.

So maybe, by me falling in line and showing up at The Winstonian, I could try to make amends. Maybe even let it be my way of trying to be a good girl to get along with my new boss for the betterment of Prism's success.

"Good evening," A young hostess greeted me as I walked across the marble foyer, glancing around at the grand specter of it all. "Welcome to The Winstonian, do you have a reservation?"

"I'm meeting someone." I replied as I got to the desk, "Tamen Bryce." She scrolled through her computer screen as I glanced around the foyer, looking for the man in question, "I'm not sure if he's here yet or not."

"He's not." She looked up, "But your table is ready, so I'll have you seated to wait for him."

"Thank you." I said, turning to a young server who appeared out of nowhere, motioning for me to follow him.

As I walked through the restaurant, my skin prickled with how out of place I felt amongst all the rich people I passed. If I was good at anything though, it was playing a part, so I kept my head high and my back straight as I walked through the crowd to a table set for two, seemingly in the middle of the restaurant.

I couldn't have picked a worse table if I had tried, and as I sat down in the pulled-out chair, it felt as if every eye in the room was on me. As if somehow, everyone knew I didn't belong with my gifted couture and rainbow hair.

"Can I open a bottle for the table while you wait?" The server asked, and I eyed the limited wine list he handed to me.

It wasn't as if I was broke, for years now I had been well off enough to stop worrying about money all together. I hardly even looked at my bank statements anymore. But that was because I didn't spend it on frivolous things.

Like bottles of wine that cost hundreds of dollars. Tamen Bryce picked the place, though, so he could pay the bill.

"I'll take the Sauvignon." I handed the menu back to him with a smile.

"Wonderful choice." The young kid nodded, "It pairs best with our halibut and caper salad."

When he left, I forced myself to take a deep breath and look around at the other guests. I hated sitting by myself, anywhere but especially in a place like this. I was a single woman living in a bustling city but stayed at home or work most times, ordering food in to avoid situations just like this one.

Unfortunately for me, I also noticed more than one familiar face in the restaurant. The familiar faces were actively trying to avoid eye contact as everyone else was rubbernecking to see the lonely female sitting by herself in the center of their space.

Johns.

Customers from The Den, who hired me or other girls for their sexual enjoyment.

Men who were sitting at sweetheart tables with women their age, wearing giant wedding rings to match their snubby noses as they stared.

My skin burned from how unjust the sex work field was and the stigmas that surrounded it. Men could cheat on their wives, hiring prostitutes to do all kinds of weird and freaky shit to them that their spouses didn't even know existed, yet when we all stood in polite society, the hired women were the ones to be ostracized.

It pissed me off. And the longer they stared at me, I felt like I could hear their whispered judgements and gossip.

When the server arrived with the bottle, he went through the big show of opening it and pouring it for me before eyeing the empty chair across from me. "Would you like me to wait to pour a second glass?"

"One is fine for now. I'm sure he'll be here soon."

"Of course." The kid gave a tight-lipped smile and backed away as I lifted the glass to my lips and took a cautious sip. I wasn't a wine connoisseur, but I sure enjoyed the lightness of my choice and went in for another one. It wasn't as if I couldn't use the alcohol to keep my lips sealed amidst the judging company tonight.

Slipping my phone from my handbag, I glanced at the time. I was ten minutes late for dinner to begin with, and had been waiting for another ten, making Tamen twenty minutes late to the place he insisted I show up.

When the invite originally showed up, I thought perhaps he was telling me to show up somewhere to fire me for chucking the glass at his face. But the longer I waited, the heavier my stomach felt, a dread settling over me like a thick fog.

Tamen was a bastard; he'd already proven that much to me. As the minute hand on my phone screen clicked by, I couldn't help but feel like being fired would have been a more merciful option, in his opinion.

Torture was more the man's style.

Eyes from other diners kept falling on me and my half empty table, lingering on the scene as though they were already casting me out the longer I sat alone in their presence.

With a disregard for proper decorum, I dialed Tamen's number and hit send. After two rings, his voicemail picked up.

Ignored.

"Bastard." I hissed under my breath as the server started moving toward my table again. Tilting my head to the side, I cracked my neck and prepared for war. Determined not to be viewed as a victim, I would not let the surrounding snobs see me as one.

I knew what he was about to say.

I knew what Tamen had done.

And I was seething under the red fabric of the clown's costume I was wearing.

"Miss, I'm so sorry. There's a strict twenty-minute reservation window. We can only hold a table for so long before we need to give it to customers who are here and ready to eat."

"Do I not count as a customer? I'm here and ready to eat." Snapping, I stared up at him, pursing my lips and daring the young twit to challenge me. "I'll take the menu now."

"But—" He stammered, looking over to the side where a man in a tux stood overseeing the entire room with a disapproving glare aimed right at me. "Your reservation was for two."

"Are you refusing to serve me?" I hissed, unbelieving of the situation I was in. Not only did I get stood up, made to look pathetic for Tamen's enjoyment. But the restaurant was kicking me to the curb as well.

"We are." The server whispered, probably as uncomfortable as I was. "I'm so sorry."

"Fine." I slid my phone back into my purse, intending to leave with my head held high, but when I stood up, the server slid a leather billfold from his pocket and awkwardly held it out for me.

"The bill for the wine."

"You have to be shitting me, kid." I seethed, but he simply shrugged. "This is absurd." Taking the bill from him aggressively, I opened the case and saw the outrageous price of the unenjoyed bottle of wine I stupidly ordered, thinking Tamen would be the one to foot the bill. "Four hundred dollars?"

"It's one of our mid-level bottles, Miss."

"Mid-level, my ass." I fished in my purse and pulled out my credit card, jamming it in his chest. "You have until I make it to the front of the building to run that before I decline the charges."

He ran away from me like he was afraid I might sprint for the exit out of spite as I adjusted my dress and forced a deep breath into my lungs for my walk of shame after slamming the rest of my glass back.

I was going to murder Tamen Bryce.

As I began my shameful exit, I gripped the wine bottle's neck bringing it with me and noticed the penguin suited man approaching from the restaurant's side. I didn't stop, if he wanted me to stop, he'd have to make me.

"Miss." He called, as I blew past him, "Miss, you cannot leave with an open bottle of alcohol."

"Why not?" I argued, raising my voice and drawing even more attention as I spun on him. "I had to buy it, why can I not take it with me?"

"It's—" He stammered, glancing around at how everyone stared. "Against our policy." He hissed in a whisper, trying to save face.

"Fuck your policy." I snapped, tipping the bottle to my lips and taking a large swig.

"Miss," He flushed, "This is a fine dining establishment, we will not tolerate this behavior from you."

"What are you going to do?" I chuckled, taking another swig. "Kick me out? Black List me? Stick a poster on your door that says I'm not allowed to come back? Fuck off."

"Call the police." He stage whispered to someone, and that was the final straw.

"Ah yes!" I turned to him, raising my voice again. "Call the police to escort the trash that is already leaving, out. How fucking efficient of you." Flying the bird at him and turning back toward the exit, I made awkward eye contact with a man that fucked a girl at the Den every single week across the restaurant.

Well, when I say fucked, I mean he hired a girl to meet him in a bedroom, tie him down and fuck his ass with a strap on the size of an elephant's dick. The woman he was dining with sneered my way as I neared their table and I—saw red. "Your husband hires prostitutes at The Vixen's Den to fuck him like a little bitch." I sneered on my way, drawing a choking gasp from the man. I pointed out another John across the way and yelled out for everyone else to hear now that the entire restaurant was silent from my first outburst. "This man hires prostitutes young enough to be his granddaughter and makes them cry when he sleeps with them." Gasps echoed out around the space while I turned and pointed one last one out, "And he likes to be whipped while he wears high heels." I stopped at the entrance to the foyer and took a dramatic bow, holding my purse and my bottle of wine up in the air. "Have a wonderful evening!"

The man-child server waited by the door for me and shakily handed me my card back as I blew past him. "Do you—" He stammered, following me out onto the street, "Do you work at Vixen's?" He asked in a hushed tone.

Rolling my eyes, I turned sharply on him. "I work at Prism." With a sharp crack of disdain, I rocked the bottle to my lips, the liquid's bitter taste a fleeting comfort. "And someday I'm going to fucking own it."

"Wow." He breathed, "Would it be okay if I—"

I cut him off and turned away toward the busy street where my hired car was no longer parked, obviously. "Don't you dare show up there and request me."

"Oh, okay."

"Fuck this place and everyone in it!" I yelled, raising both fists into the air as I walked down the dark sidewalk in the chilly evening air.

And fuck Tamen Bryce for being a weak man who needed to make me feel small, to make himself feel bigger. I'd show him just how pathetically small he really was.

Chapter 11 - Tamen

"That's my girl." I gave her mocking praise, earning a sloppy, wet kiss. Normally I'd cringe at the sensation, but for her, I endured. She was the only one who got away with making a mess of me. "Who's your favorite man in the whole world?"

"Don't even fucking try it." Maddox glared at me over the top of his beer bottle as I swayed with his daughter in my arms. "I mean it."

I rolled my eyes at him and turned us away from his angry glare. The man couldn't take a fucking joke to save his life.

Rory squealed in my arms and babbled obnoxiously as I walked around the hippy restaurant we were at, some place Liv and Peyton picked out to celebrate Maddox's birthday. I wasn't even going to show up, even though Peyton had threatened violence against me if I didn't come to the place in the city for dinner. It wasn't very often that everyone came into the city anymore, and it was expected since I lived in the city now that I would make an appearance.

Which was exactly why I hadn't planned to show up. Simply out of spite.

But then Sloane had gotten into my head and fucked around in there enough to leave me needing a distraction, and Rory's big goofy toddler personality was exactly where I'd find that.

Her little brother, Asher, was asleep in Liv's arms, completely oblivious to the noise and chaos of the trendy place going on around him. I had little hope for him ever liking me, like Rory did. The kid came out looking exactly like Maddox, and I was guessing his personality would match his grumpy old dad's.

"So," Peyton interrupted, drawing me back into the group where they all sat around a low informal dinner table as we waited for our meals, "How's Prism coming along?"

I squinted my eyes at her, as everyone else seized the opportunity to have an interest in the topic and stared at me expectantly. It was a trap, because Liv and Peyton hated that I was opening a sex club, a fact they made known every single time I came around. Which was why I didn't come around much anymore.

"Yeah," Dane leaned back, crossing one ankle over his knee as he put his arm around his wife's shoulders. "I've heard you have a grand opening scheduled for two weeks from now."

"It's fine." I shifted Rory in my arms.

"That's all we get?" Peyton huffed.

"Why would I tell you more than that? You'll just yell and nag at me about it." I scoffed.

She huffed a breath, and I rolled my eyes.

Rory leaned over my shoulder to look back out the big window, looking out over the street behind me, and threw her arms into the air excitedly as she wiggled to get down. I lowered her to the ground, completely sure that she'd throw herself to the floor to get whatever she wanted outside and, as expected, she tottered around me and slapped her little palms against the window.

"Bow!" Rory cheered, "Rainbow!"

Liv blushed embarrassedly, "Oh god, she likes that woman's rainbow hair. Go get her before she breaks through the glass."

My blood ran cold as I turned around and found a pair of molten lava eyes aimed directly at me from the other side of the window.

"Bloody hell." I whispered as Sloane's lips parted and her eyes squinted angrily before dropping to the cherub cheeked toddler banging against the glass excitedly. My Rainbow looked like a wet dream of mine, dressed in the skintight red dress I bought her, with flawless makeup and her hair styled beautifully. But I wasn't stupid enough to let her beauty trick me into missing the anger radiating off her body. I set her up tonight, cruelly sending her to dinner all alone so she'd remember that I was always in control. Bending down to pick Rory up, Sloane turned on her heel and marched back down the sidewalk towards the entrance to the restaurant. "Come on, darling. You need to have your big scary daddy holding you for this."

Maddox eyed me suspiciously as he took Rory and glanced over at the door where Sloane was all but running toward me. Liv scoffed, "Let me guess, you know the angry rainbow?"

"Yeah," I sighed, leaning over Peyton to grab my jacket. "Best I leave, now."

"Oh, no, you don't." Liv shook her finger at me. "We want to see the angry rainbow cut you a new ass."

"Rainbow!" Rory cheered, and I felt Sloane's presence behind me.

"I hate you all." I deadpanned, turning toward the woman of my dreams and my nightmares. "Sloane."

Maddox hissed behind me, "*Oh*, it's Sloane."

"Don't *Sloane*, me!" She hissed, "You weak, sniveling pathetic piece of English shit!"

Dane snorted, covering it with a cough, and Liv chuckled, "Oh, I like her."

"Fuck off, Little Hacker." I threw over my shoulder and faced the angry rainbow again. My pretty little angry Rainbow. "Let's talk outside."

"No." Sloane cried, ripping her arm out of my hand as I tried to steer her backward. "Don't touch me!"

A server appeared behind her and awkwardly tapped her on the shoulder, making my hackles raise up as he touched her. "Ma'am, we cannot allow any outside alcohol in our restaurant."

Without even glancing away from my stare, she lifted the bottle and shoved it at the man's chest. "That's fine, it's empty anyway."

"Did you drive here?" I interrupted as the server took the bottle and left. I hated that my family was staring at us like they were watching the most entertaining sitcom of their lives, but Sloane wasn't in the mood to leave. And I wasn't in the mood to embarrass either of us in public.

"No, I walked!" She snapped, "Because the car you hired to drive me to your little prank, took off, leaving me abandoned halfway across the city!"

"Tamen." Peyton sighed behind me, and I waved my hand at her dismissively.

"So, you walked drunkenly across the city wearing that?" I scoffed, "Are you incapable of ordering an Uber for yourself?"

"I swear to god!" She cried out, squeezing her fists tight like she was imagining the way they'd feel around my neck. "I hate you!"

"The feeling is mutual," I shrugged and then tossed my jacket at her. "Put that on, and I'll drive you home."

She scoffed and tossed my jacket on the floor, crossing her arms over her lush chest, drawing my eyes to it for the hundredth time. "I'd rather—"

I waved my hand at her, "Yeah, yeah, yeah, I know. Puke in your handbag and eat it." I shivered dramatically at the disgusting thought. "Let's go, anyway."

"Don't touch me."

"Let's save Tamen any bodily harm this evening," Peyton cut in, rising from her seat and stepping between Sloane and me with an exaggerated glance my way as she faced my Rainbow, "Even though I'm one hundred percent sure he deserves it. Hi," She held her hand out to shake, "I'm Peyton, Tamen's sister-in-law. My husband Dane," P motioned to Dane who smiled at her, "Is Tamen's brother. And if anyone knows how much of a pain in the ass he can be, it's me."

Liv snorted mockingly from her seat, and I glared at her, but she didn't stop. "He hit her with a car once, put her in a coma for a week." Liv said with a shrug, "Yet she still lets him come around, I don't understand it."

"I didn't drive the bloody car—"

"Shut up," Peyton argued, elbowing me in the gut. "No one cares what you have to say."

Sloane's golden eyes flicked back and forth between the girls and me, like she couldn't quite believe how they were speaking to me. "I don't understand what's going on."

"That's fair." Peyton slid her arm through Sloane's, and I groaned as she pulled her toward the couches as our server appeared with a massive tray of food. "Would you like some dinner? You can have Tamen's plate while you tell us all about what he did tonight. Chances are we won't be surprised in the least by his actions, but we can help you plan your revenge."

"I can't believe this, does loyalty mean nothing to you people?" I argued as Sloane sat down in my seat next to Peyton, eyeing me angrily still.

"Tee-Tee!" Rory wiggled out of Maddox's arms and tottered back over to me. "Eat! Eat! Eat!"

I groaned again, scooping up the annoyingly cute kid and sitting down in a chair at the end of the table next to Sloane, "Fine." I sighed, settling her on my knee. "But if the angry rainbow stabs me with her knife, it's all your fault."

Rory giggled and clapped her hands together excitedly before reaching for a French fry off my plate. "Pretty rainbow!"

Sloane glanced over at Liv holding Asher and the grizzly bear next to her, then back to me, with Rory on my lap. "You have kids?"

Liv cringed and shuddered violently, "Ew, not a chance. The babies are ours," She nodded to Madd and then glared at me. "But Rory there is obsessed with her uncle Tee-Tee and I'm afraid if we made him go missing, she'd never forgive us for it. Peyton's my sister and this is my boyfriend, Maddox. I'm Olivia. And for the record, I'm the president of the 'I hate Tamen' fan club, something I'm sure you're very willing to be a part of, so you're safe around us."

Sloane's eyes rounded as she nodded once. "Blackmailed into letting him come around by the adorable kiddo. But would take him to the train station if you could get away with it," She nodded again, grabbing a fry off my plate that I was reaching for and taking an aggressive bite out of it. "Got it. That makes total sense."

Liv cackled as I stared at them both in confusion, "God, I like her. She can take your place in our family, T."

THE LINE WALKERS

I glanced over at Sloane from my chair and watched her as she tipped her head back and laughed at something Maddox said. Christ, did she have no taste in humor? The bear was the least funny person walking the planet.

Yet Sloane seemed to enjoy his presence. Everyone's actually. She stormed into the restaurant an hour ago and melted right into the group like she had belonged amidst it for decades.

She fit in better than I did.

And the people in it were the closest thing I had to a family anymore, but they didn't even actually like me.

They loved Sloane, however.

"I have to go." I rose, pulling my wallet out from my pocket and tossing a couple of bills down on the table.

"Running away?" Dane mocked me, "Color me surprised."

Thankfully, Rory was passed out on the couch with her head on Maddox's lap; otherwise, she would have made it impossible to make an Irish exit, as the girl loved giving dozens of kisses for goodbyes.

"Whatever." I sighed, sliding my arms into my jacket and nodding once to the group, "Have a lovely evening."

I only made it a few steps from the table when I heard Sloane say something to the group that sounded a hell of a lot like a goodbye. Cringing, I quickened my pace, weaving through the crowded restaurant; I felt like I took two steps backward for every step forward as I hurried to leave.

By the time I made it to the dark hallway leading to the restrooms and the back exit, my palms felt as if red-hot pokers were running up the lifelines on them. If I didn't make it out of the restaurant and into the quiet seclusion of my car quickly, I'd snap.

And then there was no telling who would meet my knife when I lost control. Remodeling Prism had kept me too busy to relieve my stress and sate my thirst for death, leaving me on edge.

Every time I ran into someone else, I envisioned what they'd look like with a gash across their windpipe as the contents of their circulatory system emptied itself down the front of their clothes.

Fuck. I was in trouble.

Clearing the back door, I walked through the dark parking lot toward my car as a thundering echo filled my ears, blocking everything else out.

Realistically, I knew she was following me, her heels made the same annoying sound on the restaurant floor as they did the blacktop parking lot, but when Sloane grabbed my arm as I got to the side of my car, conscious thought ceased.

Rounding on her, I swung us both against the corner of the brick building, slamming her against it with my hand around her throat. "Big mistake, Rainbow."

She dug her nails into my hand, breaking the skin as she stared up at me with round eyes fighting against my hold on her. "Tamen."

"You need to leave." I growled, slamming my fist into the brick wall next to her head as I closed my eyes and fought to keep from tightening my hand around her throat anymore.

"What's wrong with you?" She hissed, and I smiled in the darkness as I tilted my head to the side and ran my nose up the side of her face, inhaling her intoxicating scent.

"So many things." I said and tightened my hand on her throat even though I knew better. "So many bloody things."

"Get off me." She cried, fighting me off with her sharp nails and swinging fists.

"Good girl." I moaned, making her fight even harder. "Finally, show me what you're made of."

"Fuck off!" She grunted and swung her knee up into my groin and I coughed at the burn, curling forward with a grin on my face, nonetheless. Her hands continued their assault, hitting my face and sides as I held firm to her, fighting through my nausea and delirium.

I should have known that my pretty little Rainbow wouldn't go down without a fight. I should have known she'd take me down with her.

But I never expected her to discover the blade tucked into my waistband while I was distracted by the sensation of her pulse throbbing against my palm in sync with the one in my hardening cock. And I sure wasn't expecting her to hook her heeled foot behind mine, dropping me to my ass against the side of my car, following me forward until the tip of my favorite blade pressed against my sternum.

She coughed, rubbing her neck as I chuckled like a maniac sitting up to stare at her mockingly.

"My, my, my." I hummed, "My pretty little Rainbow has some thunder and lightning in her clouds after all."

"Shut up!" She hissed, pressing the knife into my chest firmer. "You're a fucking nut job!"

"Duh," I licked my lips and bent one knee, laying my arm over it as I waited for her to make her move. "I told you to get the fuck away from me."

"Wrong." She leaned over me and grabbed a handful of my hair, tipping my head back into my car as she stood over me. "You keep drawing me in. You keep forcing me to be around you for your own sick enjoyment, playing with me like a sick voodoo doll."

I licked my lips, and her eyes fell to them, "And you keep playing right along. Like maybe you might win if you try hard enough." I tilted my head, pulling at her hold on my hair until I moaned sardonically at the feel. "You need to leave." I repeated.

"Why?" Sloane asked, twitching her hand with the blade in it. "Do you think I'm afraid of you?"

Leaning forward into the blade, letting it pierce through my shirt and into my skin, I grinned again. "You should be."

We were playing a dangerous game of chicken, one that might leave me on a kabob in the end, but I couldn't stop. I needed to see the depth of Sloane's mind and how far she'd go.

I ached to see her win. To defeat me. Finally, someone I'd actually let defeat me.

Leaning forward again, her wide eyes fell to the blade, watching the blood pool in the thin white cotton of my shirt before snapping back up to mine.

"Do it." I dared.

Chapter 12 - Sloane

"Just do it!" Tamen hissed, leaning further against the incredibly sharp point of his knife that I held to his chest.

"You're broken." I whispered, pulling the knife away from his chest completely and stabbing it into the earth along the edge of the building.

A sane person would have walked away from Tamen, quit their job and stayed clear of the maniac sitting on the dark ground before them. A sane person would have run for their life, especially given how quickly he had been to threaten it in the beginning.

Maybe I wasn't as sane as I thought. Letting go of his hair, I picked up his keys from the ground and clicked the unlock button on his Mercedez, "Take me home." I demanded, stepping backward as his long legs bent under him to stand up. "And you owe me four hundred dollars."

He gazed at me as though I was the unstable one before he reached in his pocket and pulled out a metal cigarette case, sticking one between his lips and lighting it up, all while never breaking eye contact.

"I could have killed you." He tilted his head to the side, pulling the cigarette from his lips and tipping his head back to blow it up into the air instead of at my face. "I still might."

Perhaps the moment frozen in time between us was my chance at setting the record straight and taking back some of the control he loved to hold over me. Or maybe I was still drunk from the bottle of wine I drowned.

Shrugging one shoulder, I pulled the cigarette from his fingers and took a drag, loving the way his eyes tracked my every motion the entire time. "And here I thought you were finally going to break the tension that's been building between us and fuck me." I popped my lips at him dramatically and then dropped the tobacco stick to the ground, crushing it with my shoe. "Take me home." I repeated, walking around his car and opening the passenger side door to get in. "Or I quit."

He rolled his jaw back and forth and then sighed, bending down to pick up his knife and stare at the dirty blade. "I should make you walk home for desecrating my favorite blade." He wiped the dirt and earth off the sharp edge against his thigh. "Do you have any idea how dull it will be now?"

I sat down in the seat and shut the door, crossing my legs as he slid his massive body down into the car with that annoying grace of his that I wanted to both mimic and tease him about. "Don't pout. It isn't very becoming of you. Though I should have guessed you were a dicktim."

"What the hell is a dicktim?"

"You in a nutshell." I mused, forcing my hands to stop shaking from the adrenaline crash now that he wasn't actively trying to strangle me and I wasn't holding him at knifepoint. "You're a dick, and then you play the victim when someone calls you on it. dicktim."

He scoffed as if the word was unimpressive, but I also noticed the slight smirk on his face as he started the car.

Slipping my phone from my bag, I pulled up my payment app and found his name connected to the contact card, typing out a scathing message. I tucked it back into my bag and waited.

His phone pinged in his pocket, and he glanced at me from the corner of his eye before pulling it out and reading the message out loud.

"*My charge for being your doll this evening. But the game is changing and you're about to be my bitch, Ken.*" He dropped his phone to his lap, "You have to be fucking kidding me." I simply shrugged as he went on, "You said four hundred dollars, but this is for five. What could I possibly owe you five hundred dollars for?"

"Four hundred for the wine I ordered waiting for your dumbass to show up before I realized what you were doing to me, and another hundred for the show I put on in that restaurant on my way out because of you." Licking my lips, "Those kinds of dramatics aren't cheap, and neither am I."

He chuckled lightly and then clicked his phone, typing something else out, and moments later, the notification of payment came through on my screen with his own message.

> *I'll take all your clothes off anytime you ask me, Barbie.*
> *+$500.00*

There was a tip added to it for another two hundred dollars with another message.

> *For the world-class performance. +$200.00*

"Pleasure doing business with you." I replied smugly as he pulled his car out into the city streets, aiming it toward my apartment building.

Silence hung between us for a while as he traversed the busy confusing streets before the questions rattling around in my head got too loud to ignore. Driven by morbid curiosity, I risked my sanity and delved into the turbulent depths of his clearly unstable mind, a maelstrom of erratic thoughts and unsettling emotions.

"You're not a good person, are you?" The question escaped my lips, a small sound in the suffocating stillness, and his grin—a silent, shadowed thing—appeared in the darkness, his gaze averted.

"You already know that." Was his reply. "I've never pretended to be good."

"But you're like—" I searched for the right words, a chilling weight settling in my stomach, but nothing captured the sheer awfulness, the blatant disregard for decency, "Criminally bad," it felt like a gross understatement.

His scoff was a sharp, disdainful sound, as if the word itself had physically offended him. "Baby, my morality no longer exists, and I'm about as immune to the law as a ghost. Especially here in the states."

"How?" I whispered in speculation.

"I'm too good to get caught. Too efficient."

"At what, exactly?" Lost in thought, I didn't realize he was pulling into the loading zone until the quiet shush of his car settling into park broke my concentration. "Whatever it is, you use that knife to do it, don't you?"

What the fuck was wrong with me that I was sitting there, waiting for him to confirm what I was sure I already knew. Tamen was a killer. He used that shiny gold handled knife I had held against his heart to kill people. I should have been ripping the door open and tossing him a 'see ya in another life' over my shoulder as I googled job openings near me. Not still sitting in his car, waiting for the verbal confirmation I didn't even need.

"I could tell you that." He slowly turned his head, the muscles in his neck tense, his eyes burning with a monstrous intensity, and I knew then what lurked within. More than just a workplace bully, he was a depraved man, his business suit masking a cruel and unsettling nature. His casual cruelty felt like a cold, sharp object. The air around him felt thick with malice. "But then I'd have to kill you."

"Jesus fuck." I hissed as my held breath released through my teeth. "You're certifiable."

His lips curled into a cruel, almost mocking smirk—a blatant challenge—before he leaned back against his headrest, eyes narrowed and gleaming. "And yet here you are, alone with me, contemplating if you should invite me up to your place so I can fuck you like the wild animal I really am."

His arrogant demeanor broke the spell, and I scoffed, shaking my head at the thought of doing what he suggested. "Actually, I was getting ready to tell you I can't work for you anymore. You're too cocky, self-centered, and cold." Opening the door of his car aggressively, I grinned back at him and got out. "Get that wound stitched before you get an infection from whatever other bodily fluid was on that knife before I pushed it into you."

The maniac just kept grinning and then winked at me. "See you tomorrow at eight for training, Rainbow."

The car door slammed shut with a sharp metallic clang, and as I walked away, my hips swayed rhythmically, a silent message for him to contemplate while the night doorman silently watched the departing vehicle.

I couldn't go back to Prism and that man.

If I did, I'd do something stupid.

Like let him fuck me like the wild animal we both knew he was. Because damn, if that didn't sound like a fantastic time.

Chapter 13 - Tamen

I was either going to fuck her or kill her.

Hell, knowing me, I'd probably kill her while I fucked her. Losing control around Sloane was inevitable, especially when I imagined what it was going to feel like to sink deep into her body for the first time.

It was after ten P.M., and she was two hours late for our training session with the girls at Prism. Last night when I had dropped her off, she told me she quit. And I had called her bluff, but apparently she felt the urge to test my limits on it. As I paced around the open floor of the new stage room, all the different ways I could make her life hell raced through my brain.

I could fire her. But she kind of already quit.

I could demand that she return to work. Though knowing her, she'd refuse.

I could blacklist her, creating lies about her, so she'd be unemployable at any other establishment. But that would only work for other bosses unless they laid eyes on her, because as soon as they saw her in person, they'd hire her on the spot.

And the mere thought of her working somewhere else, for someone else, made me twitchy. Believe me when I say there's nothing worse than a twitchy maniac. We made terrible decisions.

Mashing my thumb against her contact card in my phone, I pressed send. It wasn't as if I had a grand plan of what I'd say to her, to entice her to show up, but I was running on pure need.

Carnal need.

The need to prove to Sloane she couldn't just walk away from me. That I wasn't disposable.

But the line never even rang before I got an automated message about her number not being in service at that time, and to try my call again.

"Bloody hell." I hissed, punching out a scathing text message and hitting send, only to have it bounce back as undeliverable. "Oh, Rainbow." I cracked my neck as I pulled up the social media apps I downloaded simply to stalk her on, but her profile was gone. "Oh, my pretty little Rainbow is playing with fire."

As I closed out of app after app, only one remained unchecked. Before I even clicked on it, I knew her name would pop up, but seeing her face again finally made the game of cat and mouse that she was playing even hotter.

Last night, I had paid her electronically for the wine she bought at the restaurant and tonight, that seemed to be my only form of communication with her. Any other man might have balked at the idea of paying a woman to pay attention to him. But I was in the business of employing women to do just that, and I wasn't above it.

Typing out a message to her, I watched as it went through with the transaction.

> *Blocking me in the name of spite only turns me on. + $200.00*

A small red heart icon appeared on the transaction, telling me she fucking saw it, and was toying with me in response. I waited, daring her mentally to respond to me. Yet nothing.

I gritted my teeth and marched into the room where the OG girls were practicing some pole dancing skills that most of them perfected years before they ever slept with their first clients while the new girls we recruited from the strip club watched.

Forgoing greetings, I got right to the point of my visit. "Who here has talked to Ember today?"

The girls paused before Mya, the tattooed girl from the strip club that gave Sloane a lap dance, raised her hand. "I talked to her earlier. We have plans to meet up tonight. Is everything okay?"

"Call her." I nodded to her phone as she absently picked it up from a chair. "I need to speak with her."

Her dark eyebrows creased slightly before she shrugged and swiped her screen to dial Sloane's number.

"Wait a second." Valentina stepped in, putting her hand on Mya's arm. "Why can't you just call her yourself?"

I stared down at the blonde I had come to actually tolerate better than most of the people I interacted with. Expecting her to wither under my menacing glare, she simply raised her eyebrows at me and silently challenged me to make her.

"Because she's avoiding me." I replied honestly, feeling every pair of female eyes in the room judging me. "I was a prick."

"Shocker." Valentina winked and then let go of Mya's arm. "But she's busy getting ready for a gig tonight. The three of us are working it together."

The hair on the back of my neck rose as the bubbly blonde watched me closely, as if she expected me to have a reaction to that tidbit of juicy information. "She's working somewhere else instead of working here, at her actual job?" I snapped.

Still, Valentina watched me closely. "I'm not sure of the logistics." She shrugged and turned away, "But glory holes are kind of her kink."

Twitchy.

I was very bloody twitchy as I stood in a room full of women who were supposed to fear me simply because I was their asshole boss. Instead, they toyed with my nonexistent morals as I imagined the color of Valentina's blood across the new white marble flooring.

"Where?"

"I'm not sure of the logistics." She repeated, taking her place back at one of the poles with a smirk on her lips. "But from what I hear, Ember is the star attraction for the evening. She's going to make a lot of money tonight."

I clenched my teeth so hard, my molars cracked as I walked away, barking out over my shoulder. "Go the fuck home. We're done for today."

I sent another payment through my phone to the infuriating woman, desperate to reach her before I lost my grip on reality.

> *If you need money so badly, you should have shown up to your actual job. + $500.00*

Immediately, I groaned, knowing that would simply piss her off and make her ignore me harder. So, I sent another one as desperation morphed into something akin to anxiety in my gut.

> *Call me and I'll give you another grand. + $500.00*

I didn't wait for her call, knowing it wouldn't magically come through. Instead, I called the only person who could help me at the moment, even knowing what it would cost me.

"To what do I owe this pleasure?" My brother's annoying gruff voice floated through my ear as I grabbed my keys and jacket from my office.

"I need you to track someone. Immediately."

"Who?" He asked and then sighed, "Dammit, if you say the Rainbow from last night, my answer is no."

"Sloane." I barked, irritated that he called her by the name I used for her in my darkest fantasies. "Her name is Sloane and you know it. I need her location."

"And why can't you just ask her nicely for it?" He asked, "What did you do?"

"What I always do." Snapping in frustration as I got into my car. "Pushed. Avoided. Irritated. Annoyed. And then slammed her up against the wall by her throat." He sighed through the phone, "Until she dropped me on my ass and held my own knife against my heart."

"Hmm." He hummed, intrigued. "That's not at all what I was expecting you to say, though I can't say it's impossible to imagine that scene based on the fire she had in her eyes when she found you last night."

"Dane!" Cracking my neck, I took a deep breath. "Please."

"Fine." He sighed, and I heard him groan as he adjusted himself in his chair, no doubt working late like usual. "But answer one question for me first."

"What?"

"Is she more than just a girl that works for you?"

"Not currently." I replied instantly, pleased with his wording and the avoidance I could use to respond.

"Noted. Send me her phone number."

I hung up and instantly sent her info to him and then forced deep breaths in and out of my lungs as I imagined the situation Sloane was putting herself into out of spite.

Well, to be honest, it probably had nothing to do with me at all. She loved sex. She loved the power it gave her; I recognized that call for control the moment I saw her on stage all those weeks ago.

She wasn't mine; it wasn't as if I had a claim on her or told her she couldn't sell her body the way she had been doing for years. But fuck, if it didn't irritate my nerves, knowing she was about to let someone else touch her skin when I hadn't even had the privilege.

Other men were going to use her body, while she used them for money.

Sloane wasn't a victim, she wasn't stuck somewhere in life, forced to make these terrible decisions to survive.

Sex was her drug.

Money was her high.

Power was her kryptonite.

And she was my fucking antidote to madness. Her ignoring me and cutting me out was driving me insane, and she knew it. She just didn't know what it would cost me to lose control when it finally happened. Sloane didn't understand that someone would get hurt.

My phone pinged with a text from Dane, clicking on the link gave me a live tracker to her phone's location in real time.

"Gotcha." I whispered to myself as I dug deep into the venue she was at and the event going on tonight.

Lucky for me, I knew the man running the event. Unfortunately for me, he had been trying to get access to my particular skills for years to benefit his own business ventures. The man wanted me to kill off his biggest competition in the cocaine trade on the east coast.

Up until that exact moment, I had no interest in trading my skills for his fat wallet.

But now; now I had the incentive needed to play ball.

No one else was going to touch my pretty little Rainbow tonight.

But I sure as fuck was going to.

Chapter 14 - Sloane

THE LINE WALKERS

"It happened!" A singsong voice rang out in the crowded dressing room where I sat at a vanity, applying another layer of bright red lipstick. "I can't believe it happened, but it did! We knew it could, but we didn't think it would!"

The girls around all quieted down as the theatrical woman in a long red robe complete with a boa of feathers around the trim fluttered into the room and walked straight over to me.

Crystal was the event coordinator for the night. She worked as a middleman between high end clients and call girls for gigs like this. The woman had made quite the name for herself in the game over the years and always made sure we were safe and taken care of.

Tonight wasn't a particularly rough event, it was a casino night for a billionaire and his friends at a swanky penthouse hotel. But girls could get hurt even by well-respected men in our world, so it helped to know we had someone watching our backs.

Val nudged me with her hip as she leaned against my vanity with a smug expression on her face.

"What exactly are we talking about?" I questioned.

Crystal sat down in the empty seat next to me and tapped her fingers together excitedly. "The cap has been met. You've been booked for the entire event."

"Really?" I asked in confusion. When Crystal first raised the topic of setting a cap amount price for me, I didn't think it would actually be met. Even though the hotel was filled with millions of dollars and only about twenty girls, the men usually liked to sample as many different girls as possible.

Rarely did they ever settle for one girl all evening. Especially not with the types of girls available tonight.

Or with the theme of the party.

It was a glory hole theme.

The *whole point* of the evening was to stick your willy in any hole you wanted. Pun intended.

"Who?" I asked, looking back in the mirror to adjust the brown wig I wore to cover up my vibrant locks. Even though I fucked for a living, nights like tonight could get weird, and having a bit of anonymity after it comforted me.

Crystal scoffed, "Don't you mean how much?"

"No," Val shook her head, "She means who."

Val called me the second she left Prism, telling me of Tamen's unhinged behavior. Which I kind of expected, considering the man paid me over a thousand dollars via Venmo when he figured out I blocked him on every other front. Leaving myself only accessible to him via money felt appropriate. And to be honest, watching those dollar bills roll in electronically with his anxious messages excited me.

He was desperate.

And a part of me was wondering if he would try to fuck with my night, working for Crystal.

Crystal waved us off, "I don't know. A rich man who has a particular fetish that you are going to fulfill for him tonight." She narrowed her eyes at me with a pause, "You're here to make money, are you not?"

"You know I am." I scoffed, offended by her questioning my dedication to the night.

"Good." She stood up, patting me on the shoulder, "Because you've never let me down before, and I knew you'd be a good girl and do whatever he wanted for thirty grand."

"Thirty—" I choked, thinking surely I heard her wrong. "Total?"

"No," she smirked triumphantly. "That's your cut."

"Fuck." I hissed, deflating in my seat, knowing she was right.

For that kind of cash, there wasn't much I wouldn't let a man do to me. Damn, that kind of money made me hot.

I loved money.

I loved the power that came with it.

"Exactly," Crystal nodded and then pointed to my pink robe. "You won't be needing an outfit. He had one delivered ten minutes ago. It's to die for. I hung it in the private room he booked for you downstairs. My team is already moving one of the privacy benches down there and getting it all set up."

"That's absurd." Val groaned from beside me with comical jealousy on her face. "It's like he knows she's a slut for expensive gifts and glory holes."

"Yeah," I mused, staring at my reflection in the mirror, trying to tamp down my excitement for the night. "Seems like it."

THE LINE WALKERS

My skin felt electrified; as if the air had a current to it, flowing over my pores with a rhythm that matched the erratic beating of my heart. I couldn't remember the last time I had been so overwhelmingly excited about a gig.

Sex work had its ups and down, and I had experienced a lot of them over the years. But for me, I always got a high on a job. Even if I didn't enjoy the sex specifically, the entire experience gave me a rush, and I was hardly ever left unsatisfied when I was done.

Orgasms rarely happened for me at work, but I didn't need them during the act itself to feel fulfilled.

I had a vibrator and a tentacle dildo at home for that.

At work, I got high on the sex appeal and the power exchange that occurred. A man might hire me so he could feel like a badass and in charge, but the same thing happened night after night.

I left with a purse full of cash and a buzzing in my veins. And the man left empty handed.

I was the winner.

Every time.

Tonight, it was no different, yet it was completely different at the same time. Tonight, it felt bigger somehow. It felt like the high was stronger. Maybe it was the entire work up to the gig, and then finding out I was privately booked. Or maybe it was the way the John had provided the entire ensemble and vibe of the night himself.

It felt—thoughtful?

Intentional?

I didn't know.

It didn't matter because someone purchased my body and booked my time. And I was fucking dripping with excitement from it all. I really hoped the man could fuck. In very un-Sloane like fashion, I wanted to come.

God, I wanted to come so fucking hard.

I laid on my back, wearing a crotchless emerald green mesh bodysuit that somehow exposed my body more than being nude did. It was V-cut, and my tits were testing every fiber of its stitching with each inhale I took.

It reminded me of the golden dress from the night Tamen took me to the strip club. The fabric hugged my body like a second skin, as if made for me.

Tamen Bryce would have picked out an outfit just like this one if I gave him the chance to fuck me. I knew it.

The privacy bench that Crystal had picked out for my night was one of my favorites, if I was being honest. Sure, it reminded me of some archaic torture device, but I always had fun when I was in it.

I laid on a plush cushioned bench that ended right at my ass, leaving my cheeks hanging off the edge just enough to be completely at the John's mercy.

My knees were in slings, tied open and pulled back toward my shoulders, leaving me open and exposed, and my wrists were shackled to the sides of the bench next to my hips.

What made the privacy bench special and fed into the glory hole fetish, was the large velvet plush box that my head was in.

I was surrounded by thick padding that prevented anyone from looking in or out of the box, my head sat comfortably on a pillow. I was incredibly comfortable for being restrained for another's enjoyment.

Again, that made me so fucking wet tonight, adding to the excitement.

Essentially, I was a headless sex doll.

Yet I had never felt more powerful. Someone paid an insane amount of money to get to do this to me. To have me.

To feel me.

Like I was something special.

"Mmh," I hummed in anticipation inside of my dark captivity as it built.

A faint noise from the room caught my attention, and I held my breath, trying to hear through the thick cushion lining the headrest. I knew from experience that I could hear a man speak when he was next to the bench, but not much past that.

Still, I tried to listen intently, like I'd get some clues from the noises about what was going to happen to me.

I felt him. I couldn't see him or hear him, but I could feel his presence in the room. Spread-eagled before a stranger, I felt no shame; my body had always been my own.

The urge to speak struck me, to fill the void with conversation, which wasn't my normal routine. The man paid for a real-life sex doll, and that was what he'd get from me. I was a professional, after all.

I flinched slightly when something touched the arch of my foot before I steeled my body from the unnerving sensation of being touched without knowing where it was going next.

Hands. Big hands with rough calluses teasingly caressed my feet and then my ankles before testing the tightness of the fabric wrapped around them. Was he checking to make sure I was firmly secured, or that I was comfortable?

How did a man rich enough to spend fifty grand plus for a night with a hooker get callouses on his hands? What could he do for work that would leave those worn spots on his fingertips.

Tamen worked with his hands even though he was disgustingly rich. He tore walls out and carried materials around Prism every day.

Did this man do something like that? What were the chances of two rich hard-working men having a similar taste in lingerie?

I flexed my fingers, forcing my body to relax again as his hands drifted up my calves and to the inside of my knees. If I wasn't careful, my imagination was going to convince me that the mysterious man was my boss after all, even though I knew that wasn't possible.

Would he speak? Would he have an accent if he did? Did I want him to?

Normally, no. Yet this time, the silence felt insufferable. Perhaps having the last few weeks consumed with business work and no sex work was why I was so on edge, like I was out of practice.

A deep growl emanated through the padded box as the man's hands slowly traveled over my inner thighs, down to the exposed wetness between them. Wet lips touched the inside of my knee, and I jumped before arching into it, pressing into his touch. Slowly, one rough finger traced circles around my clit, but avoided the pleasurable spot just enough to create a need inside of me.

I rolled my hips, wordlessly begging the mysterious man above me. I thought perhaps he chuckled lightly, like he was enjoying my torment, but past the sound of my own panting, I couldn't be sure.

Then, that same teasing finger pressed into my body, inch by inch, slowly sliding inside of me.

"Fuck." I hissed, arching again, and rolling my hips to take him deeper, quicker. He withdrew it and did it again, giving me only a little bit at a time. A cold breeze flowed across my chest before warmth replaced it as the man laid slow kisses up my chest between my breasts. I could feel the fabric of his clothes against the back of my thighs as he leaned over me. His pants were soft and my fingers stretched from their pinned position to bury themselves in the material, pulling him in more.

His tongue ran a trail across the mesh fabric of the body suit over my already hard nipple and I moaned, desperate to feel more of him. Using his free hand, he grabbed my other breast and started toying with my nipple, finally pulling the fabric aside to suck it into his mouth.

Without the ability to see or hear him clearly, sensations became so much more heightened. The scrape of his stubbled jaw contrasted with the softness of his lips and tongue as he slowly sucked on each of my nipples. Never once distracted, his hands moved with practiced precision, completing each task with an impeccable attention to detail. Adding another finger to my needy pussy, he stretched me with them, scissoring them and hooking them inside of me to drive me wild.

I was no longer sure who was supposed to be deriving pleasure from the interaction. Sometimes Johns got off on enjoying themselves, regardless of pleasuring their partner. Sometimes they simply gave and never received.

With the way tonight was booked, I had no idea what his plans were, and it was unnerving because I was afraid to hope for pleasure with how badly I was desperate for it already.

If he edged me, I'd die.

Sometimes Johns were evil like that.

I closed my eyes and prayed to the divine sex goddesses that he was a giver and wouldn't force either of us to go without pleasure.

Biting my lip to stifle another moan, he bit one of my nipples, pulling on it with his teeth as his palm rubbed against my clit finally. God, the man knew how to make a woman feel good.

The pressure, rhythm, and locations were on point.

He was a giver, after all.

And I was eager to take.

"Come for me." His low, deep voice barely penetrated my cozy coffin and hazy brain, but they still hit their mark. So did the fact that there was no familiar British accent in the command. Disappointment couldn't take root though because seconds later, his lips latched onto my clit, and I came off the bench, pushing my needy body against his face as he curled his fingers upward inside of me as he sucked deeply.

Maybe it was the buildup, the excitement, or hell, maybe it was just because I loved sex so much, but I came.

I came so hard it felt like my spirit was leaving my body as I arched into him with everything I had, riding out the pleasure and begging for more as I moaned and mewled for him. He turned his lips to the inside of my thigh and moaned against it, even though I couldn't hear the noise, I felt it.

I felt him.

Needed him.

The orgasm did nothing to sate my need for more though, somehow it had intensified it as if it was just a taste of what he could give me, and I was ravenous for more.

"Please." I sighed; not even sure he could hear me.

"No." He replied with that same deep voice that made it hard to hear clearly if I didn't try. "Thank me."

No, no, no, not a fucking praise and power kink. My ultimate weakness. I silently pleaded with the sex goddesses. His perfection overwhelmed me, and I was lost to him.

"Thank you." I moaned as he palmed both of my bare breasts as his teeth nipped the inside of my ankle.

"Good girl."

Fuck, I was so screwed. The man was going to turn me into a waterfall for him with my stupid praise kink.

My hands flexed, desperate to dig my nails into something, overwhelmed me. A second later I felt him pull the buckle on my wrist cuff free. As soon as my hand was free, I found the front of his shirt and pulled him into me, until the front of his pants pressed against my bare pussy.

He chuckled and then groaned when I turned my wrist and palmed his erection through his tight pants. I tried to feel all of him, but I couldn't reach down far enough to feel the head of his dick where it throbbed down his leg.

Both of his hands landed on my knees, and he spread them wider as I turned my attention to his belt, as if he was silently giving me permission to explore him. Screw exploring him. I wanted his dick free and buried deep inside of me.

I wanted to feel it sliding in and out of me more than I wanted anything else.

More than that, though, I wanted him to feel how damn good I felt wrapped around him. I craved his pleasure as much as my own. The need to make him feel good and prove I was worthy built inside of my gut with each second of time that I struggled with his button and zipper.

It wasn't as if I could reach him easily, thanks to the padding under my chin, keeping me immobilized, but I didn't stop.

His hands roamed my body, tweaking my nipples, rubbing my clit, massaging my calves. They left my skin at one point and I bit my lip to stop a pathetic beg for them to come back from slipping free. His hips moved and then he stepped back, leaving me completely untouched and no matter how far I reached, I couldn't find him again.

"Please." My lack of willpower caused me to beg him, and he rewarded me by throwing something fabric onto my body. Using my freed hand, I felt it, lifting it and realized it was a button-up shirt, still warm from his body heat.

He was stripping for me.

Something told me he was sexy, even if I couldn't see him. His thighs and stomach had been tight when he let me explore him before backing up. Was he young or old? Tall or short? Was he the dark and broody type, or did he smile as he fucked his women?

Before I could wonder about anything else, his hot hand wrapped around my wrist and pulled my palm against his bare abdomen as he stepped between my thighs again.

Fuck—he was ripped.

My fingertips wandered over his abs like braille, reading his body for more clues before dropping to the delicious V at his adonis belt before desperately searching for what I wanted to feel most.

I heard the faint noise of his chuckle before he turned my hand over, palm up, and then his heavy cock landed in it. "Is that what you're looking for?"

I gripped my hand around his veined cock and stroked it until I finally reached the thick, bulbous head. Damn, I had seen a lot of dicks in my life, but judging by feeling only, I had never taken one with such a thick head on it before.

He stepped forward, pressing against the back of my thighs again as his heavy cock slapped against my stomach.

He shifted and then rolled a condom over the head of his dick and paused. "Tell me to fuck you. Beg me for it."

Words weren't needed, nor would they serve me or him. There was something more animalistic between us and how our bodies vibed. So, I used my body to beg him, to consent, to convince him.

Wrapping my hand around his cock, I rubbed the head against my wetness, coating it and lining him up where we both wanted him to be. And then I pulled him in, forcing him to penetrate me.

The growl that slid from his lips echoed through the padding and I smiled to myself as he stretched me open with that big head before he pulled out and pushed deeper.

I was getting paid far too much money to fuck him. I would have done it for free.

Chapter 15 - Tamen

Heaven; A resting place a man like me would never reach because of the things I'd done during my life.

And what I was doing at that very moment was solidifying my one-way ticket to hell.

But fuck if it didn't feel like Heaven for the time being.

Sloane's nails dug into my lower abdomen as I bottomed out inside of her tight, wet pussy. She rocked her hips each time I got deep, rubbing her clit against my groin, silently begging me for more.

My pretty little Rainbow had no idea it was me fucking her. She thought some random millionaire from the event had bought her.

She thought some random man had paid for the pleasure of fucking her all night long.

Which I did.

And I would.

But she'd never know it was me. Part of me wanted to reveal myself to her, to tell her exactly who was inside of her at that very moment and keep her restrained while I finished fucking her. I wanted her to hate me. I wanted her anger and violence to burn like acid on a wound deep inside of me.

I needed the pain.

I craved the torment.

My suffering was a strange balm; only then did the suffocating darkness around me become quiet, a stark and heavy solitude. And Sloane, my pretty little Rainbow, made me suffer.

Every single second in her presence, without feeling her touch on my skin, tormented me.

Every single barbed word and angry glare she threw at me tortured my desire to own her.

Tonight was a lapse in that suffering, though in a way it solidified the permeance of it in my future.

Because the moment my paid for time with her was over, she'd never let me touch her again. And I'd suffer in her presence, like a dying man staring at a cure, just out of reach.

Maybe then I'd feel sane.

Maybe with her hate toward me fixated and solid, I'd feel *normal*.

"Harder." Her muffled plea cut through my darkness and brought me back to the heavenly sensation of her body. "Please."

I slammed in deep, rocking her in her unmoving bindings. Her body rippled and swayed from the punishing thrusts, but she arched into them, taking everything I gave her. God, she was bloody perfect.

Perfect for me, yet I'd never claim her as mine.

Leaning over her restrained body, I palmed both of her perfect tits as I rolled my hips, rubbing her clit with me buried in deep. Her free hand slid up my arm to my neck and her dainty fingers wrapped around my throat, tightening as I kept the same rolling motion with my hips.

No woman had ever dared to touch my neck in such a powerful move before, but I was regretful that I couldn't stare into Sloane's fiery gold eyes as she did it now. Hell, it threw me off, but I pressed my throat into her palm more. Her spine arched and then her scream echoed through the box as she orgasmed, tightening around my dick until I saw stars.

I wanted to come; I wanted to feel that euphoria she promised me with her seduction and obedience, but I wanted more before I gave in.

I needed more of her.

I pulled the other buckle of her wrist cuff free and gave her mobility of both her hands as I pulled my dick free from her body and fell to my knees. I licked her from ass to clit and then sucked it deep into my mouth, drawing another scream from her lips as both of her hands buried themselves in my hair, pulling and yanking at it as I feasted on her.

One second, she'd pull me in tighter, and the next she'd try to rip me away like she couldn't understand what she wanted more.

Join the bloody club, Rainbow.

I licked her, playing with her body until she came twice more before her pleas and demands for my cock became too loud to ignore any longer.

What I wouldn't give for her to know exactly who she was begging for.

Burying my dick back inside of her body, we both moaned at how fucking good it felt, and I resumed the same punishing thrusts she begged for. With her claws free, she marked me up and down my arms, neck, and chest. If she could reach it, she dug in and I welcomed it, leaning into her touch knowing I'd come away bloody.

The burning of her brands built that euphoria in my brain, reminding me of my self-harm days and the rush that came from each mark left in my skin. It had been years since the last time I gave into the urge to cut, but as she dug into me, I tipped my head back and basked in the familiar old relief.

"That's it." I groaned, picking up my speed and closing my eyes as the pleasure and pain mixed, leaving me unable to hold off anymore.

The familiar feel of her tightening body and primal cry echoed as she orgasmed again, and I lost control of my restraint. I pulled out of her, ripping the condom off, and stroked my cock as I exploded all over her stomach and chest, coating her skin with my release.

Her chest heaved as I stared down at her body, wearing the outfit I bought her, coated with my brand on her skin and it was nearly enough to harden me up again for round two. Technically, I paid for her all evening, no one else would touch what I had bought. And I knew once with her would never be enough, but I couldn't take her again the way I just had.

Stumbling backward, I pulled my pants up and fastened them as she let her arms fall to her sides in exhaustion.

"Rub it in." I demanded, but she didn't move. "Now."

Lifting her hands, she gently rubbed my come into her skin, covering her lush tits with it like she knew that was where I wanted it most.

"Good girl." I praised, disguising my voice in that repulsing American accent I had perfected as a child when all I wanted was to be just like my older brother, who was always the favorite. "Thank you for tonight."

I had to leave, or I'd do something stupid like reveal myself to her so I could see her eyes when I fucked her again.

That wouldn't bode well for either of us.

"That's it?" She questioned, instantly reaching up to the box that held her captive on the bench still. "Wait."

"Good evening." I replied, picking up my shirt to leave as I heard my mistake as clear as day.

My accent, rang true through the silence of the room.

"You—" she gasped, "Wait!" Her hands moved to the latches on the box, fumbling with them as I walked away from her, intent on leaving her before she had proof of what she was sure she knew.

I crossed the large room and made it to the door as I heard the heavy weight of the privacy contraption hit the side of the bench as she freed herself.

Someday, I'd look back and kick myself for doing it. Someday, probably very soon, I'd regret giving in and giving myself up but as I crossed the threshold to the private hallway exiting the suite, I glanced over my shoulder and found her liquid lava eyes locked on me as I rounded the frame, losing sight of her completely.

"You fucking bastard!" Her scream of outrage rang down the deserted hallway as I shoved my arms through my shirt sleeves.

Oh Rainbow, you have no idea.

Chapter 16 - Sloane

THE LINE WALKERS

"Earth to the broody Rainbow that's ignoring us!" Trixie's youthful voice cut through the chaos in my mind that had been running rampant for days now and drew me back to the present.

Four pairs of eyes stared at me from around the table and I sighed, shaking off the distractions so I could focus on my friends. "Sorry," I murmured, sitting up in my chair as Raven refilled my mimosa. The only part of waking up on Sundays that I enjoyed was the weekly brunch date we had after busy Saturday nights. "I was distracted."

"About that." Val tilted her head to the side as a smirk danced in her eyes. "You know his e-payments are public, right?"

My blood froze as I stared at her across the table.

He. *Tamen*. The arrogant son of a bitch that deceived me and had sex with me against my will.

I cringed even as that thought crossed my mind, because it was a lie. One that had tried continuously to take root in my head since I saw him leave the room at the private event five nights ago, simply because I was mad.

He didn't have sex with me against my will, I was for hire, and he paid a hefty fucking price to sleep with me. And it wasn't like I was against the act itself; I was literally begging him to do it.

No, the part that I was stuck on was not recognizing it was him while it was happening.

Because I couldn't get him off my mind the entire time, sometimes even imagining him as the John I was enjoying at that time, and it had made me feel sick to my stomach that I was objectifying the act with thoughts of my broody boss. Then he articulated the last thing he said.

And I knew.

I fucking *knew*.

Right before he walked out of the room completely, I got free from the privacy bench and saw him leave, glancing over his shoulder at me with those intense blue eyes before he disappeared completely.

He left so fast, knowing I was on to him, he didn't even put his shirt on, leaving in just his pants.

Dear. Fucking. God.

That man was sinful in a business suit with the parts and pieces of tattoos peeking out above his collar and on the backs of his hands but seeing his exposed back as he fled.

Jesus.

He was covered in delicious black ink and muscles and every time I closed my eyes since that moment; I saw him with the swirly black art and those piercing blue eyes.

I was officially crazed by it.

By him.

Hence why even bottomless mimosas and carb overloaded brunch wasn't keeping my attention.

Val smirked at me again, as I tried to remember all the messages he sent to me via payments since I blocked him every other way.

The night of the private event had been mild, as he threatened me with sexual tension and sass, paying me large amounts of money to unblock him.

And then two days passed after that night before he reached out again. It had been almost four in the morning when my phone pinged with a new payment alert and his veiled message attached.

> *I'd pay the fee twice over again.* + *$1,000.00*

He didn't say sorry. Or apologize for deceiving me. Hell, he didn't even acknowledge that he was an unhinged bastard that slept with me using lies and obvious connections to get what he wanted. Tamen simply threw more money at me with his own deranged version of praise.

Did it mean he liked it? As much as I did?

Because that was the part that kept me up at night.

I loved what he did to my body. I loved the way he made me feel as he controlled the situation. Yet with other men, I usually rolled my eyes in secret and laughed at their pathetic egos when they tried to use fake power against me when they hired me.

Not with him, though. Not with Tamen. With him, I craved it.

"Sloane!" Trixie snapped her fingers dramatically, bringing me back, again. "Are you really going to sit there and act like we aren't watching the most interesting show in the world right in front of us?"

I sighed and took another large sip of mimosa, "I have no fucking clue what's going on, or what you're watching, or what I'm doing." I shrugged, "I'm out of touch over here."

"Damn." Raven whistled, leaning back in her chair to stare at me. "It's always the broken ones that fuck us up the most."

I scoffed with wide eyes, "You're right about that."

"So, what happened between you two?" Val asked, digging for more information. I wasn't one hundred percent sure I could trust her with anything related to Tamen, considering their night together the night he closed down the Den and changed it over to Prism. Not that I cared in the least that they were together physically, that didn't bother me in the least. But I didn't know her feelings toward him, personally or professionally, and I wasn't going to expose mine when I didn't even understand them.

"We hate each other." I shrugged, remembering the last payment he made late last night.

> *I think I hate you as much as you hate me.* + $5,000.00

I didn't hate him nearly as much as I wanted to, but no one needed to know that.

"Hmm." Mya held up her glass to cheers me. "If you have the energy to hate someone, it's because they meant something to you to begin with."

Looking away over the heads of everyone in the restaurant, I noticed a familiar face in the crowd of people outside and got the urge to make myself suffer even more. "It doesn't, actually." I tossed back the rest of my drink and then stood up, laying down money for the drinks and my food on the table. "He's a total stranger to me. It's purely just a case of two auras that can't stand each other or coexist in the same space without fighting for control. I'll see you girls later."

"Go ahead," Val called out as I walked away, "Leave when things get difficult, that's your specialty. Good thing we love you anyway!"

Clearing the front door of the restaurant, two matching pairs of green eyes found me and I gave a gentle wave. "Hi."

Peyton and Olivia both smiled brightly at me as they waited for me to catch up to them up the street.

"We were just talking about you." Peyton said.

"Oh?" I asked cautiously.

"We were talking about how Tamen is more grumpy than usual." Olivia shrugged, "Figured maybe you had something to do with that."

"Oh." I deflated as my cheeks bloomed red. "Sorry."

Peyton rolled her eyes and weaved her arm through mine, walking down the sidewalk and taking me with her as Olivia walked on my other side. "We didn't say it was a bad thing. We actually approve of you torturing him. More than approve, we want to help."

"More torture. Definitely more torture." Olivia grinned, and I felt like a sacrificial lamb walking between two guards on the way to the altar. "Did you know Tamen's afraid of spiders?"

"And heights." Peyton added as I fought the urge to chuckle at their tactics. "Ooh," Peyton cheered excitedly, looking around me at her sister. "And Dolly."

"Dolly?" I stammered, so lost, but had a feeling they were going to tell me so much more about Tamen if I stayed with them.

"The Feral Post Office Lady." Olivia clarified, but I was still so lost. "I'm sure he wouldn't tell us if she did, but I think she held him hostage one time. Nobody heard from him for days after that night."

"I'm so confused." I giggled, shaking my head.

"That's okay." Peyton patted my arm and winked. "Do you have any plans today?"

"None."

"Good. Then you can join us on our monthly girl day, and we can corrupt you."

"Hmm," I shrugged, "Usually it's me doing the corrupting. I don't usually meet women who are darker than me."

Peyton tipped her head back and laughed boldly. "Oh girl. You're wrapped up with a Line Walker now, you've got a lot to learn about darkness."

THE LINE WALKERS

I held my sides, trying desperately to not let sparkling water shoot out of my nose as Olivia tipped her head back and cackled loudly at Peyton's impersonation of her husband Dane running through a dark corn field years ago. I still couldn't wrap my head around a little old lady causing such mischief in a small town, but from the sounds of it, she had a thing for the hunky men.

The Line Walkers, as Olivia, kept referring to them.

Dane, Maddox, and Tamen.

Of course, there were no specifics given to me, but the way the two sisters looked at each other and kind of shrugged, sidestepping around certain topics, I was sure it was illegal.

Dark, even.

Which would fit with the brokenness I had seen in Tamen that night in the parking lot when he pinned me to the wall. The same night I held the shiny, incredibly sharp knife I found in his belt to his chest and took back control of the situation.

Before he stole that control back from me at the private event.

My phone pinged from the table, and I glanced down at it, skimming the message on the screen.

> *You get on my last nerve. + $5,000.00*

"Another one?" Olivia gasped, leaning over the screen to read it. "Damn, what's the grand total up to?"

Blowing out a breath I shrugged, "Today? Probably over thirty grand." I sighed and locked my phone screen. "He's going to run out of money eventually, right?"

Peyton snorted. "No. The man can turn dust bunnies into cash. It's quite annoying, but also obnoxiously fun to watch."

"I don't need his money. I'm not Tamen level rich, obviously, but I do just fine on my own. It was just a joke at first, but now he's relentless."

"Give a dog a bone—" Olivia sang and then leaned forward on her elbows. "There's more between you two than just work, that's obvious." She tilted her head to the side, "But I can't tell how much more than that. You're a hard nut to crack, Sloane."

I scoffed and looked away from her penetrating stare. "I'm an open book, actually. Maybe it's a hazard of the job, I don't keep much secret or hidden, I don't see the point."

"Then is it more than just a game of cat and mouse with Tamen?" Peyton questioned, "Because I want to think that maybe he's found someone to put him in his place and boss him around, besides Olivia," Her sister snorted and Peyton went on, "But I can't tell if it's just fun for you."

I blew another breath out, and rounded my eyes. "I can genuinely say with one hundred percent certainty that I hate that man. He aggravates me with every single breath he takes. My skin crawls when he tilts his head to the side in that creepy mocking mannerism that makes him look like a clown in a haunted house." My teeth clenched as I held my hands out in front of me, mimicking what it would look like to strangle him. "I want to bang his head off the wall every time he undercuts me and demeans my intelligence at work, like I haven't earned my place with more than my body. And that ego," I groaned, "God, I want to cut him so quick he can never act all high and mighty ever again. I want to scramble his brain up in a pan and put it back in his skull so he can act like an actual nice human being for once, just once in his life."

Sighing, I blinked away the rage and then froze when I saw the look on their faces, aimed my way.

"But you also want to tie him down and do indecent things to him until you can't walk straight." Peyton mused with a cautious smirk on her face, breaking the tension inside of me that built thinking I'd offended them by talking about him that way.

"God, I'd ride that man until the sun came up and went back down again." I cried, deflating even more and giving into the urge to tell them the truth about the turmoil building between their brother-in-law and me. "We hooked up, kind of, one time. It was the best sex of my life and now I can't think of anything else, but I can't decide if I want to strangle him or fuck him."

Olivia shrugged nonchalantly, "I vote that you strangle him while you fuck him. I think that's the only way to tame that beast. Isn't there an old saying about biting an alpha dog in the ear to show him who's boss?" Peyton cackled again, and Olivia went on, unphased by our hysterics. "I feel like that's the only way to get Tamen reset. Maybe it'll be like hitting Control - Alt - Delete."

Laughing so hard, I wiped away tears and doubled over in pain. I was supposed to go to the gym later, but after lunch, my abs were going to be toast.

"I have an idea." Peyton gasped, picking her phone up off the table, "Come here."

"Huh?" I stammered, fighting the tilt a whirl in my brain from the sudden change in direction.

"Come here," She scooted her chair closer to Olivia's and patted her shoulder. "Chin, right here."

"Okay," I gave into my curiosity and walked around the table, leaning down behind them and when she pulled her phone out to snap a picture I posed, smiling brightly along with the two. "Okay, explain."

"I want to test a theory." Peyton said, typing something into her phone and then laying it down with a smug look on her face. "My theory says that in about ten seconds, my phone is going to ring. And I'm going to ignore it. Then Olivia's phone is going to ring. And she's going to ignore it. And then you're going to get another money transaction, though the message accompanying it will be far less vague."

"I think I see where this is going." I mused, not sure if I loved the idea, or hated it.

"And then my guess is before we finish our desserts, one very hot and horny Tamen is going to show up here, and he's going to have to face you head on. But we're here, so he won't get away with any funny business."

"And how exactly will he know where we are?" I pondered, working through her brain.

"Easy." Peyton shrugged, "Finding people is my husband's specialty. And he can hardly ever tell his little brother no these days."

"Except that one time Dane shot the tippy top of Tamen's ear off for sneaking into your guest house." Olivia chuckled and my mouth dropped in shock.

"Shot?" I stammered, "Like with a gun?"

"Two actually." Olivia held both her hands up and made finger guns with them, pretending to shoot them at me and then blew at the barrels like an old western cowboy.

"Jesus." I passed on my water and picked up my mostly untouched glass of wine. "I think I need to hear more about that story."

Before the words were out of my mouth, Peyton's phone went off with an obnoxious ringtone that sounded like the theme song from a 90s slasher movie. "Show time." She smirked and hit the ignore button. "Time to see how much groveling that man can do."

Chapter 17 - Tamen

"Sir, do you have a reservation?"

The host called out to me as I walked through the front doors of the restaurant I tracked Sloane to. "Don't be a cunt." I threw over my shoulder at him and continued on.

I didn't know where she was, but she was here and I was going to find her.

And then I was going to drag her out by her pretty rainbow hair and get her as far away from my sisters-in-law as possible. If I didn't, then I'd lose my spot in our family. She'd take it right out from under me.

"Ah, took you far longer than I thought it would." A female voice called out from my side and I glared at Peyton, where she leaned up against the bar. I stopped, looking around for the other two cohorts in the 'Piss Tamen Off' plan of hers. "I'm almost surprised you weren't here in mere minutes."

Putting my hands on my hips, I glared at her deeper, "I was hunting."

Her eyes flicked to the crowd of customers around us before nodding her head for me to join her at the bar. She had a glass of wine in front of her and leaned her elbow on the bar top as I gave in and stood in front of her. "Who were you hunting?"

"Does it matter?" I snapped.

Her green eyes rounded slightly, but not in fear. Peyton didn't fear me, she was probably the only woman out there that didn't on occasion. Well, not since I broke into her guest house, unknowingly.

"It does." She tipped her head back, staring down her nose at me. "Dane says you've been quite preoccupied with hunting lately." She watched me closely, "He said he hasn't seen you this busy since right after Harlow House."

I rolled my eyes and looked at the bartender as he came up to us. "Scotch. Top shelf." He turned away to pour my drink, and I looked back to Peyton. "Has he finally divulged his secrets to you about Harlow House?" Her teeth bit into her lip as anger flared in her eyes, but nothing else outwardly gave away her true feelings about Dane's inability to tell her about his childhood. Yeah, well, like hell were we going to talk about my past if he would not talk about his. "Didn't think so."

"You slept with Sloane." She countered, and my skin prickled with anxiety as I stared down at the closest thing to a female family member I had in decades. Did she know the depth of that story, or just the surface level information about it?

"Are you suddenly interested in who I fuck?" I argued, "Is Dane not entertaining you at Hartington and now you need to fill your entertainment with my dick?"

"Knock it off." She hissed, leveling her finger at me as the bartender laid my drink down. My stomach rolled at her anger, hating that I took the low blow to begin with. Sighing, she took a drink from her wine as

I did the same off my scotch. "What's different about her? And before you try to tell me there isn't, just don't. Because I'm not an idiot, and I know that you've retreated to darkness to deal with something emotional. Even Dane and Maddox have noticed how often you've worked jobs lately. And it all started right after you took over Prism."

"It's an expensive take over." I brushed it all off, making excuses already paraphrased in my head. "The extra income helps with the remodel."

She stared at me for so long I had to look away. "I think that's the first time you've ever lied straight to my face."

Something akin to pain crossed her green irises before she blinked it away and looked out over the crowd. But I remained silent, because she was right. It had been a lie.

Everything felt like a lie.

Finally, I gave in, "I—tricked her." Sighing, I went on, "Into bed."

Peyton's eyebrows rose slightly as she took another sip of wine. "I thought you were irresistible to women everywhere. Why'd you have to trick her?"

I scoffed and cracked my neck. "Because she hates me as much as I hate her."

"But the chemistry doesn't care."

"Nope." I let a big breath out. "But it doesn't matter. Because it can't happen again. It won't."

"Why?" She questioned, "I can tell just by looking at the two of you that it wasn't as if the sex was bad. So, what else is it?"

Finally, I held her stare, even if it made my skin crawl to do so. I hated eye contact. I found it incredibly frustrating how effortlessly I picked up on the subtle nuances of other people's emotions, a silent language written in the depths of their eyes, their vulnerability a burden I couldn't escape. But for P, I'd endure. "Because I'm me. And I've never been safe to be around."

"You're around us and we're just fine." She countered instantly, almost like she believed that.

Scoffing, I tipped back the rest of my drink, swallowing down the expensive liquor that deserved to be sipped. "None of you have left my presence without scars. Ever. Every single one of you bears the mark of my curse."

"What is your curse?" She leaned in, intending to get the information out of me I swore I'd take to my grave.

A flash of color caught my eye over her head, and I pinpointed Sloane, where she walked around the corner with her arm twined with Liv's, laughing together. Every head in the restaurant turned to the melodic sound of her laugh, entranced by it, just like I was.

"I chose this life." Although I kept staring at Sloane, I replied to Peyton. "I chose the darkness, I walked into it willingly and never thought twice about the consequences."

"How is that a curse?" She asked, and I glanced down at her for a second before my body involuntarily went back to staring at Sloane.

"I can't un-choose it. I can't go back, and I can't get out. The darkness owns me because when I was merely a babe, I made a deal with the devil, and I'll never earn my happiness because of it."

As if Sloane could sense me staring at her, the amber glow of her eyes found mine across the crowd as I memorized every little part of her. She wore a pastel pink shirt, ripped white jeans, and gold strappy sandals.

Sloane was angelic. She was perfection.

And I was evil. I was broken.

Good and evil didn't belong together. They were made to battle each other, constantly fighting for control and power over those they inhabited.

"Tamen—" Peyton's sad voice cut through the spell, and I looked away from Sloane as she joined us, stopping Peyton from whatever inspirational sisterly thing she was about to say. I turned my back on them, unable to face the consequences of my actions face to face as I ordered another drink. It was a mistake for me to give into my anger and desire to keep Sloane far away from the only slice of peace I found for myself in my family. Now I was stuck in her perfect presence, once again coming up short of deserving to be.

Liv's snarky attitude added the cherry to the top of my self-loathing sundae. "Holy shit, it worked. You said Beetlejuice three times and Tamen showed up."

"Cut it out." Peyton snapped, "Just," She stammered, "Give it up, Liv."

"Whoa," Olivia's shock echoed through the crowded restaurant behind me.

As Sloane slid in beside me, she touched my arm and leaned around me, forcing her face into my sightline. "Hey, are you okay?"

"Why are you here?" I hissed, staring down at her. I felt raw and on edge, and that familiar call to the darkness beckoned in my mind.

Sloane's gold eyes widened at my tone, but she replied calmly. "I ran into them, and they invited me to join them for girl's day."

"You don't have other friends? Friends that aren't my family?"

I watched as a different persona slid over her features and she riled up at my question, "I do, but you've slept with all of them. So, I figured I'd hang out with the only two girls in the city that can't say that."

Smiling to myself as her bite fed at that self-loathing loser inside of me, I snapped back, "Do my sexual encounters bother you that much?"

"They didn't until I faked my way through a tiresome ten minutes with you." She flicked her hair over her shoulder, "I kind of lose my appetite for someone after something like that happens."

She turned to walk away, and I sidestepped her, boxing her in against the bar. It wasn't overly aggressive, but her lips parted, and her eyes flared with anger as she bent backwards to stare up at me. I knew Olivia and Peyton were standing right beside us within earshot, so I leaned down around her face and ran my nose up the side of her face, not touching her anywhere else, and whispered in her ear.

"Nice try, Rainbow. But I can still taste the sweet flavor of your orgasm on my tongue." Her ragged breaths against my neck showed her futile attempt to control her response. She was as fucked as I was when it came to physical chemistry. "I can still feel the way you dug your nails into my skin, branding me as you came all over my cock, begging for more."

Sloane snorted and pushed me away, breaking the connection I had desperately needed for days now, "Wrong." She huffed, staring up at me again, "Those are secrets of the trade, meant to make men like you think you're the best I've ever had." She stepped forward, and I took a step back as she raised her finger to my chest, digging her dainty black painted nail into my sternum. "The night before you, another man thought he was just as special as you did. And an hour after you left, another man swore my praises to the sky as he claimed every inch of me that you had touched right before that. You're not special. This is just a game. It doesn't mean anything."

Red.

I saw fucking red.

Imagining her letting another man touch her after I left that night burned every bit of control I had left inside, and I stepped back into her space. I would bend her over the bar right in the middle of the upscale city bar we were in to take back my claim on her, if that's what she needed to be reminded that I was the boss.

"Whoa, whoa, whoa." Peyton hissed, stepping between us and glaring at us both. "Okay, we get it. You two like to fuck each other like rabbits while pretending that you hate each other."

"We do hate each other." Sloane and I both barked out at P in unison.

"*Right.*" She droned on, pushing me back and patting my chest. "And the Feral Post Office Lady is harmless. Both are almost believable for half a second until you get close enough to see the truth. But by then, it's too late, you're in the clutches of fate by that point."

"Do not mention that untamed geriatric bobcat in my presence ever again." I snapped and Liv snickered, drawing my glare her way.

"Anyway," Peyton slid her arm through Sloane's, who looked smug as my sister-in-law once again continued to invite her into our circle. "We're headed to Duffs for wings." Even simply mentioning the rough sports bar down the street had my annoyance level already rising.

"What is that, three bars in one afternoon?" I chided.

Liv flicked the side of my face with her fingernail, "Careful what you say, mister, or I'll call Dane and have him turn off your tracker." When I gave her my attention, she raised her eyebrows at me and nudged me along after the other two. "Yeah that's right, I know all about your Mr. Hot and Cold mind fuck you've got going on with her. So act right, take us out for dinner, and then you can start winning her over the right way."

"I'm not trying to win anyone over." I argued, but she waved me off.

"Rory likes her."

"Gah," I cringed at the maternal influence she was trying to use on me. "Fuck off." She chuckled, drawing Sloane's side eye over her shoulder to me. "Whatever. But if anyone tries to do shots, I'm out." I droned, already knowing there was no way I was letting the girls go out alone. Especially not Sloane.

Which meant I was on the hook to endure the evening out with all three.

Yay me.

Chapter 18 - Sloane

THE LINE WALKERS

I giggled. Again.

God, I hated giggling. Yet around Peyton and Olivia, I couldn't stop it. Especially when they were picking on Tamen to make me laugh. It didn't hurt that Tamen didn't act like the stick in the mud he usually did when his sisters-in-law picked on him.

Since we got to the loud sports bar and found a table in the corner to sit down and people watch from, he had been almost—likeable.

Sure, don't get me wrong, unfortunately I had always actually liked Tamen. But my like for him was usually outdone by my irritation with him and his snarky, pompous attitude. It was like one minute I'd be intrigued by his brilliant business savvy mind and plans, and then the next I'd want to beat him over the head with a vase for something he said in the very same breath.

It was wild to have such a swinging pendulum of emotions around a man for me. And tonight he was holding that pendulum to one side.

The side where I actually liked him.

Or tolerated him, maybe.

Watching him interacting with Peyton and Olivia, with actual affection and caring even through his crass and sass, was making it impossible to want to pummel him.

Fuck him, yes. Pummel him, no.

And God, did I want to fuck him. But I wouldn't. Nope. I could not sleep with Tamen Bryce.

Ever again.

The man had starred in every fantasy I had when I closed my eyes since that night at the private event, maybe even before all of that. But since knowing his touch, knowing how my body reacted to him physically, not just mentally, left me unable to think of anything else.

Maybe I was just ovulating and desperate for dick, or something else. It didn't change the fact that I was horny for Tamen Bryce.

"Okay," Peyton slapped her hand on the table and giggled when a piece of popcorn shot out from under it and hit Liv in the nose. "We have to leave before we get a drunk in public ticket."

"How are you getting back to Hollowbrook?" Tamen asked with a smart mouth glare. Did that make sense to anyone but my drunk brain? It was like I could hear his glare.

"I figured we'd jump on our brooms and fly back, duh." Liv rolled her eyes as Peyton checked her phone.

"Dane is here to drive us home. How are you getting home?" She asked, looking over at me, and I hiccupped like a fool.

"Uber." I drank another sip of water. "I'm good."

Peyton laughed and rolled her eyes, "Oh, I'm sure." The girls stood up and waved goodbye as they giggled and weaved their way out of the crowded restaurant. As soon as they were gone, the loud cheers and noise from the merry crowd faded away to a buzzing noise in my ears. Tamen stared at me from his spot across the table, over the rim of his glass as he finished his drink.

The silence between us built, lingering longer and longer as we just stared. Finally, I caved and gave in. "Okay, I'm leaving. Thank you for a weird but entertaining afternoon."

"Sit down."

Nothing more. Just one command consisting of two words. There wasn't even a change to his facial expression as he said it.

"Why?"

"Because you refuse to communicate with me in any other way. So while I have you here tonight, I have things to say."

"Is that what the other night was?" I snapped, letting my buzz talk for the emotionless girl that pretended not to care for hours. "Did you stumble upon me there and say, 'What the hell, while I have her here'?"

"You don't believe that, so don't play dumb." He countered, finally leaning forward on the table between us to level me with his dominating gaze.

"I don't know what to believe when it comes to you, Tamen. Nothing ever adds up or makes sense. Every time I think that maybe for one second, I might actually have a peg on you, you flip the script, do a complete one eighty in personality and leave me dumbfounded."

"Why do you care?"

Scoffing, I let my built-up anger seep out of my lips. "Because you forced your way into my life! You bought the Den and then demanded that I play a role in your reopening. You demand, demand, demand, demand, until I have no choice but to comply! And when I don't, you threaten me and those that I work with to get what you want. You're like a spoiled little brat with all the money and power in the world to make everyone bend to your will! And the other night was a perfect example of how far you'll take things to serve yourself!"

He watched me with those piercing blue eyes for a while before he finally blinked and broke the silence. "I won't apologize for sleeping with you. You were for hire, and I hired you. Paid bloody damn well for your time, too." He started and my mouth fell open at how out of touch he was when he held his hand up to silence me before continuing. "But I shouldn't have hidden my identity from you to do it."

I snapped my mouth shut so hard my teeth clanked, and I fell back into my back rest. "No. You shouldn't have."

"Trust should be something you always have with your clients. And I broke that by lying."

"You did." I deflated even more, shocked by his admissions. Wasn't that all I wanted from him all week long? Validation that what he did and how he did it was wrong?

Then why the hell did it feel lacking now that I had it?

Still holding my stare, he rested both elbows on the table and tilted his head to the side. "But like I said, I won't apologize for finally breaking that tension between us and pushing us both into ecstasy. Because I haven't felt that kind of high in years," His pupils dilated until the blue was a thin line around the black inky depths. "And I'm guessing by the marks in my flesh that still burn when I think of you, that it was just as different for you. Despite whoever you let touch you after me."

"I didn't." I shook my head slowly, letting the alcohol rule my lips instead of my brain. "No one has touched me since. Not since I met you." He growled, the darkness of it matched everything about him I knew so far. "Show me."

"What?"

"The marks I left on you." I swallowed, "Show them to me." He leaned back in his chair, tempted but unconvinced. "Please, Tamen."

"Fuck it." He hissed, giving in to my pleas, and pulled me to my feet before dragging me through the crowded party scene at a breakneck pace.

I had provoked the bear, and I knew what was about to happen, even though I was buzzing like a light socket and high on the sexual chemistry of being in Tamen's presence all night long.

There was no turning back for me. No stopping it. No changing my mind.

I wanted whatever I was about to get.

Tamen shoved his way through the bar and out the exit without a word spoken, and when we made it to the dark parking lot, I could think of nothing more than the need burning inside of me.

This should have been how our first time together went. It should have been raw and rushed, hungry and angsty, ruled by need and excluding thought.

This was us.

"Come here." His husky voice cut through the darkness as he spun me around and pushed my back against a dropped ladder from a fire escape in a dark alley. There was an old outdoor light behind me, giving him an ethereal glow that highlighted the sharp angles of his features. "You want to see my scars, Rainbow?"

"Only the ones I gave you." I panted as he caged me in, pressing the front of his body against mine.

"Do you think I have any others?" I could make out the glow of his smirk in the darkness as he lurked over me.

"Dozens." I whispered as he took my hand in his and slid it under his shirt to his hard abdomen and I let my fingers trail over the ridges of his abs. "You're the kind of guy that doesn't go through life without getting marked by it."

He chuckled and then reached up behind his head and pulled his long sleeve sweater off over his head, revealing his upper body to my eyes. Immediately, I soaked in every defined muscle in his shoulders and thick arms, down to the veins that protruded under the thick black ink that covered every inch.

"Here, Rainbow." He guided my hand to his side, curling my fingers into claws as he ran them over the raised scrapes that were healing. My heart felt like it was going to explode in anticipation as he flattened my palm against his stomach and rubbed it up to his strong, defined chest. "And here." I dug my nails in over the marks that I could just barely feel under my fingertips.

"Damn." I licked my lips, and his eyes fell to them as I leaned forward and ran my tongue over one particularly deep gash, running straight to his nipple and bit it. His fingers buried themselves into my hair, tightening, and we both groaned. "This is how it should have been, Tamen."

"I know." He growled, tipping my head back with the hand in my hair, and his lips hovered right over mine. "I know." He hadn't kissed me before. The man had fucked me and ate my pussy like a sweet, delicious treat, but he had never kissed me. For some reason, I hesitated to lean in for it too, because it felt personal. And I wasn't sure I was ready to be that personal with him. Finally, he moved my hand to the center of his chest and pressed my forefinger over a scar that was deeper than the others, more raised and tactile.

Jesus. It was from the cut I gave him with his knife that first night in a dark parking lot. His display of all the places I'd branded him left me soaked and aching.

"Thank me for them." I purred, repeating a phrase so similar to the one he demanded of me when I was unaware of his identity at the event. "Thank me for leaving my mark on you."

I didn't think he would, in fact, I was sure he'd throw some power move over me to regain control of the situation.

His hot breath tickled my lips as his fingers expertly pulled the button on my jeans apart and slid the zipper down, all the while his eyes stayed locked on mine. My heart raced as he slipped both hands in at the sides of my jeans and pushed them and my panties down while he whispered, "Thank you, Rainbow." I didn't breathe as he pushed my pants to my ankles and off one foot before gently forcing me to sit back on the ladder step as he slowly sank to his knees in front of me. "Thank you so much for branding me with your touch."

It was like everything was happening in slow motion as he pushed my thighs apart and brought his lips to my wet center. I didn't get to watch him the last time he did this to me, and now I felt cheated out of it. Because watching Tamen Bryce feast on me was a sight to behold.

The man had a talented mouth.

Sweet, mother divinity, he was good at that.

"Yes." I hissed, grabbing the railing for support as I arched into him, dragging my nails down the back of his scalp to hold him tighter to me. Tamen growled and bit my clit before sucking it into his mouth.

I rode his face, crying out in ecstasy as I came on his tongue, I realized that my broken Duke got off on pain. Between my marks on his skin and the way he nuzzled into my tight hold on his hair, he loved the burn of pain as he pleased.

He also was a giver, which was not expected at all.

Was he a giver with all of his past partners, or was there something different about our dynamic that made him fall to his knees? Shaking my head, I brushed that thought away as he kissed my inner thigh, looking up at me from under hooded lids.

"Good boy." I praised and his body shuddered before he rose to his feet, once again towering over me as I dropped my feet to the step under my ass and sat up straight. I refused to fall beneath his power as he tried to exert it to prove he could.

He wiped his lips with his hand and lowered his face right above mine again, so I tipped it back to match. "If anyone else muttered those words to me, they'd bleed for it."

I smirked and seductively ran my nails up the tightly restrained bulge in his jeans I knew would be there, waiting for my touch. "Yet they make you drip when they come from me, don't they?"

"Guess that means we're both dripping tonight." He countered, unable to let his ego go long enough to appease me.

"Do something about it." I challenged, shaking my disheveled hair over my shoulder and hooking my bare leg around his, pulling him into my body the last inch.

"Here?" He smirked, glancing around us like suddenly a public alley wasn't suitable for fucking me.

I shrugged and pushed him back a step. "What? I've already got lines in my ass from the steps, if we change positions now, it can look like a waffle fry when we're done."

He snorted and shook his head, but pulled me up off the step and turned me to face it. "Feet up here." Taking my ankle, he lifted one foot up onto a step near my waist and I put the other one next to it, holding onto the railing for support while he kept me from standing up. I was in a weird, squatted stance with my feet spread apart, but as he pulled his zipper down behind me, I understood the game. "You want me to fuck you, Rainbow?" He asked against my ear as he tore a condom open.

Every noise was more powerful as they hit my ears. The noise of his jeans as he pushed them down, the slide of the condom as he rolled it on, the traffic on the busy city street a few hundred yards away, the erratic beating of my heart when he effortlessly lined up with my soaked entrance.

I turned my face against his, so my lips brushed his cheek as he ran the head of his cock through my arousal, coating it. "If you don't, I'll go find someone else to do the job you started."

His swift and forceful movement interrupted my words as he entered me in one abrupt and deep thrust. He was so tall; he didn't have to move at all as he pulled my hips back toward him and pushed inside of me. I couldn't let go of the railing, or I'd fall into him, and I wasn't willing to do that.

Instead, I held on for dear life as he pushed me forward again, forcing my feet further apart so I was more open to his intrusion. "Careful, Rainbow." He hissed against my ear as I moaned unashamedly. "Or my chaos will break free and wash away your pretty little colors."

"Mmh," my head fell back against his shoulder, and he bit my earlobe as I gave into the urge to lean into him. "Whatever you say, Tamen. Just don't stop fucking me. Don't ever stop."

It was probably the realest I had ever been with the man, brushing painfully close to pathetic and needy, but I couldn't stop the words as his punishing thrusts rocked my body perfectly. The big bulbous head of his cock pressed against my G-spot with every thrust, and he knew it.

"Tell me something no one else knows." He whispered in my ear, reaching under my leg to run the pads of his fingers over my swollen clit. God, he knew every secret to my body's pleasure, and I edged toward an orgasm that would leave him triumphant as I crumbled in his arms.

"No." I shook my head deliriously, "That's not what this is."

"Would you tell me if I begged?" He countered, slowing his thrusts and giving me only that thick, flared head repeatedly. "Or should I praise you to get what I want? Which route will make you squirt for me when you come, pretty girl?"

"Fuck." I moaned, tightening my hold on the railing as I fought the comfort I got from the heat of his body against mine.

"Mmh," He pushed my chest forward, so I was bent over more, presenting better for him. "I bet it's the praise." Gathering a handful of my hair in his fist, he slammed in deep, holding me still by my hair so I didn't topple forward into the stairs and bust my face as he fucked me hard. "Good girl, Rainbow. You listen to me so bloody well. You know exactly what to do to make me happy."

"Tamen." I cried, trying to bring my feet together to relieve the pressure on my g-spot that was going to make me squirt, just like he had demanded me to do. "You're a bastard."

He chuckled, and then spanked my ass cheek powerfully, before wrapping one hand around the front of my throat with the other still in my hair, holding my head down so I had no choice but to take his punishing cock. "Actually, I'm the legitimate son. But you bring out the worst in me." His tone changed to a dark, harsher voice as he bit my ear once more, bending over my back. "Come on my cock, Sloane. Give me what I fucking want."

"God!" I screeched, losing control of my body as he dominated me and I fell headfirst into a cataclysmic orgasm, riding the waves of pleasure as I gave him what he wanted.

"Not even close, baby." He grunted and then pulled out, seconds before the scorching hot spray of his come covered my ass and lower back. "Not even close."

I hung my head between my arms, gasping for breath, and then shimmied to lower my knees to the stairs, relieving the ache in my hips. I looked over my shoulder when he ran his finger across my ass, rubbing the come he covered me with into my skin. "Why do you do that? I'm not a canvas, you know. It's gross."

"Would you prefer I mark your skin in a more brutal way?" He asked, wiping my skin with his discarded shirt before pulling my pants back up so I could turn around and sit down. My white jeans were destroyed by the grimy fire escape and ground, but it was worth it for the ecstasy I got in exchange.

"Like what? Cutting me open with your spiky dagger?" I scoffed, raising one brow at him as he rolled his eyes at me.

"Funny." He droned, "You're not into receiving pain. So, I use a painless brand."

I crossed my arms over my chest and squinted at him. "You can't brand something that isn't yours."

"Sure." He nodded, and pulled his keys from his pocket, seconds before the headlights on his sporty car flashed in the lot at the end of the alley. "Whatever you say, Rainbow."

"God," I stood up, adjusting my clothes as my irritation with him started building again in place of the connection we had a moment ago. "Stop calling me that."

"Make me." He put his hands in his pockets and stared me down.

"You're insufferable." I shoved past him on the way to his car, considering I had no intention of getting into a stranger's car looking like I just got wrestled on a soccer field in April. Instead, I'd get into the Devil's car and make him drive me home after being the one to make me look that way.

Maybe I'd let him do it again before kicking him to the fucking curb once and for all when I got home.

Maybe.

Chapter 19 - Tamen

THE LINE WALKERS

There was a fantastic chance she'd shoot me.

I wasn't worried about stabbing, hitting, or any other hand to hand injuries, because I was faster and stronger than her. But firearms, on the other hand, she could most definitely get to me with a bullet before I could dodge it.

Did Sloane have a firearm in her apartment that was decorated with pink pastel wallpaper and gold furniture?

She probably had a bloody bazooka, knowing her.

I looked away from my laptop screen where I had been placing liquor orders for the last two hours and glanced at my watch—again. How on earth did someone sleep until two in the afternoon? It was unnatural.

As if my annoyed thoughts summoned her, a door clicked down the hallway and I looked over the top of my laptop as my disheveled Rainbow stumbled out of her pitch-black bedroom, bouncing her shoulder off the frame in the process. Her hair was tied up in some sort of silk bonnet my grandmother would have worn, and she wore a t-shirt eight sizes too big with the picture of some ugly frowning cat on the front of it. To tie the pathetic outfit together, a pair of pink bunny slippers on her feet scuffed against the wood floor as she shuffled her way toward me with her eyes screwed shut and her hands on the walls to guide her.

Sloane was a menace to her own safety.

Silently, I closed my laptop and watched the train wreck move through her apartment, stubbing her toe on the chair at the island and nearly taking her closed eye completely out of her head with the handle of the upper cupboard she opened blindly. As she reached for a coffee mug with her eyes still closed, the potential for disaster made me restless. The clinking of mugs and the quiet hum of the refrigerator were almost deafening in the tense silence.

"Is there a reason you won't open your eyes?" I asked, and on cue, her amber eyes shot open as a terrified scream ripped from her lips.

She found me sitting on her couch with my feet up on the coffee table and sagged briefly in relief before her favorite emotion to throw my way took over.

Rage. Her rainbow aura was red now.

"What the hell are you doing in my apartment?" She screeched, "How did you get in?" She glanced at the front door, that was shut and locked, before she continued on, hardly pausing long enough to take a breath. "Did you break my door? What is wrong with you? How am I going to lock out the crazies of this city if you break down my fucking door!"

"How am I supposed to answer any of those questions if you don't ever shut up long enough for me to speak?" I yawned, unimpressed, rising to my feet as I walked toward her. She tightened her lips and crossed her arms over her bare tits beneath the frowning cat, "God, that shirt is dreadful."

"Get out!" She snapped one arm out toward the door, and I tried to ignore the way her free tits swung under the shirt.

Tried.

"Stop it." I closed the distance between us and grabbed the mug off the shelf behind her, caging her into the counter exactly like I had two nights ago on the fire escape. Before she ghosted me. *Again*. "You're going to make your neighbors believe you're in danger in here with all that screeching."

"You bastard." She shoved me and took the mug from my hand, huffing and turning to her coffee maker. "Get out."

Placing my hands on each side of her on the counter, I leaned down so she could feel my body heat against her back and took a deep inhale of her scent at her neck. Her hands froze, halfway through programming her fancy machine as her breath hitched when I brushed my lips against her lower ear. "We both know you'd rather I gave you orgasms for your midday meal, instead."

"Why are you here?" She whispered, returning to her desired hit of caffeine like I wasn't in her space. "*How* are you here?"

"You ghosted me again." Replying as I watched her expertly work her stand, adding flavor and foam to her cup. "It's rather annoying."

"I didn't realize you had such a fragile ego."

"I didn't realize you were willing to walk away from a career of a lifetime at Prism, just to throw a hissy fit."

She turned and glared at me with her angry golden eyes before facing forward again, like she was choosing not to rile up at my words. "I can't work for you."

"Why?"

"We'll burn the whole place to the ground, on night one. You have to realize that."

"Pyrotechnics have never been my kink of choice. Dane loved to burn shit as a kid, but not me."

She turned in the small space I left for her and held her finished cup of coffee between us as she took a sip. "I'm not even going to touch that comment at this time. Because we need to focus on Prism. And you need to find someone else to do my job. Maybe Mya, or Raven can be manager. They both will work hard, I know it."

"It's non-negotiable, Rainbow. You're the only one that will star on that stage. I built it for you."

The stage that was going to be the epicenter of the club's activities had been kept secret from everyone as it was remodeled and updated. Even from Sloane.

It previously was a little over twenty feet wide, and now it was double. Where there were glass mirrored rooms above it before, there were now balcony style seating areas off each room so the guests could immerse themselves in the theme and event occurring downstairs, while still playing with what they purchased in their own rooms.

My pretty little Rainbow would shine on that stage.

It was hers.

"You hate me." She whispered and then steeled her spine with a little shake of her head, "And I hate you."

"Then what does it matter if we coexist and make truckloads of money together while we hate each other?" I tilted my head to the side, "I think we've both proven that we can get along in short bursts from time to time. We haven't killed each other yet."

Her eyes fell to a hidden spot on my chest beneath my button-up shirt, where she tried to stab me with my own knife. "That could change at any second." Her amber eyes drifted up to mine. "And probably will if we keep pretending."

"Well," I pulled back from her and stood up to my full height, towering over her. "Only one way to find out, Rainbow. Will it be your lightning that kills me, or will it be my darkness that takes you out? Which do you think will happen first?"

Sloane took another sip of her coffee and leaned up off the counter, "Call me Rainbow one more time and I'll show you just how fast lightning can strike." She walked away, back down the hall toward her bedroom without another glance as I stared directly at her lush ass as it swayed with each step under her oversized cat lady shirt. "And get the fuck out of my apartment."

THE LINE WALKERS

I didn't leave her apartment, at least not right away. Instead, I spent the rest of the afternoon working in her living room while she moved around her home, glaring at me every chance she got. At least that was on the rare occurrence that she actually left her bedroom. Sloane acted as though if she hid from me that I'd disappear. At least that was how she had started the day.

Avoiding.

Until it was time for a workout. Some sort of yoga on a sliding bed thing in her living room, to be exact. Then I was a fucking goner and didn't even try to pretend I wasn't staring at her graceful body as she contorted herself for my enjoyment.

Jesus, a man could get used to watching that.

When I did leave, she left *with* me to go to Prism, like such a good girl. Though I refrained from telling her that. I was fairly certain my pretty little Rainbow had a praise kink. At least, that's what I was garnering by the way she came on my cock every time I commended her.

Well, that and the shirt she came out of her room wearing when it was time to leave for Prism.

I had been standing in her kitchen, waiting for her when she came out, fixing her long hair back into a ponytail. As soon as I read the words on her shirt, I choked on my tongue.

"You cannot wear that out in public." I droned, as she paused, looking perplexed, so I nodded to her chest.

"What's wrong with it?"

I read the shirt aloud, "*Don't praise me, I'll cum.*" And glared at her. "That's a ridiculous shirt."

"Yeah," She scoffed, "That's the point. Besides," She winked at me as she grabbed her keys and bag, "It's also incredibly accurate."

And now we were at Prism, and I was watching her in the main lounge and bar area, working the crowd of girls hired and vetted to open Prism at the grand opening night in one week. For a while, I doubted we would have a lineup of girls worthy and capable of working with the elite customers who were already buying memberships faster than my assistant could process the paperwork. But one week out, we had a completed roster, with their trusted Ember back at the head of the crowd, settling the last details about roles, responsibilities and expectations.

I didn't even need to host the party I threatened them with at the beginning, hoping to light a fire under their asses to prove they wanted a spot at my club. They had all buckled down and worked for their position on the list.

Things felt—right. They felt good. Which should have been my first sign that they were going to go wrong, because I had nothing good in my life.

My phone vibrated in my pocket, and I opened the message, reading through the details of the job I took from the cocaine dealer that Sloane had been working for the other night. The man traded her for one job with me.

I got my side of the deal, and it was time for me to pay up. It wasn't as if I wasn't capable of the gig, or even excited by the hunt. But there was something I wanted to do with my evening that didn't include killing drug dealers.

It included tormenting Sloane. It included fucking her as she dug her sharp claws into me again, leaving more marks over my already flared skin.

But again, I didn't get what I wanted most times.

"Is that your booty call for the night?" Sloane asked as she walked around me, glancing down at my phone before I locked it and put it back in my pocket.

"I didn't realize you texted me." I chided, staring her down, "Does that mean you've finally unblocked me."

She snorted, turning away from the dozens of prying eyes actively trying to watch us interact like we were on a dirty daytime television show. "Not a chance."

"Then no, it wasn't my booty call." I replied, avoiding actually answering the question. "I have to leave. Can you handle the rest of this?"

Her eyes rounded dramatically, "You mean I get to pretend I'm actually the manager?"

Now it was my turn to reply dramatically, "Only if you actually bother to show up from now on."

"Whatever. I can handle it."

"Good. I'll see you tomorrow morning for scheduling." I stated, reminding her of our meeting to set up the roster with rooms and clients that were already requesting pre-booking. It was at ten am, which I knew Sloane hated because it was before the time she normally rolled out of bed, but she'd be there.

She was too interested in scheduling the stage acts to let me do it on my own. It was her baby, after all.

"Yeah, I know, boss." She droned on as I backed up and then gave me a salute. "Have fun on your date tonight. Can't wait to hear everything about her."

"Him, actually." I threw back and her eyebrows rose. "Though I'm sure the details of our evening together won't be your cup of tea."

I left the lounge, reveling in the shocked expression on her face as I walked away, knowing that insignificant victory would stick with me for the rest of the night. I was going to need it too, because my night was about to go to shit.

CHAPTER 20 - SLOANE

I looked at my watch again, for the twentieth time since getting to Prism for my ten o'clock meeting with Tamen. Arriving twenty minutes late, fueled by spite for the ungodly meeting time, I found his new office—his proper office, not just a table in a room—empty.

The only place I didn't search for him was the room I was forbidden to enter; my stage room. He kept that entire room a secret, which annoyed me, but if I was honest, it also excited me slightly.

No one ever surprised me with anything, let alone a whole grand theater designed for me to work from. Or at least that was my hope; knowing Tamen though, he probably purposefully designed the entire space so I would hate it. He loved irritating me for fun.

Which was why he was running late to his own meeting, I was sure. Just to irritate me and exert his dominance over me.

But as the clock neared eleven, I wondered if there was something else keeping him away. Last night before he left Prism early, he had a message on his phone, and it wasn't as if he looked overly happy about it. He didn't even rise to the occasion to tease me back when I embarrassingly pried for information about his plans for the evening. Which was very un-Tamen-like.

I paced his office, avoiding the hordes of construction crew members finishing up last-minute projects and continued to catastrophize all the scenarios possible for keeping him away. Rubbing my hands together and then wiping the sweat onto my jeans, I gave into the worry and did something I swore I'd never do.

I unblocked him.

And then I dialed his phone number.

Chewing on my thumbnail as the phone rang and rang, my heart sank further with each trill through the line. And then his voicemail picked up.

"Fuck." I hissed, grabbing my purse off his desk and walking out as the recording started. "If you're fucking with me right now Tamen, I quit. If you're not, you'd better be dead for making me worry. I'm on my way to your hotel."

The entire cab ride a few blocks over to his hotel, I worried myself into a fit.

Tamen was dark; I knew that. He didn't pretend to be normal or sane, not once. Never mind the tidbits of info I had overheard from him or his sisters when we all hung out. There was danger in his life and now that he had gone MIA, I was worried.

God, I hated worrying. Especially over a man.

When I walked to the private elevator leading to his penthouse, the doorman simply nodded to me and swiped his key card to give me access. Did he look worried?

Or was I overthinking?

"Thank you." I nodded, as the doors shut and started the long assent up to the top. "Please don't be dead." I whispered, and then the doors opened.

The last time I had been to the penthouse, it had been bright and open during our meeting, giving the best views of the surrounding city, yet today, darkness met me as I hesitantly walked out into the foyer. "Tamen?"

Silence met my greeting as I made my way toward the large, open living room. I didn't know if he was home or not, but if he was, something was wrong. "Tamen!" I snapped as anxiety grew in my chest.

I pulled my phone from my purse and hesitated, not even sure what I intended to do with it until I pushed Peyton's name and left my thumb hovering over the call button as I ventured deeper into the dark room. "Tamen, are you here?"

I ran my knee into an end table and grabbed the lamp a millisecond before it fell off onto the ground. Flicking the switch and bathing the room in light, I could finally see.

And I wished I couldn't.

"Tamen!" I screamed, covering my mouth in shock and dropping my phone as I found the man in question sprawled out on his stomach across the couch, but hanging halfway onto the floor like he had slid off.

He was wearing only a tight pair of boxers—and blood.

"Oh, my god!" I fell to my knees next to him and pushed his damp hair off his forehead as I leaned over him. "Please, be alive. Please god, be alive."

His face was cut up in different places, and the blood had crusted over, leaving hard lines across his features. He didn't even twitch as I shook him, trying to rouse him. The moment my hand touched his back, as I tried forcing him onto his side, a thick, warm stream of blood welled up from a wound on his shoulder, instantly coating my hand; it felt slick and hot.

And a weak groan slipped from his lips.

"No." I sobbed, my hands shaking as I pulled a plush blanket from a basket on the floor, its texture soft against my fingers, and pressed it to his back. "Tamen, please! Please, you have to wake up. I don't know what to do!"

"Shh." He slurred, turning his face so it was no longer buried in the cushion. "You're ruining my buzz."

"I hate you." I hissed. "Is this a bullet hole?" With trembling hands, I lifted the blanket to find a gaping, circular wound on his back, spilling blood. I slammed the blanket back down, the horrifying sight seared into my memory, praying it would somehow stop the bleeding. "What the fuck happened?"

"Bad day." He grumbled and finally cracked one eye open to look at me. It was so bloodshot I couldn't see any white.

"I have to call for help." I whispered, "I don't know what to do."

He shook his head slightly, "You can't."

"Why? I don't know how to help you. You're bleeding to death!" The sobs wracked my body as I cried in hysterics, a torrent of tears blurring my vision.

"Aw, Rainbow. Worried about me?" He slurred again, closing his bloody eye and going so still I thought he passed back out again.

"I hate you!"

A sarcastic smile graced his bloody face. "Right back at you." With a pained groan, he attempted to sit up, his arm falling limply onto the couch before his body, failing him, slumped forward into me; the smell of his sweat sharp in the air. "Christ, that hurts."

"Please let me call someone. Dane or Peyton, maybe."

"No." He scoffed. "I don't need their judgments."

"You need their *help*!" Holding him up as he once again tried to sit on his own unsuccessfully. I mustered all my strength and shoved him with all my might, sending his large body sprawling back against the couch cushions until he was sitting upright. "*I* need their help!"

"No." He repeated, lifting his chin from his chest where it rested and finally, opened both eyes to look at me. "You can leave; I'll be fine."

"No, you won't." With a shake of my head, I acknowledged the grim reality; his stubborn refusal to seek help would lead to a slow, silent death if I left. "Tell me what to do. Tell me how to help you."

His eyelids drooped, his face pale, and I was terrified he would lose consciousness once more before he let out a shaky sigh and confessed, "You have to remove the bullet so you can stitch the wound."

"Me—" I stammered as my stomach rolled at even the thought of looking at the wound again. "I can't."

"Then I'll bleed to death." His eyes opened again, "I'm honestly surprised I made it this long."

"I hate you!" From the floor, I screamed, wiping my hands down the front of my black dress as I stood. "I hate you, I hate you, I hate you!"

"I know." He coughed, "Now be a doll and go in my bathroom, and get the black leather bag from the closet. Hurry now, I haven't got all day."

I ran to his bathroom, because even though I did hate his fucking guts, especially right now, I was terrified of something bad happening to him. I was terrified of him slipping away while I wasn't there to drag him back from Hell's flames.

If anyone was going to torture Tamen Bryce with pain and suffering for years to come, it was going to me, dammit. Hell didn't get him, not yet anyway.

Sliding across the marble floor into his bathroom, I found the big leather bag that resembled a doctor's bag and ran back to him.

"I got it." I cried, laying it on the floor as he fell back onto the couch, laying on his stomach so I could access the wound. "What do I do?"

"Out of the bag, grab the rolled-up gauze, alcohol, and the long scissor looking tweezers that pinch together at the tip."

My stomach rolled with nausea as my fingers pulled the long tweezers out from the bag and imagined sticking them inside of Tamen's body. But what choice did I have? Gathering the supplies he instructed me to; I laid them out on the floor at my side and then faced him. "I don't know if I can do this."

"I slept with your friend last night." His face squished back into the couch, and he slurred. "Came so hard I nearly went cross-eyed."

"What the fuck is wrong with you?" I screeched angrily. "Who? When?"

"The brunette." He coughed, "The bossy one."

Raven. Fucking bitch!

"I hate you." I hissed, "I should let you die."

"Or you can channel that rage, using the cold, hard metal tool to dig into my bullet wound to get it out, and take it out on me that way."

I grit my teeth, knowing he was fully trying to send me into a manic rage, so I'd play a demented game of *Operation*. "I should puke into your wound, so you get sepsis. Then you'll really suffer."

He chuckled as I pushed the blanket away and stared at the wound. "Is that like gonorrhea? I had that once. That bloody sucked."

"I hate—"

"Yes!" He interrupted, "You hate me, we know. You should diversify your insults, that one is getting boring."

Without even thinking twice, I shoved the tweezers into his back and ignored the disgusting noise they made as they pushed through coagulated blood and flesh. Tamen bit the couch as I dug around to stay quiet. Silently, I worked, trying like hell to find the bullet, without having a clue what it would feel like once I did.

I was nearly hysterical, sweating and fighting the urge to puke, while simultaneously praying to a God that I wasn't sure existed, and planning out how I was going to get itching powder into Raven's G-string on opening night.

Maybe that was how people went insane. Working through high stress moments like the one I was in until they lost their grip on reality and dove straight off the deep end. I could see it.

The end of my tweezers hit something hard, and I paused, trying to tell if it was Tamen's shoulder I was scratching against, or maybe the illusive bullet. "I think I found it."

He released his teeth from the couch and took a deep breath, "Can you carefully try to pull it out?"

"What if it's your brain?" I murmured, "If I pull it out, you'll be even more useless."

He sighed, resting his forehead against the cushion, "Guess there's only one way to find out."

"Hmm." I hummed, and then carefully, trying to not let it slip out of the tweezers, pulled it out of his mangled flesh. "Got it." Holding the flattened bullet up in front of my face, I stared in awe. "All that drama for this little thing?"

He scoffed and looked over his shoulder at the piece of lead. "Care to close me up before I lose any more vital heart lube?"

Rolling my eyes, I dropped the bullet onto the coffee table and looked back into the bag of sadistic tricks to find the suture kit he was talking about, but saw something else that looked faster.

"Got it." I replied, eyeing him up as I poured the alcohol into his wound and wiped away the excess. Tamen was mansplaining to me how to stitch up the wound, like I didn't take sewing in eighth grade

Home Economics class; I even won first place for my quilt pillow that semester. So, as he spoke, I nodded my head and gave the occasional 'Yep, got it' to keep him calm.

"Make sure the stitches are close and tight, but not too tight. The wound needs to be able to breathe—"

The deafening click of the staple gun cut him off as I started closing his wound as aggressively as possible for all the emotional turmoil he had put me through in the last thirty minutes. "Yep, got it." I reassured cheerily.

His growl sounded animalistic, and I smiled bigger as I went. "You." *Staple.* "Fucking." *Staple,* "Cunt." *Staple, staple, staple.*

Let's be clear, the last two were frivolous additions, completely unnecessary to closing the wound. But by the time I was done, I felt *way* better.

"All done." I slapped his back and rose to my feet as he glared daggers at me from his prone position. "Tight, but not too tight. Just like Raven."

"You're insane." He glared at me over his shoulder and then pushed himself up onto his ass again. "Clinically committable."

"I was normal before I met you!" I pointed the stapler at his face and the intrusive thoughts almost won out, leaving him with an extra staple in his forehead, but I dropped it back into the bag before I could tempt that monster anymore. Crossing my arms over my chest, I grimaced as his blood started to crust between my fingers and on the front of my dress. "I might still hurl."

"Come on," He stood up, swaying on his feet and leaning into me heavily before walking us both toward his bedroom. "You can help me get cleaned up."

"I'm not helping you with anything." I snapped, irritated all over again at the entire situation. "Not until you give me some answers."

"Answers." He hummed, walking slowly and falling into the wall until I had no choice but to wrap my arms around his slim waist and help support him as we went. "The sky is blue because of reflections off the oceans. The dung beetle does, in fact, eat dung. And no, Olivia doesn't really like you. She just hates me so much she's willing to pretend."

I paused and glared at him, contemplating dropping him on the floor completely. "Take that back."

He groaned as we started walking into his bathroom and he sighed dramatically, "Fine, I don't know if she likes you or not. But she does *really* hate me."

"Because you hit her sister with a car." I deadpanned, remembering what the girls said that first night.

"Meh," He shrugged, leaning on the stone shower wall as he reached in and turned it on. "Probably has more to do with the fact that I kidnapped her and stood by as a mad doctor tried to cut Rory out of her stomach to sell her. But that's just speculation."

I dropped my arms from him, and he fell forward into the stone, glaring at me. "You did not."

"Did." He shrugged, and then half grimaced, half winked at me as he pushed his boxers down, revealing the cock that I had dreamed about non-stop. Forcing myself to look away, he smirked at me and stepped backwards into the hot spray, sighing. "But in my defense, I didn't know she was Peyton's sister. I never would have allowed anything to happen to P's sister."

I scoffed, flapping my arms out at my sides, at a complete loss. "We'll come back to that later, but I want answers to what the fuck happened to you. Who shot you?"

"Join me and I'll tell you." He countered, placing one hand against the wall and staring at me. It was hard to look at him, still covered in blood and grime, while he simultaneously tried to seduce me in his weird way that kind of worked.

"I don't understand you." I stated plainly, feeling vulnerable by even admitting that.

He apparently felt more vulnerable by that statement, because he responded with a jab. "Even the most educated shrinks don't understand me, Rainbow. I wouldn't expect a hooker to figure me out."

I hated that it hurt.

I hated that at some point, I had allowed him the power to say things to me that hurt.

So instead of joining him in the game where we lob insults and digs back and forth for fun, I turned and walked away.

"Wait!" He called after me and I paused right outside of the bathroom door. "I didn't mean that."

"Yes, you did." I replied, because we both knew the truth.

"I'm cranky." He admitted, sounding tired. "Blood loss has a way of doing that to a man. Even one as invincible as me." Turning, I chanced a look back at him, noting how weak and tired he looked standing there in the large shower, calling for me. "Please stay."

"Why?" I asked, opening myself up for yet another insult, but hoping for something more, anyway.

He shook his head and shrugged slightly, "Because I want you to."

"You'll tell me what happened?" I reiterated, hoping he'd play nicely.

"Yes." He nodded, but held his finger up a second later. "But I don't want you to think that it's going to reveal some big super-secret answer to the inner workings of my brain if I do. Because it won't. Hell, you'll probably just be more confused."

Taking a step back into the bathroom, I pulled the dress up over my hips and then shimmied it up off over my head. "I'll take my chances."

Nudity had never made me feel vulnerable before, or at least not in my adult life. It was why I was so damn good at my job.

But stripping myself bare, for Tamen, even though he had already seen most of me at one time or another, felt powerful. It didn't make me feel powerful like being nude in front of a man usually did. But it felt like the act was powerful.

Raw.

Real.

Kicking my panties to the side, I walked into the shower until we were toe to toe, and his blue eyes traveled back up my bare skin to my face as he spoke. "Thank you."

"For what?" I whispered, caught up in the moment.

"For staying." He tilted his head to the side as he gently slid his fingers through mine, pulling me flush to the front of his body. "For helping me."

"Tell me the truth now." I said, and he smirked as he backed us up into the spray of the shower more fully. He rinsed the blood from his face as I took the cloth off the rack and poured a gallon of soap onto it. It would take more than that to clean his skin of the mess, but it was a good start.

"Well, you see what happened was," He started, pausing to watch me as I started rubbing the cloth across his chest and stomach. "There was this girl, in a glory hole—"

Chapter 21 - Tamen

Did I blame the bullet hole in my back on Sloane? Kind of.

Was she currently wearing one of my shirts and nothing else, sitting on the kitchen island ordering room service? Also, yes.

I'd call that a win.

And a loss, because it was torture having her nearby. The best kind of torture.

She swung her legs back and forth while curling the phone cord around her finger absently as she ordered almost every plate on the menu. She insisted I needed to eat red meat to help build back the blood lost last night, and while she wasn't wrong, I didn't think one ribeye was going to make a big enough difference to go through the trouble.

But I didn't tell her that; having her taking care of me was reason enough to go through with it. And I was so bloody tired. It was only two in the afternoon, and I was desperate to crawl into bed and sleep until the next sunrise. That's what my body needed to recoup.

Not steak.

As she hung up the phone, she stayed on the counter, staring at me silently. Any other day, the silence would have led me to make some snarky comment or insult. Today, though, I simply didn't have the energy.

So, we just sat in silence, staring.

Her face was washed free of any product, her hair pinned up in a simple twist and the white button up she wore added to the fresh and simple look. It was odd to see her so *bare*, it made her look vulnerable. Untouched by life.

"Are you in danger?" She asked after a while, breaking through my silent obsessing over the way she looked in my clothes, in my space. "Is something like what happened to you last night going to happen to you again?"

In the shower earlier, I had given her a very watered-down explanation of what had happened, leaving me with a bullet hole on the floor. I told her I had traded a job for the privilege of keeping her to myself at the private event. And that it went sideways.

"I don't make it a habit of allowing bullets to rip through my body, if that's what you're asking." I replied, in avoidance.

"Do you take jobs like that often?"

"I used to." I admitted. "It used to be my whole way of life. Now it's more of a recreational sport. A stress reliever."

"Killing people." She stated, not quite asking, though I never spoke of life and death. "You kill people, don't you, Tamen?"

I eyed her, holding her stare to acknowledge that this wasn't a normal conversation two people usually had so candidly. "If that's what the job calls for."

"How does one go from murder-for-hire to sex club owner?"

I chuckled, sinking down further into the chair as the fatigue became a heavier burden to carry. "Sex, drugs, and money, baby. They all go hand in hand. Surely you know there's darkness all around your world, whether you see it firsthand or not."

"Sure." She shrugged, and then leaped off the counter, gracefully walking toward me. "But I'm usually more focused on the pleasure when I'm in that world."

"You have my attention." I adjusted myself in my lounge pants and she smiled softly down at me as she came to a stop between my spread legs.

"I still hate you." She murmured. "You traumatized me with that whole dramatic event."

Swallowing, I let her words seep into my mind, so I had no choice but to acknowledge them. She deserved to have her feelings validated, because she was right.

"I never wanted you to see me like that. I never would have exposed you to this if I'd had a choice in it all."

Sloane slowly placed one knee next to my hip and seductively straddled my lap until her body heat blended with mine through the thin clothes between us. "I'm glad I found you before it was too late." She gently placed her hands on my abs, sliding her fingers over the ink that covered every inch of my torso like she was tracing a map. Unable to resist, I held her flared hips in my hands, fighting the urge to rock her forward on my already rock hard dick. "But that doesn't mean I don't want to strangle you for my troubles."

I grinned, and lifted one of her hands to my neck and she instantly tightened her fingers around the front of my throat. "Go right ahead, Love. Take all your frustrations out on me." Tipping my head back against the chair, I stared up at her and gave into the urge to rock her hips onto me. She licked her lips and rolled her hips a second time for another grind across my erection. Judging by the scalding heat branding my dick, she was naked under my shirt, and I struggled to think of anything else but sliding up into her body.

"As if you could ever let me top you." She smirked, lowering her lips to hover right above mine. "Both times we've been together, you've dominated me effortlessly."

"I can be a switch if the incentive is right." I swiped my tongue over her plump bottom lip, teasing us both. "Whatever you want, it's yours. I won't even pretend that I don't like it."

Her teeth latched onto my lip and bit down, making my dick jump between us as she slowly started grinding on it. It was as close as we had gotten to a kiss. Why hadn't I fucking kissed her before now? "You'd submit to me?" She hummed, "You'd give in and let me have my way?"

"You submit to me." I replied, "And I know that's not your norm. So why not? I'll try anything once."

"Oh, baby." She moaned seductively as her arousal started soaking through the front of my pants. "You're talking to an over achiever here, be careful what you say."

"Would you prefer I beg?" I countered, fully willing to beg to get inside of her sinful body again. "It wouldn't be a hardship on me."

Sitting up in my lap, she teasingly started unbuttoning the shirt she wore and the whole time, she rocked her hips, pleasing us both. "I want you to beg." Pulling the shirt wide, but keeping it on, her delectable body played peek-a-boo with my hungry eyes every time she rolled her hips. I was entranced by the femininity of her body and how she used it like a weapon and a promise at the same time.

Sloane was a professional, after all. And I was in awe of her skills.

"Whatever you want, I'll do it." I said, looking away from her perfect nipples to her flawless face. "Tell me how you want me to beg."

Was I topping from the bottom? Kind of. But as she lifted my hands from her hips to her breasts and used my fingers on her hard nipples, just how she liked it, I didn't think she minded.

"Ask for permission to kiss me." She breathed. "You've never kissed me."

"Please Sloane, let me taste your lips. I want to taste perfection." Not a single word was a lie or an act. I was suddenly obsessed with her mouth and needed to kiss her. "Please."

Leaning forward again, she hovered right over me and admitted, "I've never kissed a male client before."

"Good thing I'm not paying for this, then." I pinched her nipples harder than I had been and she sagged into me, getting closer to my lips.

"You're paying for this." She chided, "You just don't realize it."

"Then make it worth my money." Countering, I challenged her, and she grinned.

"The customer is always right, after all." She whispered and then gently laid her soft lips against mine.

Jesus, fuck.

I tilted my head and let her set the seductive and teasing pace as she worked me over with her lips. Provocatively, she ran her tongue over my lip but wouldn't let me in when I tried playing a game of will and power.

Every interaction between us was a chess match, both of us fighting to win the unspoken prize at the end. This one wouldn't be any different.

Tonight, we were playing for control.

And I happily intended to let her win.

Finally, she gave into my needs and deepened the kiss, moaning when I instantly met her moves with my own eagerness. Her fingers moved back to my throat and tightened, pushing my head back into the cushions as she dropped her lips to my neck, biting and licking a trail down to my chest.

"Why did I enjoy that so fucking much?" She hissed, tightening her hand on my throat, restricting my air, and I grinned.

She could kill me exactly like this, and I'd still smile as I crossed the threshold into death for good.

"Because it's me." I teased, and she bit my ear hard enough to draw blood. She was playing with fire, though, because I loved every burning touch she graced me with. "I'm quite irresistible."

"I know." She groaned, "I've heard the rumors."

A sour taste filled my mouth with the conflict I heard in her voice as I remembered the lie I told her earlier.

"I never slept with your friend." I said, and she paused, leaning back to look at me skeptically.

After a moment of silent contemplation, she asked, "Why would you lie about that?"

"To make you mad." I replied plainly, "So you'd turn your energy from fear to anger, and use it to help me."

She swallowed, but didn't say anything right away. Finally, she broke the silence. "Why would you think that sleeping with other people would anger me?" The quick shift of her amber eyes to the side spoke volumes, revealing a hidden truth I chose to ignore. "We're not together. You can sleep with whoever you want to."

I didn't believe her words, but rather than call her on them, I admitted something. "Because I know how it makes me feel every time, you tell me about the other men you've let touch you since I fucked you the first time."

Should I have shown my cards like that? No.

Was I hoping that maybe, just maybe, there'd be some sort of benefit to come from the admission.

Sitting up to her full height, she stared down at me with her hand on my throat, scowling. I dropped my hands back to her hips, anticipating her throwing herself from my lap at my pathetic admission. Finally, she cocked her head to the side and glared at me, "Don't ever lie to me again, Tamen Bryce. Especially about other women." She reached between our bodies and pulled my aching cock free of my pants and fisted it as I fought the urge to thrust up into her hand. "Promise me that."

Licking my lips and fighting the lack of blood flow to my brain, I gave her what she wanted. "Yes, Ma'am."

Sloane moaned and tightened her hand around both my neck and dick in sync, before shoving herself off my lap in my distraction, even as I grabbed for her, but she avoided me. "In the name of honesty, I have something to admit." She walked away from me to where her purse laid on the counter and fished something out of it. At first I was afraid she was leaving, going to walk out and leave me hard and aching for her as a punishment for my deception.

I would have deserved it for sure, but damn, that would be cold.

As she walked back across the space on the balls of her feet like a dancer, my shirt swaying and open down the center of her body, I caught the flicker of something gold in her hand.

"I lied to you." She said, drawing my eyes back from her hand to her face as she stood between my legs once again. "But from now on, I'm going to be honest with you, as long as you return it."

"About what?" I demanded, anxiety crawling up my neck as I tried to remember everything she had ever said to me.

But thinking got hard as she slid my shirt off her body and gracefully sank to her knees between mine. Pulling on the waistband of my pants she removed them until we were both bare and then she ran her nails up the length of my tattooed thighs, barely avoiding the space where my secrets hid, as she gripped my dick and stroked me with both hands.

"There are no others." She whispered, staring up at me with her mystic golden eyes as she stuck her tongue out and twirled it around the tip before sucking the head into her mouth and letting it pop free. "Not since before the night we met. I lied about letting others have me to rile you up."

"Minx." I hissed as she sucked my dick back into her mouth. Bloody hell, she was a magical being with skills unmatched. "Diabolical, really."

She hummed with a smirk and pulled back, licking her puffy lips as she flashed the golden Magnum condom she got from her purse, slowly rolling it onto my dick.

"Like knows like." Sloane purred, straddling me again and sliding directly down onto my dick. I was fighting to keep my eyes from crossing, and she was riding me hands free like a master. She was so far out of my league it was comical. "Mmh, I thought if I was in control, it'd feel normal. And then I'd be able to get over this infatuation with you." She cracked her neck, letting her eyelids flutter closed as she gave into the pleasure as she slowly rode me, rolling her hips rather than thrusting herself on and off of it. I couldn't care less what motion she used, so long as she let me stay buried inside of her heavenly body.

"There's nothing normal about me, Rainbow." I replied, before sucking one of her nipples into my mouth and drawing a breathy cry of pleasure from her lips. "This isn't normal."

"Maybe it's that adage that we all want what we can't have. Maybe that's why it's hotter." She said and then grabbed both of my wrists in her hands and pinned them to the chair by my head. My shoulder burned as she stretched my flesh around the staples she mutilated me with, but I didn't stop her. My cock throbbed harder as she restrained me as she rode me. I could have easily overpowered her, flipping the script and pinning her down as I fucked her hard, but she wanted to be in control.

She wanted proof that this differed from anything she shared with anyone else.

I didn't need the proof, I already knew it was.

Fate wrote the connection between our souls long before we ever met.

It would be the very thing I fought at every turn simply because once I gave into it, I'd be lost and I'd bring her down with me when it all ended. It would end, eventually.

All good things did.

"Or maybe it's just better." I countered, taking the opportunity to thrust up into her when she lifted herself fractionally and her tits swayed from the violence in it. "The infatuation runs in both directions, Rainbow."

"Again." She breathed, staring at me as she held herself up. "Hard."

"Gladly." I winked and did it again, making her eyes roll as I found the pace and rhythm she sought after. I could do it all day long, slamming up into her body as her tits jiggled and her lips parted in pleasurable cries while she held me down like she was in control. Whatever my pretty little Rainbow needed.

She was in control; I was on bottom with my arms pinned behind my head, yet I fucked her like we both knew who belonged to who.

Right now, she was mine. And I was going to take care of whatever she needed. With each plea and demand that fell from her pretty kissed lips, she told me exactly what those needs were.

It was the first time I fucked her while staring at her beautiful face, and now that I had seen the color of ecstasy kiss her skin as she orgasmed, I'd never take her any other way. She was magical, and entrancing, I could stare at her all day long as she came on my dick.

Or my face.

Even as she dug her nails into my wrists, branding me, I ached to taste her orgasm on my tongue again. But I knew my pretty little Rainbow would behead me if I tried to take my dick away from her right now, even if I was simply trying to trade it for my tongue.

So, I gave her everything she demanded from me, watching her lose control and come over and over again. Until I couldn't hold back any longer either.

"You're close, aren't you?" She gasped, staring down at me through hooded eyes as she rocked against my pubic bone. "I should make you come in the condom, since I know you hate it so much."

Glaring up at her. "I have nothing against coming into a condom." I uttered, and slammed up into her, "I just prefer to see it on your skin."

"How about my tongue?" She ran the tip of her tongue over her top teeth and then released my arms and scurried off my lap to her knees again. "Come on my tongue, *Mr. Duke.*"

Pulling the condom off and tossing it to the side, Sloane sucked my cock deep into her mouth and I rested my chin on my chest and watched the show. God, it felt bloody amazing and if she wanted to swallow my come, I wasn't going to tell her no.

Within no time, I was there, fighting the urge to blow and wanting the experience to never end. Pleasure won out.

"That's it, Rainbow. Make me come." I feathered my fingers into her hair and held her head as she worked her mouth up and down me until I was lost to the sensation altogether. She sucked me down, never once letting my orgasm deter her until I was melted in the chair, and she sat triumphantly at my feet.

"Good boy." She purred, licking her lips with a smug shimmy. "I knew you could be a good little submissive for me."

I snorted and shot forward, wrapping my hand around her throat and leaned over her as she laid her hands on my thighs for leverage. "Careful baby, I don't fully submit to anyone. Ever. But if you play your cards right, I might let you pretend I do from time to time."

"Tamen." She whispered, running her hands down my thighs with wide eyes. At first, I didn't catch on to the sudden shift in the emotions clouding her bright amber eyes. And then I felt it.

Her fingers.

On my scars.

"Are these—" She stammered, pulling her neck back out of my hold to look at the texture of my skin under the black out tattoos I used years ago to cover my weakness. Tears muddied the shimmer of her irises as she shook her head in confusion. "Cutting scars?"

"No." I stood up in a flash, pushing her backward so I could walk around her.

Gone was the euphoria I had been feeling from my orgasm.

Gone was the excitement I had been feeling from being close to her.

Gone was the comfort I had been feeling in her presence from letting my guard down and relaxing around her.

I forgot; no one was safe.

No one was equipped to handle all of me.

Momentarily, I let myself forget I was supposed to stay hidden from everyone. Monsters like me couldn't reveal themselves. Monsters like me couldn't coexist with normal people.

My father had taught me at a young age that I was the worst kind of beast out there, because I wasn't redeemable. There was no good in me, never had been. I wasn't a machine he had created over time to be useful; I was just demented from the start.

A willing participant in all his sick games.

And now Sloane saw a bit of the boy that had tried like hell to bleed the monster out of his soul, unsuccessfully, all those years ago. Which meant she had worn out her welcome.

Now, she had to go.

CHAPTER 22 - SLOANE

Tamen told me to leave. I flipped him off.

He told me to get out of his life. I rolled my eyes.

He told me I was fired. I laughed.

And then the room service boy arrived in the foyer with all the food I had ordered. Thank God too, because if he hadn't interrupted our face off, who the hell knows what we would have done. I was as stubborn as the day was long, and Tamen was hiding secrets. Which meant neither of us was going to budge on this.

I was bunkering down and staking my claim; he wasn't getting rid of me. Not now that I finally got to see a real, raw piece of the man inside of him. Of his scars. His pain.

He wasn't evil like I had thought, like he had wanted me to think.

He was a product of something evil, something dark. It lived in him.

But I wasn't sure he wanted it to.

So now we sat in silence, on opposite sides of the living room, eating our food while he actively ignored me. Tamen Bryce was about to figure out how fucking annoying I could be when I chose to.

It was why I lived alone all of these years; I could annoy a statue into moving.

I took another obnoxiously big bite of my Reuben, smacking my lips together as he glared at me over the rim of his beer glass, but he remained silent. Breaking the tension, another dinging of the elevator in the foyer alerted another guest was arriving.

Tamen's blue eyes intensified as I clapped my hands and stood up, still wearing just his shirt, to go get my next delivery.

When I came back with my small paper bag, I knew he wanted to ask what the heck I ordered, but refrained. His goal of absolute silence, like a monk in a monastery, was annoying at best, but it wouldn't rile me up.

I'd annoy him back with my ability to over-talk if I had to.

I set the bag down on the counter and cheerily began unpacking it, laying down baggies of different herbs and glass bottles of different tinctures. As I lifted the fat smudge stick up and cradled it in my hands like a precious gift from the divine goddess herself, his curiosity could no longer be contained.

"Getting high?" He droned on like he was uninterested, but we both knew better.

"This would be one hell of a doobie if I was." I grinned and then picked up the crystals I ordered and started placing them around the room.

"What are you doing, exactly?"

"Resetting your space." I answered, "You've got bad juju here."

"It's fine." He sighed, "It's a hotel, I'm sure it's seen stuff that would make even you blush."

I brushed off his dig and continued my task as he silently watched me from the chair. As I lit the smudge and blew out the flame, creating the smoke needed to clean his space of all his evil darkness, he scoffed.

Moving around his space, I wafted the smoke into all the corners and nooks as I envisioned the black aura around him getting smaller and smaller, making space for a peaceful one. When I passed by him, I blew the smoke directly onto his head and he coughed dramatically.

"That shit burns." He grumped.

"I bet it does, Satan." I replied flippantly, as I kept going. "That's rich coming from someone who smokes a pack a day."

"Only around you." He snapped. "You stress me out."

"Oh boy," I mimicked Mickey Mouse and then shimmied my hips at him. "Such a sophisticated insult."

"Excuse me." Tamen yawned and stood up, shaking his body like he was removing the sage smudge from his skin. "I'm too fucking tired to entertain you right now. Lock up when you leave."

With my back turned to him, I pursed my lips in annoyance but refrained from calling him out. Barely. He was shutting me out, or at least trying to. But he was underestimating my persistence when I got a plan in my head. "Yeah, yeah, yeah," I waved at him. "Sure thing, Boss."

It grated my nerves to call him that, because before he went all Jekyll and Hyde on me after we had sex, things had almost felt—comfortable between us. Familiar even.

Stupid me for thinking Tamen Bryce could keep up his nice boy attitude for long. He disappeared into the bedroom and part of me wanted to stay and find other ways to annoy him for the fun of it, but I wasn't that heartless.

The man had been knocking on death's door when I found him this morning. I couldn't add to his misery.

But that didn't mean I didn't know someone who could.

I put my dirty dress back on but wore his button-up shirt, tying it at my waist to make an effortless, casual look that really just hid the blood coating my dress until I got home and could throw it all away. Walking out of his space, I dialed the phone number for the only person who could torment him and get away with it, and she picked up on the second ring.

"Hey girl! We were just talking about you, were your ears ringing?" Peyton asked with a chuckle.

"They weren't actually, but I hope it was good things being said."

"Oh, they were," She reassured, "What's up?"

"Actually, I was hoping you could help me out. Or Tamen, rather."

"Uh oh." Her voice dropped as she got serious. "What did he do now?"

"Well," I paused and then went full send. "He got shot last night, and I'm worried about him being alone as he recovers. He kicked me out of his hotel after traumatizing me by making me take the bullet out of his back when I found him passed out and bleeding to death. But you know how he is, he won't let anyone actually help him for long before fucking it up with that stupid mouth of his."

"Jesus Christ," She whined, "Dane! We're going to the city. Tamen's being a drama queen again!"

Chuckling at the absurdity of the fact that she wasn't surprised he was shot but that he was being a dick, I rode the elevator to the ground floor. "I appreciate you checking in on him. I'll cover for him at Prism, there are meetings with contractors that can't be missed if we want to open this week. But I'd just feel better knowing he's not bleeding out in his stubbornness."

"Oh, he'll be bleeding when I'm done with him." She sassed and then sighed, "Thanks for calling me, Sloane. I know he's probably not been overly kind to you today, or any day, for that matter. But I appreciate you still looking out for him."

"Yeah," I hummed, remembering the way I had ridden him in the chair with my hand on his throat, feeling slightly guilty for using him after all he went through. Not that he had complained at all until I found his scars under the ink on his thighs. "No problem. Actually, do you mind if I ask you one more question. And feel free to tell me to fuck off, because I know how out of line this is, but has Tamen always been—" I struggled to find the right word to describe him, "troubled?"

Her sigh was one out of love and I knew asking her was the right thing to do, "The way that Dane and Maddox tell the story, is that Tamen has always wanted to be different than he is. When he was younger, he wanted to be like them, doing—" She hesitated, "*bad* things we'll say. And then, when he was older and doing the same things as them, it was almost like he wished he had stayed away the whole time. I think that's why he spends so much time building businesses up, even given the fact that they're not always the best kind of mess to be in, I think that's his way of trying to do something else with his life. But at the end of the day, a cheetah can't change his spots, and the world has left its mark on him."

"Thanks for sharing that." I replied, imagining a younger Tamen, tall and lanky chasing after a younger Dane and Maddox in the streets or wherever they all learned their dark skills. "I appreciate any knowledge I can get to help me figure the man out."

She chuckled lightly, but there wasn't much humor in it. "Hey if you figure him out completely, let me know, would ya? I'd love some more answers into the mind of Tamen Bryce."

Ending the call, I battled with my inner angel and demon, trying to decide what I was going to do about the infuriatingly sexy man that weaseled his way so far into my life that I couldn't remember the normalcy I'd felt before him.

Wasn't I some independent boss babe who ran my shit without worrying about anyone else?

Then it was time to get her back. And I'd start by finalizing decisions at Prism that Tamen had left until the last minute.

That was my right as a manager, right?

CHAPTER 23 - TAMEN

It was opening night at Prism. There were times I wasn't sure I'd polish up the pile of shit I found at Vixen's Den enough to make it to opening night. I probably wouldn't have if it hadn't been for Sloane, either.

I hadn't seen her in days; my doing, of course. Though I was pretty confident that she was avoiding me as well. We'd been busy enough that it didn't matter, until now.

Now, I paced my luxurious new office on the second floor overlooking the large entertainment spaces below, and fought the urge to go seek her out in the crowd. The way my office was built, I had one-way mirror access to both the stage room and the large bar and mingling spaces, even though they were separated by many private rooms.

Every room was booked tonight, and every night on the schedule moving forward. Memberships far exceeded what we could actually facilitate if everyone showed up at the same time. And the amount of money the girls of Prism would make was astronomical.

In just over an hour, Sloane would take center stage of her brand new exhibition space, yet I still hadn't let her see it.

It was a gift to her, but I couldn't bring myself to show her. I couldn't bring myself to face her.

So I texted her instead.

> Make sure you check out the stage before your show.

Her reply came instantly.

> As soon as these magic hands are done with me, I'll get around to it. Your sisters give the best gifts.

And then she sent a winking face.

"What the fuck does that mean?" I asked out loud, like someone in my empty office was going to garner me some wisdom into the complex mind of my pretty little Rainbow.

> Explain that further.

But she didn't reply fast enough for me as my tie suddenly felt like it was choking me out. I panic dialed Peyton's number and cursed when two rings in it went to voicemail. Hanging up, I dialed Dane, and he sighed as he answered.

"Hang on, she's right here." He said in place of a greeting, and Peyton cursed at him in the background, but he cut her off. "I want nothing to do with any of this. If there's bloodshed tonight, it's on you and Liv."

"What did you do?" I barked into the phone as Peyton finally answered it.

"Change your tone with me or I'll block you."

"Peyton!" I snapped. "Tell me what you and Liv did."

"What did Sloane tell you?" She paused.

"Something about magic hands gifted to her by you two asshats."

Her snippy voice conveyed her annoyance with me as clearly as her words could have, "Masseuse, Tamen. We scheduled her a sensual deep tissue massage with a highly rated Kamasutra masseuse before her big opening night to help relax her and get her in the mood."

"Bloody hell, Peyton!" I hung up the phone and a picture message came through at the same time from Sloane.

She was on her stomach with her eyes closed and a goofy smile pulled her lips back as some fuckwad had his hands buried in her hair, pulling her head back.

Twitchy.

Twitchy, twitchy, twitchy.

The fuckwad was going to lose those fucking hands.

I glanced back at the picture as I grabbed my jacket off the back of my chair and tore off through the building for Sloane's office. The room's dimmed gold chandelier betrayed her location, yet when I reached her door, down the hall from mine, it was locked.

Good thing I had override privileges on all the electronic locks.

Within a breath, I shoved the door open and found the subject of my fury laid out in the middle of a massage table covered in a piece of fabric the size of a washcloth.

Moaning.

Cracking my neck, I stepped inside, and slammed the door shut behind me as the fuckwad looked up from where he was stroking up the length of Sloane's long leg, ending indecently high and then repeating the motion. Did he truly not understand how close to death he was?

"Oh, what an unwanted surprise." Sloane spoke, muffled through the table's padding, before she lifted her face and laid her chin on her crossed arms. "What's the matter, TeeTee? Something bothering you?"

"Rainbow." I seethed through clenched teeth as she let her eyelids flutter closed as the man bent her knee to lift her foot as he began massaging it. "You're playing with fire."

"No, I'm not." She replied dismissively. "I'm simply enjoying a present that your thoughtful sisters sent to me. Considering you wouldn't let them attend tonight in person." She finally opened those golden eyes again and stared at me. "Besides, what do you care about how I get in the mood for a show? It's not like you were volunteering to help me."

"Get in the *mood*?" I uttered as the word left a foul taste in my mouth. Did she really plan to allow this nobody to get her in the mood when I was right down the hall the whole time?

She chuckled and sighed, "Yes, Tamen. Believe it or not, if we're sexually aroused, we tend to make more believable partners for the night."

"Sloane." I snapped, flexing my hands at my sides. She wasn't booked for any private sessions tonight. Or in the future, for that matter. In fact, her name wasn't even listed in the system to book for anything other than the stage room.

And only I booked the stage room.

"No." She countered forcefully, pointing her finger at me. "This is my space. In here, I'm in charge. And right now, I'm doing what is necessary for me to go out there and be on top of my game to entertain all our customers. Which means you don't get to invade my space and start any of your shit. So, you can either leave," She stared me down, "Or you can sit in that chair in the corner." Raising one eyebrow, she dominantly finished. "And watch. *Silently.*"

Fucking hell.

She was dominating me.

And I couldn't do anything about it.

There wasn't a chance in hell that I was going to leave her office while she was naked with a stranger touching her skin with the literal intent of arousing her. She'd kick me out on principal alone if I gave her even one reason to, simply to get back at me for the other day at my hotel when I had kicked her out for getting too close.

"Fine." I shoved my jacket off my shoulders and sat down in the chair she pointed at, staring at her the whole time as I did just what she said.

I sat.

And watched.

Remaining silent the entire time.

Like a good fucking boy, just for her.

I had dabbled in letting women be in charge in the bedroom before, I wasn't a total Neanderthal. But allowing Sloane to dominate me when my dick wasn't actively inside of her body was uncharted territory for me.

She was used to being in charge though, and as she held my stare, moaning as the guy bent her leg up on the table, stretching her hamstring, I could see how much she was enjoying herself. Sloane was thriving, having me as her plaything while enjoying her massage.

Truth be told, I didn't mind either. Even though I wanted to throw my knife into the side of the bloke's neck for having what I was sure was an unobscured view of her naked cunt, it didn't matter.

Because her eyes were on me.

He didn't matter to her; I knew that.

How many other men came and went through her life, meaning nothing to her past the exchange of money at the end, leading us both to this exact moment?

And why did that somehow make what was burning between us for weeks now even more powerful? Without a second thought, I let my body have control, feeding the need to be near her.

As I watched her, the glow around her burned bright yellow. Power.

Sloane was a goddess by her own right, and when she felt powerful, she was vibrant.

Her lips parted as I stood up from my time-out chair and stalked toward her, lowering myself to her level. Capturing her wild hair in my hands, I held her head still and pressed my lips to hers without a single word.

The shock held her immobile for a moment before she melted against me, opening for me as I pressed my tongue into her mouth. "Dismiss him." I rasped against her lips, biting her bottom one when she didn't reply. "Let me be what you need tonight."

In any other situation, I would have felt pathetic for allowing myself to be subservient to anyone, but not to Sloane.

Not tonight.

"God." Her silky voice exposed her need as much as my actions did mine. She waved her hand in the air. "You're dismissed, thank you! Go. Now!"

I didn't bother pulling away from her lips to make sure the man listened, he silently vacated the space like a true professional as she kissed me again. Rising to my feet, I kept kissing her as she rolled over on the table, until she was on her back, exposed to my hungry eyes and desperate hands.

"I can't come." She stammered, digging her nails into the back of my hand as I slid it down the front of her chest to her lush tits. "It will ruin my high for the night."

"I'm not going to make you come." I assured her, kissing my way down to her nipples, and sucking them into my mouth as her back bowed off the table. "Not until tonight is over and we've both earned it."

"Tamen." Her strangled voice ended in a whine as I pushed my fingers through her wet cunt lips. "Yes." Sloane's legs fell open as I played with her body, working her up into an inferno and then slowing down to let it lessen.

"I can be everything you need, Rainbow." I uttered, pulling back to stare down at her perfect face, dotted with perspiration from my attentions. "All you have to do is let me."

"All you have to do is earn it." She countered, opening her clouded golden eyes and nibbling on her lip, running her hands up my chest and clutching at my shirt. "God, I want you to earn it, Tamen."

"I don't know how." Admitting what we both knew, I replied, "I'm not a nice man. I'm not romantic."

Sloane chuckled breathlessly and shook her head as she sat up on her elbows to stare at me. "I don't want romance or fake words from you, nutcase. I know you're a sadist who gets off on making me miserable." She grinned and rolled her eyes when I glared at her. "Bullying you gives me the same high as when you torment me back. I just want you to be honest with me about it. I need you to respect me as an equal if you're going to demean me for foreplay."

I let her words weave through my damaged brain, trying like hell to make sense of them. What woman in the world wanted barbs and insults instead of flowers and gentleness?

The answer was right in front of me, though.

Sloane.

My pretty little Rainbow wanted vulgar words and sass I offered her out of spite to begin with, because the fire in it felt right. To both of us.

"I'll try." I rasped, fighting the warning bells that were telling me to abort the mission altogether. "That's all I can promise."

"I'll take it, for now." She sat up, swinging her legs over the edge of the table and pulling me between them with my belt. "Now do something else for me." She purred, pulling my pants open until my hard dick was in her palm as she leisurely stroked me.

"What?"

"Torture me." Her purr vibrated through my body as she gently pressed the edge of her nail against the hole at the end of my dick. "Make it feel," Lining me up with her wet entrance, she brought her knees up and pulled me forward. "Like you hate me each time you don't let me come." Her head dropped back when I was deep inside of her, bare and free of anything between us for the very first time, like an unspoken truce had been called. "That way I know I'm torturing you the same way every time you don't get to come."

I growled, fighting the urge to give in and come already just from how good it felt inside of her without a condom. I never fucked bare, and I knew she didn't either.

Yet this. Right now.

There was no other way I would want to take her right now than like this.

Wrapping my hand around her throat, I forced her to lay down across the narrow bed until her head hung off the other side and slammed into her aggressively. "I've been tortured every single second since I saw you on that stage for the very first time." Sloane moaned and let her body hang free as I savagely fucked her, giving into what we both wanted. "You didn't know it, but at one point that night, you stopped and stared up at the mirrored glass, like you could see me through it, watching you."

"Yes." She cried, "God, just like that. Tell me about it."

"I had planned on using a faceless woman for the entire night. I was stressed and in desperate need of something to break through that overwhelming feeling, so I didn't lose my mind once and for all." Knowing she'd be onstage soon, I bit her chest, leaving a mark on her skin for everyone to see, and smiled when she screamed for me. "And then I saw you. God, my pretty little Rainbow. You were majestic on that stage, commanding dozens of people in the throes of passion and entertainment without even raising your voice. Your body moved in sync with theirs, and you captivated everyone. Me included."

"You fucked Val that night." She moaned, "I want to be jealous of that, but I'm not."

"Why?" I licked up her neck and slowed my thrusts when I felt myself getting dangerously close to coming. "I'm jealous of every man who's ever even spoken to you."

She smiled and lifted my hand to her mouth, sucking two of my fingers into her mouth so deep I could feel the tightness of her throat on my fingertips. I pulled my dick free of her cunt that was strangling it in perfect sync to her mouth and she gasped, falling back when I kissed my way down to her clit. "Because I know you were watching me." Her fingers dug their way through my hair, and she held me against her by handfuls as she rode my face from below. "I could feel your stare, even if I didn't know what it was at that moment. I felt you."

"That's right." I pushed my tongue into her body and then slapped her clit before pausing completely as I sensed how close she was to orgasming. Walking around to the other side of the table, I lifted her head and cradled it in my palm as she eagerly started sucking my cock upside down. "I came while I stared into your golden eyes, unable to see anything else in the world. It's been that way ever since, too."

Gasping, she pulled off and stared up at me, "And you hate that."

There was a rawness to that statement, it wasn't something she took personally, but she wanted to know why.

"No." I replied, caressing my way down the front of her exposed body until I got to her clit to distract myself. "I resent it." She shuddered from my touch and slowly played with my dick as we practiced restraint, edging ourselves closer to that fall. "Early on, I learned that weakness takes many forms. And my obsession with you is my biggest one."

Sloane rolled over, bending over the table as she stared into my eyes with an intensity only she could pull off, naked, stroking my cock and begging me to torture her. "I don't have to be your weakness, Tamen. I could be your greatest asset if you earn me. Your best friend and loudest cheerleader. I know you've mastered this total dark and depraved lifestyle on your own. But you could stand to let a little light into your life."

"A little Rainbow, maybe?" I thumbed a strand of her hair as I leaned down to kiss her again. The minx sucked my tongue into her mouth and bit it.

"With a pot of gold and everything." She licked her lips and then fell onto her elbows, popping her ass up across the table to twerk it enticingly. "All you have to do is catch it."

I prowled around the table to her and spanked her ass, watching it ripple as she watched me over her shoulder. Lining up, I pushed back into her heaven. "As long as no little red-headed fucks come chasing me when I dip into it for another piece of gold."

She chuckled and then moaned when I spanked her again, peppering her skin. "Mmh, keep the rainbow happy and everything stays all sunshine and pleasurable."

CHAPTER 24 - SLOANE

The second my heels touched the obsidian black stone stage, I was home.

Every set of eyes in the room was on me, warming my skin with their attention and waiting to see what magic I'd weave for them. And it hadn't lessened through the entire performance I gave either. It was a high like no other.

"Harder." My assistant called out, and I nodded to the masked man standing on the stage with us, wielding the whip. Her echoed cry of pain and pleasure made goosebumps break out across my skin. "Thank you, Ma'am."

"You're very welcome." I purred, walking around the stage, engaging the audience, who watched with bated breath as I picked up the candle from my tray of goodies. "You're doing such a good job."

"Thank you, Ma'am." She repeated from her spot in the center, rigged up with a red rope tied in the Moon Tie pattern, holding her up in the air. Defenseless.

And perfect for her Domme to play with.

Tonight's show for opening night was Shibari or better known as rope play. Bondage.

It was one of my most favorite things to teach, because almost anyone who walked in the front door could find some part of bondage that excited them. For most, it was a simple pair of handcuffs, or a silk tie around their wrists, tied to the headboard while their partner teased them for foreplay. For more adventurous guests, it was a spreader bar or some more in-depth restraints that held them open in a certain position. And for players like my two assistants who were in a loving and healthy relationship for over fifteen years now, it was suspension Shibari on the main stage of an exclusive sex club for a sold-out crowd to watch.

Everyone had their interests.

And I loved nurturing them in a safe and controlled environment with experienced knowledge at the head of the trialing.

The balconies surrounding the stage room were mostly full, customers leaving private rooms they spent thousands of dollars on by the hour, watching me. The responsibility of that gift didn't go unnoticed.

I was working for everyone tonight. Including the man in the mirrored glass right off center stage. I couldn't see Tamen in his office, but like that first night, I could feel him. Yet he wouldn't walk out onto his balcony for me. He was hiding.

"As you can see," I announced, letting the natural acoustics of the space and the tiny microphones hanging over the stage in the lights and rigging carry my voice to everyone as I neared my bound assistant, "Lyra's rope rigging is transitional," She was currently *sitting* in her rigging, with her knees bent up to her chest, legs spread and arms tied to the small of her back behind her. She elected to remain nude aside from the ruby red rope, so the room had a view of her vulnerability.

Using my free hand not holding the lit pillar candle, I shifted her forward, and gravity did the rest, tipping her forward in almost a somersault move until she hung upside down with her ass in the air and her head facing the floor. An audible gasp of fear rang out from the crowd as she plummeted before the ropes caught her without injury. I loved that part. "Meaning you can play with so many different toys and positions from one simple rigging."

I lifted the candle to the sole of her foot, keeping it just far enough away from her skin to avoid a burn, but giving her nerves the heat needed to create a panic response.

"Ah," She cried, unable to move her foot away on her own thanks to her position. "I'm sorry, Ma'am." She apologized for speaking out of turn and I nodded my head once, seconds later the whip landed on her upturned pussy right next to my shoulder. "Thank you, Ma'am!" She screamed on autopilot.

"This rope tie is called the Moon Tie, and it's one of endless possibilities you can learn here at Prism in our exhibition series on Shibari Rope play. You can find the schedule of events here in our stage room on any of the flat screens around the club and online. Or better yet," I winked with a seductive smile over the crowd, "Ask one of our lovely ladies in residence to assist you in your exploration." Knowing chuckles replied as I gave one final wave, "Thank you, good night!"

THE LINE WALKERS

"Ahhh!" Trixie sighed dreamily as she twirled on the stool at the bar. Prism closed half an hour ago, and all of us congregated at the bar like none of us were ready to end the magical first night. "What a night."

"It was so much more than I could have ever dreamed it could be." Val agreed, sipping her martini. "I can't believe we get to do this every day."

I snorted and took a sip of my chardonnay, "I remember you ready to quit altogether before Tamen bought the place. Isn't it wild how things have changed?"

"I can't even describe it." She shook her head, "Tonight felt so freaking empowering. Like for once, we were in charge and not just at face value, but of everything. They all came here for us."

"And they'll all keep coming back," Tamen's booming voice carried across the crowded space as he came down the stairs. "All of you were wonderful tonight, and the customers are raving about their night just as much as you all are."

After my warm-up session in my office earlier, he had disappeared, managing the night and mingling with the big-name clients. I knew he was watching during my show, but I hadn't actually seen him until now.

God, why did a man have to look so damn good in a tailored suit? It was unkind to my lady bits that were vibrating with need even before he joined us.

"I didn't even have sex with anyone." Mya chirped up, with a comedic shrug, "And I made more than I did in a week of tips tending bar at any other club."

"You almost sound disappointed about getting by with no sex." Trixie giggled.

"I kind of am," Mya chuckled back. "I've never had sex with a millionaire before. I was excited to check that one off my bucket list."

The girls all laughed, understanding her point in a way that anyone else in the world could never grasp. So many of us chose to be here, yet the world expected us to hate it. Simply because society thought we should.

Sure, some of the girls would probably have taken a different path in life if their fate had taken a different direction, but that didn't mean we couldn't all choose to embrace the good fortune we'd found here at Prism under Tamen's ownership.

After my show, I spent the rest of the night networking in the crowd. Meeting clients, introducing myself and facilitating introductions between them and the girls they were interested in. It was pretty similar to what I was doing as one of the highest paid escorts at Vixen's Den before Tamen bought it, but now I was official.

I had the title, and the beautiful glitzy new office to host meetings in and so much pride in what my girls were building for themselves here.

What I was *helping* them build. Stability and security in not only their finances but also their happiness and self-worth were truly priceless things. This could empower many of them, shifting their perspective from feeling victimized by life's circumstances to celebrating their resilience in achieving their success.

It was a beautiful thing.

"So, we all get to come back tomorrow, then?" Raven asked him with a grin. "We passed the test?"

"You did." He nodded, walking to the bar and taking the offered rocks glass from the bartender, before turning to face everyone holding his glass in the air. "You've all proven yourselves these last few weeks, working hard to learn the new ways of the business I was creating and implementing them flawlessly this evening. There is nothing you can't do with this kind of dedication and gumption behind it. So, this is to you, all of you," He glanced at everyone, pausing briefly on me with an added nod, "To your success and prosper here at Prism."

"Here, here!" Trixie and others cheered happily, clinking glasses and tipping them back.

"Now get out of here." Tamen announced good heartedly, "It's late and we're back at it with doors open tomorrow at noon. If you have any questions about schedules, contact me or Ember. Good night!"

I stayed in my seat as the crowd dispersed, everyone on a high from opening night and the excitement for tomorrow, until it was only Tamen, and I left in the vast room.

Silently, from his spot on the other side of the large round bar, he stalked toward me, those bright blue eyes penetrating every wall I'd ever built in my life until he stood right in front of my crossed legs. After my performance, I returned to my office to find a beautiful designer dress hanging in the attached bathroom, another silent, unmentioned gift from Tamen that fit perfectly. It was silver and shimmered with diamonds on every inch of space, down the fitted bodice to the long skirt. Oh, and four dozen vases of wildflowers in a varying rainbow of colors and scents. But I would never mention those, I wouldn't want him to think I thought he was a romantic or anything. Instead, I'd silently enjoy them and let them continue to make my heart race every time I saw them in my office. Just like the man who bought them did to me.

And as he finally got within reach again for the first time in hours, I suddenly ached to get out of his newest gift and feel his skin on mine. Almost as if he felt the same way, he silently grazed the backs of his fingers over the bare skin of my knee, peeking through the slit as he pushed them higher, opening the fabric as he went.

The piercing blue irises I was obsessed with finally rose from where they stared at the skin of my thighs to my face as he spoke, "I was in complete awe of you tonight during your show." He licked his lips as I remained still while his fingertips continued wandering over my inner thigh. "Could you feel my obsession with you through the glass?"

I gave in and smiled at his words, feeling the warmth of them on my needy core. "Almost as if you were touching me like you are now."

"You were magnificent." He affirmed, leaning down and gently kissing me as he nudged the inside of my leg, telling me to open for him. "Perfection." His breath on my lips created goosebumps on my skin as he slid my dress up my hips to stand between my legs. "Breathtaking."

I sighed into his touch, unfamiliar with the gentleness of it, but not hating it either.

"I'm not sure I'm a fan of this pleasant side of you." I admitted, even as his fingers trailed up to the band of my panties and tugged.

"Maybe that's how I plan to torment you." He laid soft kisses down my neck to my shoulder, but intensified none of his touches. "How long until you beg me to bully you, I wonder?"

"Hmm..." I hummed, tightening my hand around his tie and pulling it until he looked at me. "Be careful Tamen, or I'll leave you tied up on my stage for all the girls to find tomorrow. Now be a good boy and give me what we both want. Give me the burn we both need." His perfectly white teeth flashed before he leaned back in and bit my neck hard enough to draw a startled scream from my lips. "Good boy."

CHAPTER 25 – SLOANE

"Tamen?" I called out one week later, cautiously entering room forty on the second floor. It was one of the darker themed rooms, with various BDSM tools and goodies. The man of the hour designed most of it himself, though he never admitted why he cared specifically for this room above all the others. "What's going on?"

Val told me ten minutes ago that I had been booked for the evening and should report to the room. I recoiled at the idea, but her cheerful grin and the unexpected revelation that Tamen was behind it all quickly eased my apprehension. He was the only man allowed to book me for a private session. Which was exactly how I wanted it to be.

"Hello, My Pretty Little Rainbow." Tamen's thick accent drew my attention to the side of the room as he stepped out from behind a silk screen set up as a changing area. He looked magnificent striding across the room; the black fabric of his shirt shimmered against the charcoal of his suit pants as he walked, the undone shirt revealing a glimpse of his inked chest. With one of his favorite cigarettes burning between his fingers, he stood barefoot at the edge of the room, staring intently at me; the sweet scent of his tobacco hanging in the air between us. "Thank you for meeting me here."

I crossed my arms over my maroon body con dress and watched him speculatively. "I wasn't aware I had a choice."

He grinned, taking a puff of his cigarette. He tipped his head back and blew the smoke up to the ceiling in that powerfully dominant way that always made me wet. "Tonight is all about you."

The club was nearly at capacity, with a million different things he and I could both be doing to keep things running smoothly. "Why?" I asked. "Why are we here?"

"To recreate a night that was one of my favorites. But one that desperately needs a redo, nonetheless."

"I'm so confused." I shook my head with a stupid smile on my face. "You're talking in riddles."

"The first night I had you." He replied, reminding me of the night at the private event when he tricked me into thinking he was a faceless John using my body for his own pleasure.

"I thought you said you'd never apologize for that night."

"I won't." He shook his head, taking another drag off his cigarette before pinching it out with his fingers. "That's not what this is."

"Then what is it?"

"It's me giving myself to you, completely, without limits. Just like you gave yourself to me that night." He undid his cuff links and nodded to the room where different implements were all waiting to be used. "Pick your poison, Rainbow. I can't say no. I'm at your mercy."

"My mercy." I spun around, looking at all the fun items I could use on him if he were truly my toy for the night. "This feels like a test."

"Does it?" He questioned, sliding his shirt off and hanging it up on a hook on the wall. "It feels like a gift to me."

"I sure love getting gifts." I hummed, desperate to give in to it. What I wouldn't do to have Tamen in my clutches for a night of fun on my terms.

"So, pick your gift tonight, Rainbow." He leaned over my shoulder, whispering in my ear as I took another appraisal of the room. "How are you going to use me tonight?"

"Fuck." I moaned and then pointed to my favorite toy in the room. "St. Andrew's cross."

I could feel his smile against my cheek before he kissed my neck and walked around me toward the cross in the corner of the room. He pulled it out into the center of the room and eyed up the shackles already attached at the four corners. "This is your pick?"

"It is." I crossed my arms and stared down my nose at him slightly. "Are you still brave enough to give yourself to me?"

Tamen chuckled with a sinister grin and pulled the fastener of his pants open. "I'm all yours, darling." Holding my stare, he pushed his pants and boxers down, stepping out of them and adding them to his pile of discarded clothes. "How do you want me?"

I crooked my finger at him, walking over to the cross and looking up at the wrist cuffs at the top. "Tied up and silent."

He tried to hide his grin as he turned his back against the cross, holding his arms up to the cuffs, waiting for me to fasten him.

Slowly, I shook my head and twirled my finger in the air for him to turn around. "Facing the cross."

Raising one brow at me in question, he chuckled lightly and turned around, facing the cross and revealing his backside to me. "Like this?"

"Just like that." I murmured, locking his left wrist first in the cuff and then moving around his body to do the right. When I was behind him, I laid a kiss directly between his shoulders and he took a deep breath, like it gave him life. "Nervous?"

"Anxious." He replied, glancing over his shoulder as I hooked his other wrist to the cross before slowly lowering myself to the floor to attach his ankles. The cross was more of an X than a cross, and it made him have to spread his feet pretty far to reach the cuffs, leaving him unstable and on edge.

Exactly how I wanted him to be.

Having been detained appropriately, he silently watched me as I walked around the cross, looking at him through the V between the armbars. "I'm not sure how far to push you."

"Are you afraid of breaking me?" He grinned monstrously. "I'm unbreakable."

"Safe word of your choice."

He rolled his eyes and glared at me before adjusting himself to stand as upright as possible. "Black."

I let the word tumble around in my head for a moment, wondering why he chose that to be his saving grace, but I kind of already knew.

Tamen Bryce had a black soul, or so he thought at least. I wasn't as convinced, but it didn't matter.

"Black." I repeated, walking back around the other side of the cross. "Limits?"

"None." He replied instantly, following me as best as he could. "Do your worst."

"I thought this was about pleasure."

"Yours." He countered. "And trust."

"And yet you want me to hurt you, don't you?"

Pausing before he answered, I knew he gave me his truth. "I expect you to."

"Interesting." I hummed, reaching behind me to tug the zipper of my dress down and shimmy out of it, letting it pool onto the floor. "I'm not a sadist, but I am into degradation from time to time."

"Oh, joy." He joked and then went silent when I went to the side of the room and took out a couple of different tools he couldn't see. Wearing only a matching black set of lingerie left me feeling bold and empowered as I picked my weapons against Tamen.

This was my element.

"We're going to play a game." I sang, letting the click of my heels echo around the sound proof room as I circled him. "Questions." I announced, glancing at him as I passed his face again. "If you answer all of my questions, I'll reward you with pleasure." I faced him head on and brought the satchel of clamps out from behind my back. "If you refuse, or lie, you'll receive a punishment."

His blue eyes dropped to the bag in my hand as I waited for his consent. "I hate this game already."

"Afraid of a little pain?" I mocked him with a smirk, and he scoffed.

"Afraid of what questions you'll ask is more like it. I get hard on pain."

"Good." I hummed, calling his bluff as I lifted a small metal clamp up in front of his face. "Because these are going on your balls each time you refuse or lie. Let's get started."

"Evil." He replied, but he didn't tell me no, and we both knew I'd respect his decision if he did.

"Let's begin." I walked back around behind him and slipped a black blind fold on over his head, blocking out his sight so he couldn't study me like he usually did. When he was blind and restrained for me, I started. "How many people have you killed?"

He snorted, and I fought the urge to attach a clamp to his ass cheek just for the fun of it. "Hundreds, Rainbow. I don't keep count."

I mulled that over, imagining him killing that many people. The longer I imagined it, the longer Tamen's face morphed into a sinister villain from a movie, splattered with red and smiling a grotesque evil sneer.

Not my Tamen.

"How many people have you spared?" I asked.

Instantly he replied, "None."

I picked a clamp from the bag and attached it without a noise, making him buck and hiss from the pain it caused his sensitive groin. "Fucking hell, woman!"

"I don't believe you, and I told you what would happen if you were dishonest with me."

"Fuck!" He gasped, before taking a few deep breaths while I admired the tenseness in the long muscles along his back. "You have no proof I wasn't honest."

"It doesn't matter; this is my game, remember?" I walked around to the front of his body on the other side of the cross, loving the way he cocked his head to track my steps with his ears. "Next question. How old were you the first time you killed?"

He sighed, but answered. "The moment I was born."

I paused, running that scenario through my head as sadness for the little baby Tamen used to be, filled my heart. "Your mother died in childbirth?"

"So, they say." He replied. "My father always said she saw how evil I was when I came out and her heart broke from the regret of having me."

"Tamen." I whispered, but stopped when he bucked against the chains.

"Ask something else. Something not about my childhood."

"How did you get into this life?"

He groaned, "That's my childhood, Rainbow!"

"You don't make the rules, asshole!" I called back, reaching around the cross and attaching another clamp to his tight sack, making him cry out again in surprise. "Answer me."

"I've already gotten the clamp, woman. Why would I still answer it?" He snapped angrily.

My intention hadn't been to anger him with my game, but it was inevitable at the same time. He refused to share anything of meaning with me. Nothing of depth or importance ever passed his lips when we were together. To have something more than surface deep, I needed to know his brain and his reasoning.

My whole adult life I kept everyone at arm's length, living like a cast member in a show, always on and hiding the real me. But with Tamen, I saw his darkness and his scars.

Now I wanted to know the story behind those parts of him.

"Why do you cut yourself?" As soon as the words passed my lips, I saw the grief in his body open up, threatening to swallow him whole.

"I don't." He replied in a strangled voice, "I used to."

"Tell me why."

"Why wouldn't I?" He argued defiantly. "My life was shit."

"Tell me why, though." I urged, "Please."

He growled and tightened his hands into fists where they were bound above his head. He wanted to deny me, but he wanted to avoid further clamps. I stayed silent, letting him decide his fate. Eventually, he parted his lips and admitted the truth, "To bleed the evil out."

"How old were you?" I asked, praying my voice would stay firm and flat to hide my sorrow as he told me about his pain.

"I don't know. Grade school to high school, I can't remember."

There were dozens of other questions I wanted to ask, but I knew he was teetering on the edge of losing his mind to his memories and if I pushed, he'd shut down out of spite.

"Did you do it anywhere else but your thighs?" I asked, silently lowering myself onto my knees so I could kneel between the bottom part of the cross and come face to face with the blackout tattoos covering his thighs.

"Why do you care so much about them? What does it matter, it's done. They're old and I've moved on." He snapped again, letting his anger take control of him.

"Because I want to kiss every single scar you gave yourself." I whispered, before leaning forward and laying my lips directly over the raised flesh on his inner thigh. Using my flat palms against his legs, I grounded him to my presence as I slowly and erotically laid kisses over every inch of skin that he had marred in his painful childhood.

"Sloane." He gasped in a pained voice, bucking against my touch like each touch of my lips branded him again. "Are we done?"

"No." I gingerly rose to my feet, sandwiched between his big hard body and the padded cross at my back. "I'm just getting started with you." I kissed my way up his abs and to his chest, running my hands over his flesh as he growled and groaned. It was the first time I touched him so freely, over every inch of his body. I pulled his head down so I could kiss his lips, and he hungrily ate from them as if my kiss could soothe his demons. "You aren't evil, Tamen."

"You don't even know me." He argued and pain bloomed in my chest, but I forced it down. Tamen lashed out on a good day, not to mention when he was tied up, forced to expose his inner struggles to me in a power switch. Of course, he'd lash out and try to hurt me to match his own pain. "I don't know you."

"If you truly believe that, then I guess this is done." I replied, sliding my body to the side, but he instantly pressed me into the cross harder, immobilizing me as I dragged my nails through the hair on the back of his head, holding him to me.

"I can't—" He shook his head as his body trembled, "I don't know how—"

"I know." Kissing his face, I soothed him gently. "But you can't shut me out when I try. One of us has to try."

I held him just like that, and after a while, he broke the silence. "I was sixteen the first time I killed someone on purpose. My first job, for my father. Dane and Maddox were on a different job and something came up he needed me to handle. So I did it. I killed a person for him and came back to Harlow House, and sat down to dinner like everything else was fine. Yet the entire time my brain was screaming and bouncing off the inside of my skull like it was trying to convince me to run away from that life, even though I had spent a decade trying to prove I could handle it." Lifting the blindfold off his eyes, I stared up at him as he shared parts of himself with me willingly. "My reward for doing such a good job was his hired whore for the night. I was a virgin even after I became a killer, and he thought I should cross off two big items on the same night."

"He didn't." I gasped, as if that was the worst part of the whole story. My composure was a mask, carefully constructed to prevent Tamen from seeing my disgust at his part in the events he was describing, the stench of his sick childhood heavy in the air between us.

Tamen smirked slightly. "I guess that's where my fetish for prostitutes started."

"And I guess I'm where it ends." I countered, tsking my teeth at him snidely. "Thank you for sharing that with me." Though it left me with way more questions I ached to have answers for. What was Harlow House? Why was his father running these jobs he kept talking about? And why couldn't he leave if he wanted to?

"I'll share more with you." He backed up, releasing me from captivity against the cross. "But not like this. I want to do it in my own time. My own way."

I groaned and rolled my eyes theatrically, knowing he was right. "Fine. But that's a shame because your reward tonight was going to be—" I hummed and licked my lips seductively, "So fucking worth it."

I went to slide out from my spot to release his bindings, but he held me tight again, pressing his body into mine. "Wait, I answered your questions. I earned my reward."

I grinned and pet his chest mockingly, "You didn't answer all of my questions. There are so many more. And they were far more fun than the difficult ones I wanted to start with. I was going to get through the dark stuff and into more of the—" I hesitated like I was trying to think of the right word, "pleasurable stuff."

"Rainbow." He growled regretting his call to end our game. "We have the room all night."

"Hmm." I hummed, glancing around the room. "Answer this for me and we'll see where we go from here."

He nodded in agreement, though I was pretty sure he'd agree to just about anything at that moment.

"Why did you show special interest in designing this room? Are you just that into BDSM or is there something more?"

Tamen grinned and leaned his body up off of mine to release his hold on me as he nodded to the wall. "Go look out the window and you'll see why this room was important to me."

Squinting at him, I hesitated and then untangled myself from him and walked toward the large one-way mirrored glass to look down at what I already knew was down there. "My stage?"

He rested his chin on his bicep as he winked at me. "This room sits right at the front of the stage, with a perfectly clear view of you as you run your shows. It was also the room I was in the night I met you. I watched you for the first time, from that very window."

The man, the myth, the legend.

Walking away from the window back to my caged man, "Sometimes I think you're perfect." I scraped my nails down his spine to his firm ass and dug them in, leaving a mark on both perfectly taut cheeks. It should be illegal for a man to so effortlessly have a perfect ass. "But then I remember your flaws. Like the fact that this is the room that you fucked Val's face in that first night."

He grunted and groaned when I reached around his gigantic body and stroked his cock. The thing had been hard and ready since he stripped down; I was pretty sure it even got harder with each clamp placed on his sack. "I'm a flawed man," He shrugged, "What are you going to do about it?"

"Fuck you." I replied, biting his shoulder and leaving another mark. "Maybe when I'm done, you'll finally be a good boy."

His dick throbbed in my hand and he flexed his hips to push it deeper into my palm. "If you were trying to punish me, your pussy wrapped around my cock is never a hardship."

"Jokes on you, Bully." I chided, dropping his cock and pulling off one clamp aggressively.

He howled and bucked wildly as I walked away to the chests of toys available with a special saunter.

I was in my element again, back on top, and ready to dominate him and the scene. Tamen was in for a wild night of true submission and pleasure.

"I'm not the one taking it tonight." I purred, lifting the lid on my favorite chest in the room. "Tonight, you're going to fifth base."

"Fifth base?" He questioned, and I could hear the anxiety in his voice as the cuffs rattled against the cross. "What the hell is fifth base, and what kind of baseball do you watch?"

Chapter 26 - Tamen

"Oh, you sweet, innocent boy." Sloane's thick, honey-like voice, low and resonant, carried across the room as I craned my neck, nearly breaking it, to see what she was doing at the mysterious toy cabinets.

"Innocent?" I stammered, trying to keep her talking. "Were you not paying attention earlier?"

"Oh, I was." With a little humming sound, she turned, the weight of what she held heavy in the air; I saw it, and the blood ran cold in my veins — I had made a grave mistake. "I've paid attention to everything you've ever said to me. But have you done the same in return?"

"What does that mean? Of course I listen to you!" I struggled as she held out a black leather strap on harness and gracefully stepped into it, sliding it up her legs and tightening it around her tight waist. "Sloane."

She pouted and cocked her head to the side, "No more, *My Pretty Little Rainbow*? I'm offended. And I was going to go easy on you for your first time taking my strap." She paused and tapped her finger to her chin, "Have you ever taken anything up your ass before?"

My cough was a desperate, choked sound, and I turned from her, my eyes tracing the patterns in the ceiling as my inner conflict raged.

Black.

Fucking say it, Tamen.

Black.

Safe word out this mess before you get fucked up the ass by her toy.

"No." I replied, still staring up at the ceiling. "No, I haven't taken anything up there."

"Mmh," She hummed in a seductive voice, drawing my curious eyes back to her. "I'm so glad to hear that, baby. God, I'm so wet already and I haven't even started."

Against my better judgement, my cock jumped, throbbing from her seduction and sass. I was too manly to admit she terrified me at the moment, but my body couldn't hide its excitement either. "What is your plan, exactly?"

"Well, first and foremost," She reached behind her and undid her lace bra, letting her big tits free. As if that wasn't distracting enough, she reached up and palmed them, letting her head fall back as she massaged them, letting sexy little sighs and moans slip from her lips as she toyed with her nipples. "I'm going to suck your cock until you're cross-eyed." She dropped her head back down to look at me and licked her lips. "And I'm going to prep you to take me until you're aching for me and can't take it anymore. That's when you're going to beg me. You're going to promise to be my good boy and tell me all the things you'll do for me if I just take you out of your misery and fuck your virgin ass for the first time."

She grabbed the dildo of choice and a bottle of lube from the cabinet and set them down on the bench next to the cross. Admittedly, the dildo was far smaller than I imagined she would choose. I thought for sure she would have come back with a massive monster dick to make me miserable, but it was only four inches or so long and slender. Except for the big mushroom head on it. That would fucking hurt.

Sweet, lingering kisses followed the soft touch of Sloane's hands on my skin, a gentle dance of caresses across my back and sides. I leaned into her touch, desperate for it, feeling so on edge and uncertain. With a swift movement, she pulled the blindfold back down, the sudden absence of light disorienting me in my distraction.

I thrived in the dark—normally. Right at that very moment, however, I hated it.

"Have you done this before?" I asked, hating that she was going to tell me yes.

"Not like this." She replied instantly as I heard shuffling in front of me seconds before her lips landed on my inner thigh, making me jump and then instantly lean into her touch. "Never like this."

"What's different?" I fought to stay grounded as her fingers wrapped around my dick seconds before her wet tongue slid down the length of it. God, her mouth was so wet and hot.

"I'm enjoying it." She purred before taking me deep into her mouth and gagging on it. I bloody loved it when she gagged on my cock. "My panties are soaked right now, and my clit is so swollen. You can't see it, but I can't stay still, I keep rocking my hips to rub my pussy on the strap of this harness."

"Rainbow." I moaned when she gently pulled one clamp off my scrotum, it burned as blood returned to that part of my skin, but it hurt far less than the last one she pulled off. Minor victories, I guess.

"What about this excites you so much?" I questioned, and I could feel her smile before she licked the shaft of my dick.

"This is more, Tamen." She asserted plainly and cupped my sack, rolling my balls in her palm. "You're more. I've never had feelings for anyone I've been with like this before. The connection excites me."

I processed her words as she continued her torture on me, using her mouth and hands to make me lose my mind. "The connection." I hissed when her fingers traveled behind my balls to that place I never wandered. "Right. That's it."

She chuckled and I could almost see her snarky grin in my mind's eye as I laid my forehead on my arm and fought the urge to push back against her fingers. Why the hell did it feel so good?

"I hope you know how hot it's going to be for me when you beg the first time."

"Still don't think that's going to happen," I growled, "I'm willing to give you control, but begging isn't something I do easily."

"Ooh," She sang and then I heard the cap of the lube bottle open and tensed. "Does that mean you've begged another woman before me?" When I didn't reply, simply because my tongue was stuck somewhere down my throat as her cold wet fingers started rubbing themselves across my taint, she went on. "Do I know her? Does she work here, should I go ask her for pointers?"

"Fuck you." I hissed, losing control as her fingers found their target and started that same teasingly pleasant motion against my back door.

"Nah, baby." She moaned, rubbing her lips on the swollen head of my cock in rhythm with her fingers until I could not stop my hips from jerking, seeking more from her skills. "But I can't wait to fuck you."

"Then get to it." I demanded arrogantly.

"Beg me, Bully. That's the only way I'm going to give you what you obviously are too manly to ask for. You should see how insane your body looks right now; it's telling me everything your words won't."

"Tell me." I fought to distract myself as she somehow had me pushing my legs apart even more than they already were. "Describe what you see."

"Mmh," She hummed, fisting my dick and letting her saliva glide it over my flesh. "You're red. Everywhere. Like you're burning up."

"Hot. Yep." I nodded, "Very hot."

"And tense." She added, laying her lips against my inner thigh once again on those scars I hated most that she seemed to be obsessed with. "Your thighs look like they could crack a watermelon."

"I have no idea what that means. You Americans are so weird."

"You seem to spend a lot of time here in America for someone who constantly complains about the people."

Shrugging, "I have dual citizenship, but I don't know anything about this land outside of the dark city dealings I've taken part in since infancy. Everything else is foreign to me."

"Does the UK feel more like home?"

"Nothing feels like home. I'm a nomad with a British accent. That's all."

"Shame." She tsked her teeth once more before removing her hands and mouth from my body completely. I sensed her standing up onto her feet on the other side of the cross before she spoke again. "I liked the idea of telling everyone I was fucking a Royal." As she said it, Sloane moved behind me and laid another one of her burning kisses between my shoulders. "Call it a fantasy."

"Please, Rainbow." I hissed, sagging into the cross from the overwhelming weight of the sensations in the room.

"You can do better than that, Mr. Duke." She whispered, leaning into me so I could feel the cold of the leather against the back of my thighs. "Use your fancy words to beg me."

"Fucking do it already!" I barked, gritting my teeth when she pushed her hand against the back of my neck, bending me into the cross. "Yes."

"What do you want?" She questioned, pouring lube down my crack and creating a mess. "If it's too much for you, just say *black*. Say it and I'll stop."

"I want to come! Punish me as you see fit for my actions that first night. I'm not stopping!"

She snickered and then I felt it—the toy against my ass. I wished I could see her wearing it in her high heels and panties, but that would have to wait for another time. I could scarcely form a thought as it was. "You're getting closer, Bully. You're so close to being a good boy and begging for me. Let me hear it. Beg me."

"Please!" I roared as she put pressure on the toy until I felt like I'd never take another deep breath again. "Fuck me, Sloane!"

"Who do you belong to, Tamen?" She asked, pressing the thick head of the toy into me. It felt like I was going to rip into two, a cold sweat broke out across my skin as my head swam. "Tell me who you belong to, Bully, and I'll make you feel so good."

"You." I grit out, clawing at the cross with my fingers as she pulled out and pushed back into me. "I'm yours, Rainbow. Your good boy. Your toy. Bloody hell, just let me come, please. Please Rainbow, please!"

"There he is," she purred, pushing the toy into me all the way and biting my shoulder. "That's my good boy taking my toy. You're so perfect."

"Fuck." I held on for dear life as she slowly started fucking my ass, speaking those annoying words repeatedly as she dominated me. The toy itself wasn't painful like I thought it would be, and she was a master at her trade, reading my body as she fucked me. Twice she added more lube, mere seconds after it began to burn past pleasure and brought me back to that headspace between enjoyment and torture where I wasn't sure if I wanted to beg her to stop or beg her to fuck me harder.

My body shook, trembling in my bindings as I moaned incoherently, feeling pleasure past anything I'd ever experienced before.

"Sloane." My breath caught, her name escaping my lips in a mumble as she quickened her movements, pushing harder and faster against me, forcing me to sink further into my restraints to accommodate her.

"You're doing so good, baby. You're so perfect taking this like a good boy. Tell me how it feels each time I thrust into you."

"Like I'm going to lose my mind." I bellowed, fighting my bindings. "I must come, Rainbow. Please, can I come, please?" I fell into the submission she ached for so effortlessly it should have alarmed me. I had no problem letting a woman top me, but I never begged. Never like this.

"You want to come for me, good boy? You think you've earned it?"

"Yes! Oh, bloody hell, I can't—" I tipped my head back and roared as my body felt like I touched a high voltage wire, spasming and locking up tight as fire erupted in my cock. "I can't stop."

"Come for me, baby." She cooed, digging her nails into my side to hold me how she wanted as she fucked me through the painful orgasm. She never even touched my dick as I came, which made the orgasm nearly painful from the unfamiliar sensation, but damn, it was divine. Leaving me convulsing against the cross, she withdrew just as I was about to reach the end of my orgasm, almost causing me to black out from the overwhelming sense of relief.

Relief from the orgasm breaking over my body.

Relief from letting everything go and giving myself to Sloane in a way I'd never done with someone else. It wasn't just the act of getting pegged, but being vulnerable with her that left me shaken and broken.

Or healed.

Lost, or was I finally found?

My arms fell to my sides, heavy and free, as she released the cuffs, and a padded bench pressed against my legs as she pushed me down before removing my blindfold. She thought of everything.

"Jesus." I let out a croaking sound as she released my ankles; the world swam into focus as my eyes opened, her face was the first thing I saw. "You're bloody perfect."

Sloane let out a big breath of what looked like apprehension when I tried to grin at her. "Lay back and take some deep breaths." She instructed, pushing me onto my back on the bench

With a dopey grin stretching my face, eyes squeezed shut, I lay there, a well-behaved dog following orders, trying to process the events that had just transpired. The lingering warmth of my climax slipping from my limbs.

When I felt her naked warm body gently straddle my stomach and curl forward to lay on my chest, I wrapped my arms around her back, clinging to her as the unspoken change between us settled in my brain. "Did you hate that?"

I snorted and rolled my head from side to side in exhaustion. "I've never come that hard before. And without a single thing touching my dick."

She chuckled, kissing my chest over the scar on my sternum from that night she held me at knifepoint. "I'm quite impressed by your ability to do that. It was very entertaining to watch."

Without opening my eyes, I cracked my hand onto her backside, causing her to shriek and buck against me, but I kept my arms tight around her body, immobilizing her. "Careful, Rainbow." With a low, gentle warning, I sat up straight, and she settled onto my lap, her legs circling my waist, her eyes fixed on me. "Now, I think this has been a fun experiment and all—" I lifted her and carried over to the massive bed with red satin sheets on it and threw her into the center before walking away to the cabinet of toys I picked out specifically with a night like this in mind.

"What are you doing?" She sat up on her elbows, watching me cautiously as I grabbed what I needed and stalked back over to the bed with my loot.

The pile of things made an interesting combination and when she saw them, she tried to scurry away from me, but I expected that move and caught her before she made it to the floor. I had both of her wrists tied to the top corners of the bedposts with minimal effort, but her ankles were proving to be harder to capture as she kicked them at my face repeatedly.

"Stay still." I barked. "It's my turn to play."

"Fuck you, asshat!" She cursed, landing a blow to my face and wincing when her toes cracked under the impact. "Ow!"

"Should have just been a good girl and done what I said the first time." I chided, tying one of her ankles to the corner and getting the second one restrained, leaving her in a starfish position on her back. "Good girls get to come faster than bad girls."

"This was supposed to be about you! To settle the score!" She screeched when I wrapped one of the leather cuffs around her thighs and she could not resist, though she tried to shake me off the best she could. She had so much fight in her, it made my dick hard again.

Already. Who knew that was possible.

"That was the plan until you fucked me in the ass, you monster." I accused, even though I didn't feel that way in the least. "Now it's time for me to be the Bully you hate, all over again. I can't stand being the good boy you made me into."

"You fucking cock twit!" She screamed as I attached the second leather cuff to her other thigh. When I lifted the Hitachi wand in the air and turned it on she balked again, fighting like a wildcat caught in a trap as I fastened it into the cuffs, laying the vibrating head directly onto her clit, even going as far as spreading her pretty pink lips to make sure it had direct contact.

Her body twisted in pleasure, arching off the bed as she let out a guttural moan, completely at my mercy.

"Now," I stood up and clapped my hands together before retrieving my last trick for the night and standing over her. "We're going to play a game. A game of *questions*." I announced, and her face whitened even as her hips writhed against the toy she couldn't escape. "If you answer all of my questions, I'll reward you." I kneeled between her spread thighs and brought the satchel of clamps out from behind my back. "If you refuse, or lie, you'll receive a punishment."

"Jesus fucking Christ." She cried and then her back bowed off the bed as she orgasmed, screaming my name as she climaxed in surprise. When she opened her eyes again, I could tell she was expecting me to admonish her for coming without permission, like she would have done to me. But I just smiled down at her sinisterly.

"Oh, did you expect me to withhold pleasure from you, Rainbow?" I tightened my lips disappointingly with a shake of my head. "See, you think I'm a sadist or just a surly cold Englishman, but in reality I'm a depraved monster who loves to make you come." Her back bowed again as the toy brought her closer to another painful precipice of pleasure. "I hope you're comfortable there, Love. Because you're going to be my little toy for a very long time tonight. I can only imagine how many times you'll orgasm for me before the sun comes up."

"I hate you." She hissed, biting her lips to stifle the moan that leaked through them.

"I know." I whispered, leaning over her and attaching one of the clamps to her hard nipple, and nearly salivating at the scream she gave me in response. "And I fucking love that."

Chapter 27 - Tamen

"What exactly is your plan here?" Dane asked with a bored expression from the passenger seat.

"You don't need to know, because you're not coming in." I repeated for the fifteenth time since he ambushed me outside of my hotel, getting in my car. If I had been in London, I would be on my bike and there would have been no room for him to tag along. Despite England's reputation for unpredictable weather, Boston's was even more erratic; the constant change made it impossible to ride, and I yearned for the open road on my bike.

"This is a revenge hit, isn't it?" Dane pried, eyeing me. "Those hardly ever go well, brother."

I hated when he called me that. We weren't brothers, not anymore. The time for that was long past, which made his intrusion into my life even more annoying. "It's not revenge. It's simply finishing something I couldn't last time."

"So, who is it?" He moved forward like I hadn't tried dismissing him at every turn.

"Don't you have a wife you should be spending your time with this evening, instead of bothering me?"

He shrugged nonchalantly, "She's busy with Liv and the kids. They're having a whole evening at Hartington, complete with bounce houses, a chocolate fountain and endless martinis courtesy of Mrs. Straight's impeccable ability to host a party. I think there was even a cotton candy machine."

"So, you ran away from a happy house to sit in my dark car and annoy me?"

"No, I saw that I wasn't needed there, so I left to find something else to do."

"I don't need you." I snapped back, firmer than I should have. His answering sigh nearly gave him the entrance needed to slide into some brotherly role of wisdom and support that I wasn't interested in. "It's a simple in and out job, no assistance required."

"Bummer." An intrusive voice whispered from outside of the car as a dark bear leaned down into my open window. "I was promised fun."

"Jesus fucking Christ!" I cried out, slapping my wheel and glaring at my brother and then over to Maddox where he squatted next to my car. "This isn't a field trip for bored house husbands."

"Good." Maddox shrugged, "I'm not a husband."

"Yet." Dane smirked, and I rolled my eyes and slammed my head back into my seat.

"Leave." I hissed, shoving my car door open and sending Maddox onto his ass as I got out. Dane followed suit and leaned his elbows on the roof of my car as I glared at him. "Both of you, leave. Now."

"Oh, come on," Maddox brushed his hands off on his jeans and smirked in the darkness that somehow always seemed to cling to his features. "We won't take any of your fun away. We just want to watch. We won't even touch anything."

"Remember the last time you said that?" Dane chuckled and Maddox grinned as I threw my hands up in exasperation.

"I didn't technically touch anything first." Maddox pointed out, "That dude touched me."

"You put an explosive up his ass and tied him to the top of a light post." Dane deadpanned.

"Best Fourth of July to date, too." Maddox stared off as if he was remembering fond times. "Pyrotechnics are such a lost art these days."

"You guys are fucking nuts." I shook my head, grabbing my bag from the trunk and walking away from their circus sideshow, headed into the woods towards my target. Did I think they'd stay in the car and leave me be? Not a fucking chance.

But if I had to stay to watch their middle-aged pathetic bored house-husband comedy show any longer, they were going to be in danger. And we all knew, even in my prime, they'd team up against me.

They always teamed up against me.

Walking through the woods with barely a snapped twig between the three of us, Maddox finally broke the silence, asking in a hushed tone. "So, who's the target?"

They weren't going to leave, that was obvious. And they weren't going to shut the hell up either, unless I gave them something. "Max Halmer."

"Max Halmer." Maddox repeated questioningly, "Why does that name ring a bell?"

"Startup tech guy, Max Halmer?" Dane threw in.

"No," I replied, stopping at a ridge and looking down at the impressive estate below. "Coke addicted, prostitute beating, slime ball Max Halmer." I held my finger up to my brother before he could even start. "And no, this has nothing to do with Sloane."

"Why would I automatically think that you targeting a man who's notorious for trafficking and killing off sex workers across the East Coast would have any link at all to your girlfriend?" Dane scoffed, "So far-fetched."

"Ridiculous, really." Maddox shrugged, "You know, the only jobs I ever botched were the personal ones, come to think of it. But good thing this isn't one of those."

"It's not!" I snapped. "He's competition for someone I made a deal with. I was supposed to take him out weeks ago, and he got away. That's it."

"Was that before or after he shot you?" Dane crossed his arms and glared at me like only a disappointed male figure could.

Fuck him.

"I hate you both." Walking away, I started my descent down the hill.

"That seems to be a trend for you." Maddox chided as he followed. "I've heard you say that about Sloane a handful of times myself. So luckily for you, I know that means you really love us and couldn't imagine your life without us in it."

Twitchy.

I was so fucking twitchy again.

Max Halmer was probably one of the most pathetic men I've ever faced, and dying men were usually always pitiful, so that was saying something.

His security team lacked muscle and skill, relying solely on his high-tech system to alert.

But not to deter.

Security had to be a two-step process, and he forgot the second step.

"Come on, Maxi Pad." Dane chided as the sniveling man tried to scurry away from his approach. The overdone tape job to the chair, courtesy of Maddox's boredom, prevented any real movement though. It looked as though he wore a body suit of tape, he probably had a better chance at tipping over and getting a head injury than getting away. "You had to know we'd come for you."

"I—" He stammered, slurring his words through his new dental work courtesy of my fist as he tried to run away at first, "I don't even know you!"

"You shot me!" I scoffed, letting the theatrics of the night finally loosen me up to play along a bit. I was usually the one who loved a good mental warfare game before the execution, and watching Dane and Maddox have fun eliminating the security team *had* actually been fun. "In the back, nonetheless. Who does that?"

"I—" He choked on the blood pooling in his mouth and fell into a fit of incredibly embarrassing sobbing. "I'm sorry!"

The three of us paused, standing over the man, as his hysterics grew in volume. "Has anyone ever cried this hard before?" Maddox nudged me with his shoulder, "I mean you've hardly even touched him," Max's eyes opened a crack, before Maddox finished, "Yet."

The sniveling simp fell back into more sobbing as I shook the cringe worthy feeling it gave me to watch a grown man cry. "I don't know how much more of this I can take." I opened my bag and stared down at the array of tools laid out inside.

Originally, I had planned to turn him into a piece of Swiss cheese with my knife, but the more he cried, the more dramatic I wanted to be about it.

"Well," Dane interrupted, looking down at his phone a second before an alarm sounded from somewhere inside the house. "You're going to have to wait a moment more, I'm afraid." He looked up at me and pointed at the front door down the long hall to the foyer. "Because you are not going to want to miss this show."

The three of us crowded together as the front door flew open, banging off the wall before a smoke grenade rolled in through the opening.

"Is that—?" Maddox hissed as we watched the smoke turn a bright orange color.

"A drop zone marker?" Dane tried but failed to hide his chuckle behind his hand. "Oh, but wait until you see the masterminds behind it."

Seconds later, dark figures dressed in tight black outfits paraded in through the opening. And by paraded, I mean, one rolled in with some sloppy Catwoman move, one ran at the speed of a clumsy snail, and the other one crouch walked like a crab, making a beeline to the table against the wall to hide behind.

"Oh, my god." I groaned, covering my face as I realized what kind of spectacle I was witnessing. "No, they didn't."

"Oh, they did." Dane chuckled as Maddox bent forward, hands on his knees, laughing as the clumsy snail ran into the doorframe of the hallway and cursed in a very familiar voice.

The next noises were coughing. Lots and lots of coughing as the drop zone marker smoke filled the large foyer, coating the three stooges in iridescent orange dust.

"Damnit, Liv!" The clumsy running snail who I now recognized as Peyton gasped, "I thought you said this was fog."

Wheezing, as she fought with her tight black facemask, the crouching crab pulled it off and revealed a tuft of crazy red hair as Liv gasped for breath, "I must have grabbed the wrong one."

Meanwhile, my eyes found the roly-poly Catwoman fighting for her life as she tried to slink down the hallway toward us.

One. Somersault. At. A. Time.

Like a bad kindergarten level somersault—and that was being kind.

Halfway down the hall, she gave up, sitting on her ass in the middle of the floor as she removed her mask, letting her crazy rainbow curls free. "This all played out much cooler when we made the plans between drinks four and five." Sloane said with a lopsided grin.

"Yeah," Liv chuckled, walking next to Peyton toward us, where we still stood in utter shock. "But that was like six drinks ago."

"Good God," Dane laughed, "You three are menaces to your own life expectancies."

Leaving our now silent and surprised victim of the night where he was, I stood over Sloane and held my hand out to her, helping me up and glancing down at her lush body in her outfit. "Is this latex?"

She giggled and shrugged, "My on-hand costume choices were limited, it was either this or sheer black lace."

I wagged my eyebrows at her, "I don't hate that option either." Turning to join the group, surrounding my hit for the night, I watched Sloane's face as she came face to face with the reality she so desperately fought to be a part of.

I expected her to be grossed out by the blood and gore on Max's face, or even just somber to the fact of what I was here to do. But she wasn't.

She simply looked at the man, crying again as we all stared down at him and asked. "This is the man who shot you?"

"It is." I replied, looking over her head to Dane, who nodded approvingly as he held his wife to his chest.

Liv hunted with Maddox pretty regularly, in some weird middle aged date night adventure they did to keep their sanity amidst raising kids. Even Peyton went with Dane on some hits, but having Sloane with me at one, never crossed my mind.

Maybe it was the liquid courage that gave her the idea to tag along tonight, or something else, but I didn't hate having her here. "And you're going to kill him for it?" She asked, looking up at me.

"A hit was put on his head long before he shot me, for his own actions. He just bought himself some more time by trying to take me out." I replied honestly.

"He traffics women." Maddox added, "Prostitutes and drug addicts. And then he funnels the money through his tech company to wash the blood and tears off it." Holding his hands up, he indicated the luxurious mansion we were all standing in.

"Jesus." Sloane murmured, glancing back down at the man. "I thought shooting you made me mad enough to want him dead. But this—" she swallowed, "on top of that, makes it even worse."

"You don't have to watch this part." I nodded to the bag I'd abandoned when they arrived with their fantastic entrance.

"I want to." She took a deep breath and backed up, giving me space. "I feel like for the girls that don't get to see their justice being served, I need to watch for them."

Peyton took her hand in hers, squeezing it as they moved off to sit on the steps as Liv piped up, "If you're not going to do it, can I?"

Maddox chuckled and pulled her back toward the stairs, "Let the man have his own trophy."

"What?" She shrugged, "I'm just saying, he's dragging his feet a bit."

I turned back to my victim as Dane stood at my side and suddenly the need to draw it out and make it personal no longer consumed me. I just wanted to make it *right*. But I was also a maniac with a blood thirst that had gone unquenched for too long lately, so I settled on a quick slit of his throat.

He thrashed, and gurgled, and gasped, until he simply didn't exist anymore. No longer able to hurt anyone or profit from their pain.

And my vendetta for the bullet Sloane had to dig out of my shoulder was settled.

"So," Maddox asked after a while as we all walked back through the woods towards my car, "Wanna hit up IHOP?"

"Jesus, that sounds delicious." Peyton moaned and Dane chuckled.

"You three stooges going to change first, or are you going there like that?" I asked, nodding down at their ridiculous outfits. I was pretty sure Liv had black tube socks on in place of actual shoes.

Sloane scoffed and smacked my chest, "We were aiming for Charlie's Angels. And you'll take us out, however we look, got it?"

I kissed her.

Easily.

Uncaring of the others staring.

Their opinions on it did not matter to me. I just wanted to kiss her.

"Got it."

Chapter 28 - Sloane

I rolled over, stretching my arms out above my head and groaning at how good it felt. There was simply nothing better than that feeling of a first stretch in the morning after a wonderful night's sleep.

Well, maybe there was something better.

Many things, actually.

Things that all came from Tamen's expert body and mind. God, the things that filthy man could think up to do to me. And say! Oof, the man's dirty talk game in that pert British accent, made me quake.

Prism had opened a month ago, and we both had been working non-stop every day, figuring out the new business kinks and hiccups, leaving us only very limited time together in between my obnoxious need for beauty sleep, and his awkward inability to lie in bed past eight am. Morning people were so weird.

My phone buzzed next to me and I grinned, feeling stupidly giddy the way I did most mornings when I woke up to some sort of good morning text.

These were not cutesy or romantic texts. These were texts from the mysterious man who always evaded daylight like a vampire.

Tamen didn't do romantic things; at least not in a conventional way.

Swiping my phone open I read his words and snorted to myself at how far out of touch he was.

> **I heard you were talking shit about me.**

I rolled my eyes and typed back a witty response.

> **Do you want me to repeat it all for you, or did you hear enough?**

> **Pack your shit, we're going to Vegas.**

Romance? Who is she? Not with Tamen. He was all whiplash and windburn from his mood swings.

Throwing my legs over the side of the bed so I wouldn't be tempted to fall back asleep before my Pilates class across town, I replied.

> **I don't take orders, asshole. I give them. Try again.**

Unblocking Tamen had been a necessity to run Prism in tandem, but I sometimes missed making him work for access to me. His reply came back too fast to build up the fun of the game.

> **Sloane, you get on my last bloody nerve sometimes.**

I replied and got out of bed, heading into my closet.

> **The feeling is mutual Bully, now say please.**

As much as he tried to pretend he was a big boring pain in the ass, Tamen actually enjoyed sparring with me like this. In a way, I think it made him feel like he could be nicer to me in person if he was a jerk digitally.

I stumbled through my clothing options, trying to decide on my outfit when my phone went off again, this time signaling a different notification. This time, it was an e-payment made by my very terrible, bully of a boss.

> *I'll pick you up at ten. + $1000.00*

His text reply came in right after that.

> **See you in an hour, Rainbow.**

Well shit, since he asked me so nicely. Truth be told, I didn't want to go to Pilates, anyway. And I was always down to go to Vegas, it was the only place on earth that made me feel slightly normal compared to the others in the crowd. Sin City was the place that the weirdos and the outcasts went to feel a sense of acceptance.

And the dry heat was my personal favorite.

Abandoning workout clothes, I did what any sane person did when their insane fuck buddy offered a trans-continental trip up on a random Tuesday morning.

I exfoliated, duh.

It was Vegas, after all, with Tamen. I wasn't planning on staying clothed for much of the trip if I could help it.

THE LINE WALKERS

"Explain to me exactly what we're doing. You didn't even tell me how long we're going for." I chatted as we soared through the sky, somewhere over the Midwest.

"We're taking a trip." Tamen replied, barely glancing up from his phone. "I don't have our return flight booked yet, but a few days."

I glared at him, which he didn't see, because of the attention whore his phone was being at the moment, and pursed my lips, looking back out the window to my right. We were flying in a private jet, and while it was not my first time on a luxurious flight like this, it was my first time as an actual client.

Usually, I was the entertainment for the flight, or at the very least, for wherever we were flying to.

The flight attendant came back to our seats, handing me another strawberry mojito and topping off Tamen's club soda. She was efficient and didn't seem bothered by the fact that she was being actively ignored by Tamen for going on the fourth hour straight.

Well, that made one of us, I was over it, however.

"Do you think she ever goes the extra mile to make her clients happy?" I asked, staring at the way her tight waist almost sat on top of her flared hips as she walked away. She'd look divine in a white garter belt set that accentuated the stark difference between the two parts of her body.

"I'm sure she's excellent at her job." Tamen replied absently. Again.

"So, if I asked her to help me join the mile high club, she'd do it?" I didn't look at him on purpose, but I watched his head snap up from his screen, finally, out of my peripheral. We were facing each other, though it was probably the first time he had looked at me all flight.

"Excuse me?" He cautioned, with a low baritone in his voice.

"You know," I shrugged, still staring at where she disappeared into the galley between the cabin and the cockpit. "Do you think she'd let me kill some time until we land?" Finally, I glanced at him briefly, "Or maybe one of the captains could step away. Does it really take two people to fly the jet? That's just an in case of emergency kind of thing, isn't it?"

He drawled, in his British accent, "Rainbow." I loved hearing it aimed my way.

"What?" I sat back in my seat and stared at him head on, sipping my drink. "I'm bored."

"You're going to get yourself a spanking to kill time, if you're not careful."

Ah, there he was. My bully was finally paying attention to me again. "Well," I uncrossed my legs, loving the way his eyes instantly fell to the short hem of my white and blue sundress as it rode up, "if I'm going to get a punishment, I'd might as well get my reward first." Rising to my feet, I stepped out into the aisle like I was going to follow the sexy brunette to the galley when Tamen's big hands shot out, wrapping around my waist like a vice and pulling me down to his lap. The plush leather chairs easily accommodated my knees on the sides of his hips as I straddled him, finally getting his eyes to focus on only me.

"You're acting like a spoiled brat," He chided, rocking me forward until I was pressed firmly against his lap between my spread thighs. "It's very unbecoming of you."

"You kidnapped me and then ignored me." I purred, unbuttoning the front of my dress as his eyes battled between following my fingers and staring at my face. Tamen hated eye contact, but I noticed he worked hard to maintain it with me. Only with me. "Why do you always avoid eye contact with everyone but me?"

Everyone else only got fleeting glances of attention from time to time. But with me, each moment of focus felt like a direct power exchange, filling up my bank with his affection, knowing it cost him greatly to do it.

He groaned and looked away, almost like he was proving me wrong for the fun of it before he answered. "I spent a lot of time studying people. Through eye contact."

A snippet of his past. I tried hard not to pant in his lap like a dog eager for another treat. But I was salivating over more information. "What do you mean?"

He sighed and ran his hand over his face, but I ran my hands over the wide expanse of his chest, forcing him to ground himself to me. It worked, his blue eyes moved back to mine, and he held on there. "I can find anyone's vulnerability in their eyes. Sometimes right away, sometimes it takes a while, but the end result is always the same. I know their weakness in the end."

"So why do you always look away? I would think knowing someone's weaknesses would serve you well in your—" I shrugged, "choice of recreation."

He didn't take my joke lightly, though, tightening his hands on my waist as he took a deep breath. "There's an incredible burden that comes with knowing someone's biggest fears. It's heavy and most of the time, I don't want to know it. But I have no choice because of the time spent warping my brain to learn how to discover it through eye contact."

"Your father made you learn it." I stated, not actually asking, and he gave me a small nod.

"It was one of my first *skills* to learn." He glanced out the window, but I didn't take it personally. "Sometimes knowing how to hurt someone in the worst ways is a curse fit for the devil himself. Not a man like me."

"What's my vulnerability?" I asked, swallowing down my fear as I took a chance for him to actually hurt me. Did I have a weakness? Was there one definitive thing that would destroy me if exploited by a man like Tamen?

"Don't, Rainbow." He shook his head. "Drop it and let's move on back to the mile high club. You want to join, I'll induct you."

"Please," I pressed, using my hands on each of his cheeks to force him to look at me. "Answer my question and we can move on. I promise."

He groaned like the war waging in his head was too much and then sighed. "You really want to know?" He asked, "You want to know what part of your insecurities I'd exploit if you were just a job to me? You want me to tell you how I'd destroy you?"

"Yes." I whispered, not completely sure after all. But I couldn't turn back now, not since seeing the intensity in his eyes as he asked.

"I'd make you love me." He replied, leaving me breathless, as if my lungs were frozen. "Because that's your weakness, Sloane. Your biggest vulnerability is you believe you're incapable of loving anyone. Of being loved back. So to destroy you, I'd trick you into loving me. Then I'd own you. And then I'd ruin you with it."

"I—" I stammered, sweat beads grew along my spine as his words swirled around the surrounding air. Just because he could, didn't mean he would. I knew him better than that. "You wouldn't—"

"Enough." He cut me off with a pained shake of his head. "I said I'd tell you and then we'd move on. No more."

"Tamen." I tried once again, unable to just let it go. But he was ready to move on like he hadn't just cut me from throat to belly button, exposing my biggest fears to a monster capable of using them against me.

"I just wanted to relax for a few days with you, Sloane." He sighed, closing his eyes and leaning forward to rest his forehead against my sternum. As if the move was a natural one I'd been practicing for years, I wrapped my arms around his neck, holding him to me as I dragged my nails over the back of his scalp. "I just wanted to spoil you in Vegas for everything you've done for me and for Prism. That's all." He said in a pained voice as he tightened his arms around my waist. "I just wanted to treat you like a Goddess for a few days in one of my favorite cities. I didn't want this."

I swallowed, forcing air into my lungs and blinked away the tears that angrily burned along my lashes as I fought to get control of my emotions and fears.

"Ooh," I shimmied, and bit my lip. "Tell me more. I love being spoiled."

Hesitantly, he leaned back and stared at me, before choosing to move on, just like I did, even though it felt wrong. Finally, he cracked a small smile and slid his hands under the skirt of my dress and relaxed back into his seat. "You've been incredible the last few months, taking on new tasks and surprising me at every turn with your magnificent mind and dedication. And I want to spend a few days doing whatever pleases you."

"Whatever—" I mused, leaning in to brush my lips over his, "Anything I want?"

He chuckled and deepened the kiss I was teasing him with. "Just know that whatever you torture me with for your enjoyment, I'll get revenge on you with my form of enjoyment."

"Deal." I agreed instantly as his fingers brushed over my panties. "You've got yourself a deal."

Chapter 29 - Tamen

THE LINE WALKERS

"I have regrets." I yelled out over the music as Sloane tipped her head back and laughed loudly as she climbed up onto the bar. "So many regrets."

"Oh, come on, cowboy." She yelled, lifting the straw hat off her head and tipping it to me like in some old western before turning on her heel and shimmying for the loud crowd. "Live a little!"

I clenched my teeth to keep from ordering her off the bar as a loud thumping song switched over, making the crowd go wild as the bartenders all abandoned their drink making to join Sloane on the bar top.

As if it was something pre-rehearsed, all the women began dancing in sync to the tune, kicking their boots and stomping their heels in rhythm. Sloane was right in front of me as she moved back and forth over the sticky top, and even though every eye in the room was on her, she only looked at me as she danced.

She was perfection in her short white shorts and black tank top as she shimmied and shook her ass up and down for the crowd.

Part of me wanted to make her get down and stop displaying what was mine for everyone to see, but I knew better than that. If I made a show of trying to control her, she'd rebel.

And we were in Vegas.

Sloane would probably end up marrying an Elvis impersonator at some twenty-four-hour chapel just to spite me if I even tried. And we could have none of that. It wasn't like we had talked about exclusivity or rules now that she ended up in bed with me every night after work, but the unspoken rule was obvious.

No one was going to touch what was mine.

Not after that moment on the jet on our way to Vegas. The moment that things shifted between us from good hearted sexual fun to something far, far deeper than I shared with any other human on earth.

We didn't speak on it after that moment, but I knew we needed to at some point. She was mine, and I wasn't letting go.

Her boss babe exterior didn't fool me anymore either; my possessiveness over her turned her on. My wild and crazy Rainbow enjoyed being taken care of. She enjoyed running a show on her stage for everyone to watch, but when the lights went off and the curtain closed, she always came right back to me for more.

"Do we sell water in this bar?" One bartender screamed out from the bar top and the crowd erupted in cheers and boos alike. I glanced around and a few people made a fast exit away from the bar where they were fighting to get a drink just a moment ago. Other customers held their arms up in the air and opened their mouths, shaking their faces back and forth like they were waiting for something to fall from the sky.

What the fuck was wrong with this place?

All together, the crowd started chanting with the bartenders, and I looked up at Sloane as she jumped up and down, taking the soda gun nozzle from the original girl that created the frenzy. "Hell no H2O! Hell no H2O!"

Sloane's mischievous grin made my stomach drop, seconds before she hit the button on the nozzle, spraying water out over the crowd, myself included, as everyone screamed and cheered.

"Bloody hell." I grunted, pulling her feet off the bar as she laughed, tossing the nozzle to another girl as I threw her over my shoulder and pushed my way through the crowd. "This place should be shut down." I cursed, finally breaking through the crowd and hitting the pavement outside as Sloane's melodic giggle rang out in the dry desert air.

"I haven't had this much fun in years!" She cheered, throwing her arms up in the air as I slid her down my front to let her stand on her own two feet. "I love Sin City!"

Onlookers hooted and cheered her on as the party lived on all around us, but I was ready to take her back to our hotel and stop sharing her with every other party goer in the city like I had been for the last six hours. She was drunk; I was in desperate need of a shower since I was pretty sure that was Sprite she just covered the bar with, and if I was lucky, I might get her to eat something before she started puking her brains out all over the ensuite.

"Yeah, yeah, yeah." I nodded, pulling her toward the curb and hailing a taxi. "You say that every five minutes."

"You know what else I think, but don't say every five minutes?" She purred, sliding between me and the cab as I desperately tried to get her inside.

"What's that?" I played along, pushing a random lock of pink hair behind her ear as she grinned up at me through blurry eyes.

Her aura was pink as her cheery smile made my own try to form. Her happiness was infectious.

"I love your cock." She giggled at the end. "More importantly, I love what you do to me with it."

"Is that so?" I caged her in, forcing her to step down off the curb, getting her closer to the inside of the cab while distracting her. Her words were making me hard, but if I didn't get her back to the hotel soon, both of us were going to be indecent in public, just for two very different reasons. "Be a good girl and get in the damn cab, and I'll treat you like a goddess for the rest of the night with my cock."

She giggled, and then moaned when she palmed me, finding me hard and ready for her. "Oh, the way I'm going to make you eat those words tonight, Mr. Duke." I hesitated and frowned at her as she slid into the cab, looking up at me. "I hope you know, I chanced an incredibly awkward encounter with TSA, just for this reason."

"Jesus Christ." I cursed as she slid into the seat, leaving me to wonder exactly what kind of toys she loaded her suitcase with for this trip. "You're going to be the death of me, Rainbow."

THE LINE WALKERS

"Will you help me with something?" Sloane called from the bedroom.

I was sitting on the couch, answering emails while she got dressed for dinner. It was our second day in Vegas, and today we had spent the entirety of our time in relaxation mode thanks to Sloane's hangover from day one. Which was perfectly fine with me, actually. First, she tortured me by making me stay in bed until ten o'clock. My body hurt so bloody bad from laying there that long, that it was a good thing the next event on our schedule was the spa.

That was where I could really enjoy spending some time. Not that I needed or enjoyed all the weird mud masks, or the slimy seaweed wraps she insisted we do as a couple. But watching Sloane relax and smile dreamily at me as all the different spa employees pampered her was worth it all.

And now we were getting ready for a divine dinner at one of the top-rated restaurants in all of Nevada.

I wasn't going soft or romantic on her, though. When we got to our suite yesterday, the rose petals I ordered to be placed out lovingly on our bed spelled out, *You annoy the shit out of me,* instead of something sappy.

And Sloane had laughed so hard she had tears in her eyes.

"With what, exactly?" I replied, glancing up from my phone as she came out of the bedroom, holding something behind her back. She wore a tight, strapless white dress that was see-through around her torso with white lace, showing off the boning of a corset before the tight fabric hugged her flared hips and ended right at the top of her thighs. Her rainbow hair was pinned up in a fancy updo that made it look like a spiral rainbow on her head. She looked angelic, but I knew she was anything but.

"Putting this in." Bringing her hand out from behind her back, I choked on my tongue as she tossed a furry tail that matched her rainbow hair into my lap.

"Rainbow." I warned, lifting the tail and swinging the heavy metal plug part around as she simply stared at me. "You're not wearing this tonight."

"Since when do you get to dictate my wardrobe?" She cocked her hip out and pretended to be offended, but I knew better. "I'm wearing the pretty dress you bought me." Bickering with me was foreplay for her, and she was looking for some fun.

"Since the restaurant I'm taking you to this evening is so fancy, I'm not even sure this dress will pass their dress code. If you show up with a tail hanging out of your asshole, I'm positive they'll deny you entrance."

A seductive smile decorated her face as she ran her hands down her body with a gentle pout, "You'd let them be so mean to me?"

Oh, my pretty little Rainbow.

"You want to cause a scene, so I have to cause one back?" I questioned, eyeing the plug in my hand, knowing that I was more than interested in helping her put it in, but not if everyone knew she was wearing it. I was more interested in exploring her body at the end of the night when I finally took it out, though to be honest.

"Maybe." She purred, "I didn't get to see enough the other night. I want to see you like—that, again."

I palmed my aching dick, and her golden irises flicked down to the movement before snapping back up to mine. Standing, I towered over her and brought my hand to her throat, holding her by it as she tipped her head back to look up at me. "Are you going to purr for me like a good little kitty if I do it?"

She moaned, melting into my hold, and licked her lips. "So good. I'll be the best little pet."

"Pick a different toy if you want to play, Rainbow. And I'll agree. Something no one else can see."

"Fine." She sighed and pulled her other hand out from behind her back. In her palm was a metal butt plug with a pretty pink flared end on it. "No tail included."

"Good girl." I smirked, releasing her throat and taking the plug. She had a packet of lube with it and I knew the whole tail thing was just a setup to rile me up. Sloane knew I'd never let her out of the room with a tail hanging between her thighs, but part of me wondered if she'd do it if I called her bluff. "How do you want to take it?"

She grinned her cute little seductive smile at me before spreading her feet and bending over so her hands were on the seat of the chair I had vacated, with her plump ass up in the air. "Just like this, Sir."

My palm cracked across the back of her upper thigh for fun as I lifted her skirt to reveal a pretty white thong, barely covering her holes. Flicking my wrist, I glanced at the time; we had less than seven minutes before the time we needed to be leaving the hotel to make our reservation. Which meant I had seven minutes to play with my pretty little Rainbow before I spent the next few hours playing with her in public.

"Tell me something, Rainbow." I spoke as I pulled her thong down her thighs, leaving it there to immobilize her. "Do you actually enjoy anal, or are you one of those girls who do it simply because you know men enjoy it?"

"Mmh," she swayed her hips, glancing over her shoulder. "I usually come harder with something in my ass." I groaned, but she continued to tease me. "To be honest, I'd rather have both filled. Two toys, a toy and a dick, two dicks, you name it, I want it."

I spanked her again and ran my fingers up through her wetness and circled her clit before moving up to her ass. "I can't wait to stuff you full and feel you come harder than I've made you so far."

"Then let's get this party started, baby." She hummed seductively, arching her back harder. Silently, I sank to my knees behind her and spread her cheeks, running my tongue up from clit to ass.

I loved the way she moaned when I touched her, like she couldn't help the noises that escaped her lips when I pleasured her. It felt real.

I ate her pussy as I started playing with her ass, rimming her and teasing her as her legs shook and quivered beneath her.

Sloane reached back and slid her fingers through my hair, pulling my face in against her pussy more and I growled, loving the bite of her nails on my scalp as I pushed my tongue in deeper. "That's it, baby," She purred, rolling her hips to find a rhythm she liked as she used my face for her enjoyment. "Damn, that feels so good."

I pushed one finger into her pussy and used my tongue on her ass, pushing against the tight resistance as she mewled and moaned for me. She was the perfect vocalist for me. Readying the lube, I poured some onto her ass, watching it drip down to coat her before I started giving her my finger. As expected, her desperate pleas ramped up as I fingered her tight ass. Her pussy dripped, clenching around nothingness each time I penetrated her ass, and I ached to fuck her.

There were only a mere four minutes left, though, and they were all for her and her pleasure. That was the whole point of me bringing her on vacation; to please and spoil her.

And I was currently doing both.

Coating the plug without the tail, I started inserting it into her ass as I circled her clit, teasing her with indirect pleasure and pressure until she was gasping and pushing back on the widest part until it was fully inside of her.

"Cock!" She gasped, leaning up to look over her shoulder again. "I want to come on your cock."

It wasn't a request. It wasn't even a plea.

My pretty little Rainbow wanted to be filled with me, and I wasn't going to deny her.

Yanking my belt and zipper free, I fisted my aching cock as she pushed me down into the chair and then sat in my lap, facing away from me. She reached between her spread thighs, still with her panties tangled around her knees, and lined me up with her wet pussy, sinking down onto me in one quick thrust. "Fuck, Rainbow." I growled as she started rocking back and forth in my lap, the plug making her pussy impossibly tight as she rolled her hips.

"Clit, baby." She brought my hand around the front of her body to her clit, and I wrapped both arms around her, holding her as she worked herself towards her orgasm. I played with her how she demanded, bit her neck and told her all the dirty ways I was going to fuck her ass all night long as she shattered into a million pieces, crying out my name as she came.

"That's my good girl. You love what I can do to you, don't you?"

"Mmh," Her head flopped back against my shoulder, and she tentatively rolled her hips again and I flexed my cock inside of her still spasming pussy. "Bend me over and let me return the favor."

I chuckled, biting her ear around her sparkling earring before lifting her up by the waist until she was on her feet in front of me. Her golden eyes found mine as she looked at me in confusion when I stood up and tucked my unsatisfied dick back into my pants. Her offer was enticing, it would probably take me less than thirty thrusts into her perfect tight pussy to blow my load, following her into ecstasy. "I have other plans for my orgasms tonight."

Her eyes rounded slightly as I slid her panties back up into place and then pulled her skirt back down over her plump ass. "Is that so?"

"It is." I stated plainly, kissing her lips before adjusting my tie and nodding to the door. "Tonight is going to be one of the best nights of your life."

She smiled up at me with glassy eyes, "You sound pretty sure of yourself, buddy."

"I have faith in our ability to find fun wherever we go." I countered, "It will be a night we remember forever."

CHAPTER 30 - SLOANE

"Where am I?" I croaked, holding my head to keep it from exploding as I tried to slide off the bed.

Tamen groaned somewhere from his side of the bed, but it sounded weird, so I forced my eyes to crack open enough to look at him. Only, he wasn't there. One foot was on the bed, but the rest of him was missing.

Slithering like a pathetic newborn reptile on ice, I made my way to his side of the bed and peeked over the edge. If it didn't feel like my head was going to explode into a red mist, I probably would have laughed at what I found.

Tamen laid in a heap, naked as a jaybird tangled up in the sheet, using an empty bottle of champagne as a pillow.

"Good god, I'm still drunk." I grunted, flopping back down onto the bed, daring to look at the windows to see if there was any sunlight coming through the cracks, but the curtains were shut so well I couldn't tell. "What time is it?"

"What country am I in?" Tamen shot back in a cranky voice, "What day is it?"

"Fuck all if I know." I laid there as shuffling came from the ground, a moment later, one very disheveled Tamen threw himself up onto the bed, landing next to me as he swallowed me up with his thick arms and the sheet, cocooning us both back into comfort. "What the hell happened?"

"You got me drunk." He whined into my neck, but I could feel the ghost of a smile on his whiskered face. "I think. It gets kind of—blank after dinner."

"Dinner—" I tried to think back to what we were doing last night and remembered the way he bent me over in the living room and ate me out before putting my plug in. "Oooh, dinner." I giggled, getting flashbacks of the indecent things we did to each other at dinner.

He snorted and tightened his hands around my waist, pulling me in tighter to his body. Dragging my nails over the back of his hand, something snagged against the sheet, creating a foreign feeling on my skin, so I pulled the fabric aside and lifted my hand to investigate.

I stared at the foreign object for a heartbeat, and then two, by the fourth or fifth panic was building in my chest as I tried to make sense of what I was seeing. "Tamen." I croaked, and cleared my throat when he hummed in response, but didn't pay any attention. "Tamen!"

"What?" He leaned over my shoulder to look at me as I held my hand out in front of his face.

"What the fuck is that!" I cried, desperately trying to remember what exactly happened after dinner last night.

"Oh, bloody hell." Tamen groaned, taking my hand in his and holding it still where it had been shaking from fear. "I thought the Elvis man at the wedding chapel was just a dream."

My lips parted in exasperation as I stared at him over my shoulder before glancing back at the offensive item on my hand.

Or rather, my finger.

My ring finger.

On my left hand.

Chapter 31 - Sloane

Eighteen Hours Before

I stared at my reflection in the mirror above the sink, the steam from the hot water fogging the glass slightly, but my radiant energy shone through; never had I looked so alive. Sure, I was a master with my makeup, and I truly believed the power of positive thinking could turn any situation into a positive one. But the glow in my eyes was from something else tonight.

It was something real. Something physical I could touch and hold on to. It was mine.

Tamen was mine.

Since meeting him, I felt invigorated, thriving as I hadn't in a long time. Sure, most of the thriving existed out of spite and scheming to get back at him for something, but that was the fun of it.

I was having fun with life.

It didn't feel like I was living simply to exist anymore. I was prospering.

In ways I didn't know existed for girls like me. Which led me to the bathroom in a loud club on the Vegas strip. My belly was full of the most delicious food I'd ever tried before, most of it had been hand fed to me by Tamen from his spot next to me in the booth tucked in a corner of the romantic fancy restaurant. It wasn't exactly how things were normally done in polite society, but we didn't care.

We could have fucked on the table, but refrained.

Barely.

The plug I was wearing was making me crazy the longer I wore it, without any real stimulation to any other place in my body. I smiled to myself as I remembered the look on Tamen's face when I tossed him the furry tail plug, asking him to put it in for me.

The accessory made for a great photo op when I posted to my cam site years ago, but I never actually wore it for pleasure. But the pleasure I got from watching Tamen trying to figure out how to tell me no was worth it all.

He didn't want me to be embarrassed by rude people in public who would criticize my decision to be so bold. So, he told me no, but was okay with the other one that didn't have the long pastel tail attached.

But it wasn't without its own tricks, and Tamen was about to find out exactly just how bold I loved to be in public. Luckily, we were in a place far more accepting of our particular flavor of bold.

Still, I was about to have fun with him.

I freshened up my lip stain, leaned over the counter when a girl came out of the stall behind me, and I watched her step falter for half of a second when she looked at my ass before a bright smile crossed her face. Joining me at the counter, she nodded to me with a smirk, "I like your style."

"Thanks." I winked, tucking my cosmetics back into my clutch and heading back out into the dark club where Tamen waited for me.

He leaned against the wall, with his ankles crossed and one hand in his pants pocket, looking like a GQ model. His usual suit and tie were absent, replaced by sand-colored slacks and a white cotton shirt, yet his dark and dangerous aura remained, despite his relaxed appearance. He looked up when he sensed me getting close, and the dark cut of his eyebrows over his bright eyes gave him that demonic gaze that bloomed fear and excitement in my belly every time I found myself in his presence.

The whites of our clothing matched, but my rainbow hair and his dark and dangerous vibes contrasted with each other perfectly.

We were worse than oil and water.

We were light and dark.

Night and day.

Good and bad.

Yet we were both imperfectly perfect together.

"Let's go dance." I called out over the loud music, nodding to the crowded dance floor in front of the stage where the DJ was putting on a wild show.

He glanced out at the chaos and rolled his eyes, leaning up off the wall. "One dance. And then we leave."

"Two dances." I countered, leaning in to kiss his neck as he bent down so I could get to his ear. "And then a blowjob in the bathroom. Maybe a few drinks after that."

With a snort, he spun me around, pressing my back to his chest, and then bit my neck. "One dance. One fuck in the bathroom. One drink. Then we leave."

I grinned, a smug feeling settling in my chest, and nodded, knowing I held all the cards, regardless of his response. "Yes, Sir."

Walking forward, I headed toward the dance floor but looked over my shoulder to find him staring straight at my ass, finding the fun little party trick of the plug as he saw it for the first time.

He caught up in two steps and plastered himself to my back as we joined the crowd, speaking into my ear. "Your ass plug is blinking a rainbow of colors in time with the techno music."

"I know, isn't it wonderful?" I giggled, grinding my ass into his groin and making him grunt. "Now everyone will know where your cock is going to be tonight."

"Rainbow." He warned with that deep growl but stopped when I took his hands and wrapped them around my waist, moving him with me until he gave in and stopped fighting the urge to dance with me. "You're a troublemaker."

"I know, isn't it wonderful?" I repeated, kissing his cheek when he brushed his cheek against mine. Dragging my nails over his scalp, I held him there, talking into his ear. "Thank you for tonight."

He paused slightly, turning his face to look me in the eye like what I said was serious. I hadn't meant for it to be heavy with anything other than an acknowledgment of how happy I was. But it seemed even that was serious for him.

"Thank *you*, Sloane." He replied almost ominously.

"For what?" I turned and faced him, wrapping my arms around his neck to keep him close. In a flash, he ran his hands down my backside, his touch lingering at the edge of my dress; the neon glow fighting for attention through the thin white fabric, as he seemed torn between protecting me and letting me enjoy myself.

He settled on resting his gigantic hands on my ass and moving in time with the music as I stared up at him. "For literally everything." Tamen replied, "You'll never understand it, and that's okay. But you're literally everything, Rainbow."

I let his words wash over me as the vibes from the club warmed my blood and mixed with the wine from dinner, creating the perfect buzz in my veins.

Pulling his face down to mine, I kissed him deeply. "I love that I hate you." I said, and he smiled against my lips, knowing what I was saying in my own way.

"I hate that I love you." He replied, saying exactly the same thing as me, even though it was in reverse.

They both meant the same thing to us.

We loved each other.

In our own weird way.

It was completely us. Even if he believed love was my biggest weakness.

"Sunny!" A cackled voice called out through the music and Tamen tensed, squeezing his hands around my body.

"No bloody way." He growled, refusing to pull away from me.

"Is that you, Sunny?" The voice called out again, and I pulled back to find a cute older woman standing next to us. "I knew it!" She clapped her hands excitedly up at Tamen, and then to me. "I can recognize that ass anywhere! Across the room, or across the country!" She patted Tamen's ass for added emphasis, and I choked on my breath, giggling at the way he jumped and moved around behind me.

THE LINE WALKERS

Four dances. Seven shots. Three Godfather cocktails. And zero bathroom blow jobs or fucks later, Tamen was finally enjoying himself. Or he was at least no longer glowering in the corner.

I had been enjoying myself all night long, but it took that long for him to catch up. It took me longer than it probably should have to realize who the woman was that interrupted our moment on the dance floor, but once I recognized the feral post office lady Peyton and Olivia had told me about, it all made sense.

Turns out, Dolly, as Tamen called her, was on her bachelorette trip to Vegas. It was also her seventieth birthday bash.

And the old biddies from her bowling league that came with her on the trip were a hoot and a half. So, of course, I instantly invited them to join us at the bar for a celebratory round of drinks, much to Tamen's annoyance.

Three hours later, the old ladies were drinking me under the table and the way my sides hurt from laughing was just continuing the vibrancy I had felt in life the last few weeks.

"Can I ask you a question, dear?" Martha, Dolly's sister, leaned around the table where we were sitting in VIP, thanks to Tamen's more relaxed nature and wallet. We moved to a quieter club somewhere between shot four and five, so we could hear ourselves think.

"I suppose so." I nodded, preparing myself for something unhinged, simply because these ladies had no filter at all, and alcohol was seeming to make them bolder.

"Is that a disco ball flashing under your dress?" She sipped off her lemon drop martini, "Is that a fashion thing you young girls wear these days?"

I snorted, and Tamen tipped his head back and chuckled, sipping his cocktail. "Oh, I can't wait to hear this explanation."

"It's a butt plug, Martha." Dolly droned on with a wave of her hand dismissively. "They do all kinds of things these days."

"A—" Martha looked between me and Tamen, blinking. "A what?"

Dolly interrupted, "Do you like taking it in the ass?" She said it so flat-faced I couldn't help but grin. The conversation wasn't something I expected to have with strangers, though I wasn't embarrassed. "I mean, that's the point, isn't it? To take it in the ass?"

"In a way." I stammered through the uncomfortable explanation. "It's a sex toy; it's meant for pleasure."

"But you're not having sex right now." Janice, Dolly's best friend, quipped from where she sat next to Tamen, eyeing him up like a piece of meat. "What's the point?"

I shrugged, sipping my Cosmo. "Well, on the practicality side of things, prep time. And on the fun side of things, it builds anticipation."

Janice cackled and patted Tamen on the knee, "I knew you had a big dick."

Dolly scoffed from the other side of the man-meat sandwich, leaning around him to glare at her. "I already told you he did."

I choked on my drink and alcohol came out of my nose as Tamen pulled a pack of cigarettes from his pocket, lighting one up and blowing the smoke into the sky. "I'm sorry, what?"

Dolly winked at me, rubbing her hand over his knee. "It was before you, I'm sure. And if it wasn't, don't worry, I won't steal him back from you. I'm going to be an honest woman in an hour."

Tamen chuckled, "Way before you, Rainbow."

"Good god." I scoffed, shaking my head, already imagining the story I was going to get out of him at some point.

"My Raymond is big in the drawers, too." Dolly added like anyone asked, "Not Big Ben big," she nodded to Tamen, "but he gets the job done."

Attempting to turn the conversation away from my butthole and my boyfriend's big dick, I asked Dolly about her favorite subject ever; herself. "How did you meet Raymond?"

She lit up like a light bulb, "He's the handyman that the Post Office calls when things break around there."

"I bet they were breaking all the time, weren't they?" Tamen asked her with a side eye, and she chuckled like a schoolgirl.

"Sure were." She ticked items off her fingers, "My favorite was breaking the key off in the lock, because that had to be fixed that same day, so he was always quick to come running for me. But then there were other things too, like the toilet."

Martha grimaced, "You clogged the toilet to get your crush to come over?"

"No, honey," Dolly pursed her lips, "I broke the porcelain bowl with a hammer." She whooshed her arms out in a frenzy, "Water everywhere!" The girls all fell into giggles as she continued with her list. "The door hinges came off easy with some WD-40. The windows got stuck really well thanks to that fancy orange glue from the hardware store." She rubbed her fingers absently as she shrugged, "So did my fingerprints, but it was worth it."

"How long did you do these things for?" I asked.

"Years!" Her eyes widened. "It took that man years to realize what I was doing and just ask me out. He said he was tired of fixing everything around there three times over and if it would get me to stop, he'd take me to Mario's for dinner." Dolly's shoulders shrugged in pride, "And we've been inseparable ever since."

"And getting married tonight!" Janice raised her glass, and the girls all cheered loudly.

"Wait, you're getting hitched tonight?" I asked, surprised, given that it was already after midnight. Didn't old people go to bed early?

"At two forty-four am on the anniversary of our very first kiss." Dolly sighed happily.

Martha leaned over to me and then stage whispered, "And by anniversary she means two months later. She's a ho."

With understanding, I cackled and raised my glass; I was a ho for a man, too. I mean, technically I *used to be* a ho for hire, but now, I was just a ho for Tamen.

"Ooh," Dolly lit up like a Christmas tree, "You have to come. It's right down the road!"

"To your wedding?" Tamen scoffed, but she ignored him.

"It's perfect! You guys can help celebrate with us! You can bring your disco ball butt plug and everything!"

"Oh, my god." Tamen held his face in his hands, shaking his head as he laughed at her antics.

"I mean," I shrugged, glancing at the man who promised to do dirty things to my disco ball butt after one dance, yet here we were, hours later, having the best time. "I don't see why not."

"Perfect!" Dolly cheered and held up her glass for everyone to toast. "Let's go! You're going to love Elvis. He's so handsome."

I cocked my head to the side in confusion as Tamen tried to walk to me, but Dolly and Janice both weaved their arms through his, holding him hostage, "Don't you mean Raymond?"

Dolly snickered as they walked past me and Martha toward the exit. "No, I mean the man dressed as Elvis that's marrying us. He's about twenty years younger than Raymond and smells like sin. If we get there before Ray and the guys, maybe Elvis and I can sneak off for one last rendezvous."

"And if Elvis says no, you've got Big Ben to stand erect," Janice hiccupped, "I mean in!"

CHAPTER 32 - TAMEN

THE LINE WALKERS

"Hold on, one second." I rubbed my temples as Sloane paced around the room. If the raging hangover in my head wasn't taking away my ability to think, it would be my raging erection from watching her pace naked. "There's no way we're married."

"Then what the fuck is this?" She screeched, throwing her hand in my face on her way by. "You remember the chapel!"

Shrugging and forcing back bile, I tried to reassure her. "I remember *a* chapel. Vaguely. In bits and pieces of time. Not the whole thing."

"Well, what happened then?" She cried out, stopping her pacing to stand in front of me with her arms crossed over her abundant tits as she angrily glared at me. "Because I don't fucking remember anything after dinner!"

"Why are you yelling at me like I'm the bad guy?" I hissed, walking around her for a bottle of water from the table. Blimey, my throat was dry.

"Because you let us get married in Vegas!" She screamed, no longer able to hold back her panic. "I was drunk! I shouldn't have been able to consent! Isn't there a rule for wedding day sobriety!"

Her aura was bright orange as she started crumbling into her terror.

I scoffed with a shrug, "The Vegas wedding chapel market would crash if there was, I suspect."

"I hate you!" She hissed, resuming her pacing.

Her words spurred a memory to come back to me, and I froze, remembering it.

"What?" She asked when she saw me lost in thought. "What do you remember?"

"You told me you love me." Grimacing, I replied, the taste of regret bitter on my tongue as I realized my words weren't helping to dispel the image of us, stumbling drunk down the aisle, hitched by a cheesy Elvis impersonator.

Fuck, I remembered the Elvis man. It was looking worse and worse the more I remembered.

"I did not." She snapped. "I said I love that I hate you!" She froze and covered her mouth, remembering it firsthand as she whispered, "And you said you hate that you love me."

"Same thing." I stated, but she wasn't listening to me.

She was lost in a memory.

"Oh my god, what if we actually did this moronically stupid thing?"

"Then we undo it." I replied, walking out of the room.

"Undo it?" She chased after me at an alarming speed for someone who looked like they were going to blow chunks five minutes ago. "You want to undo it?"

I glared at her over my shoulder as I searched for another bottle of water. Jesus, the room cost me nearly five grand a night, why was there no bloody water anywhere?

"A moment ago, the idea of it happening was the last thing you wanted." I chided, grabbing the open bottle of champagne off the table and chugging it. Alcohol was the last thing I needed right now, but my mouth felt like I spent the evening licking a donkey's ass. I was desperate.

"I don't." She paused, "But—"

"Just stop and take a second." I wiped my mouth with the back of my hand and offered her the bottle, but took it back when she turned visibly green without even looking at it. "There's absolutely nothing that panicking is going to do right now. If we did or if we didn't meet Elvis at the chapel, it is done. Let's just take a second, wake up, *sober up*, and try to piece together what happened."

She huffed and then took a deep breath and glared at me. Sloane might not be very happy with me at the moment, but she knew I was right.

"Okay." I hit the button to open the blinds, letting the midday sun into the space and grimaced when it made my headache intensify. "Headache meds, water, and food. In that order. Then we can talk about who, if not me, put that tiny rock on your finger."

She grimaced at me again, lifting her hand to inspect the pathetic ring on her finger, but stayed silent.

It wasn't necessarily tiny, but it wasn't what I would have picked out for her if I had intended to get married.

The idea of being married to the woman should have alarmed me, but it didn't. Realistically thinking, she was probably the only woman I'd ever feel even slightly comfortable tying myself to legally, but still.

I wasn't husband material.

Besides, were Vegas marriages even legally binding?

THE LINE WALKERS

Sloane hesitantly took a bite of her avocado toast across the table from me, but she wouldn't meet my eyes. Was she afraid of what I'd see in them if she did? People weaved in and out around us on the patio of the hotel restaurant as we tried to eat food that would absorb the alcohol without making us throw it all back up.

An hour ago, we had woken up in hangover bliss. Somehow my ass was on the floor, and she was naked in bed and beckoning, and I had easily and happily accepted her call.

And then everything went to shit because of that small golden band on her finger.

Now, she was silently creating God only knows what scenarios in her head, more than likely blaming me for them, and avoiding me like the plague.

I took her silent treatment and tried to focus on what I remembered. Bits and pieces of fuzzy memories were all I had after dinner, and they all seemed too farfetched to be believable.

What if the whole thing was literally an alcohol induced bad dream, and none of it had actually happened?

What if she wasn't my bride?

What if she wasn't my anything?

Why did that scare me more than the alternative?

I fought through the haze, trying to remember what we did after dinner or if we went anywhere else beside our hotel.

"Well, well, well, if it isn't the newlywed couple out in the sunlight for the first time!" The crackly old voice of the woman who haunted my dreams assaulted us.

Sloane's eyes rounded to the size of oranges as she wiped her mouth as the feral post office lady, Dolly, sidled up to our table.

As if she was the catalyst for unlocking all of my blacked-out memories, the bits and pieces of what happened last night fell into place, filling the gaps in vivid, colorful images.

Jesus fuck, Sloane and I got married.

"What?" Dolly paused, when neither of us acknowledged her. "Hungover, aren't you?"

"We—" Sloane cringed and then held her head in her hands. "Oh god."

"We blacked out." I admitted, leaning back in my chair and finally looking over at the scary woman. "But you just confirmed what we were pretty sure we already knew."

Dolly chuckled and patted my arm, making me cringe slightly. "Oh, don't fret, I'm sure with a little sunshine and time, you'll see what we all saw last night."

"Which was what, exactly?" Sloane asked, breaking her self-imposed vow of silence.

Did I care what the predatory old lady thought about us, no.

"You two are soul mates." Dolly replied, catching me off guard. I chanced a glance at Sloane and she peeked across the table at me before turning away again. "Look, I've been around long enough to recognize the connection of two souls in that deep way that defies any other logic or reason. It doesn't happen often, surely you can agree with that. But with you two, there's something that needs no words or titles to make sense. So, what if you two drunkenly put a title to it in Vegas?" She put her hands on her hips and glared at me, "I'm sure you've done far worse in your life." I looked away. "Sit on it. See how it feels for a few days and then go from there." Dolly finished with a wink, "Besides, they say the newlywed phase is the best time of your life."

"Is that how you're feeling this morning?" Sloane asked, chancing a small smile as she looked at Dolly. "You were drunker than us last night and you look like you're standing in a photo shoot, all glam and happy as a newlywed yourself."

Dolly chuckled and shrugged, "My liver is so pickled at this point in my life I hardly ever get a hangover. Besides, I've waited a hell of a long time to find a good man willing to put up with my floosy self. I'm not wasting a second of it. And you shouldn't either, you two. Life passes in the blink of an eye when you've got a good thing, and it drags out at a snail's pace when you're lonely. Don't waste the opportunity you've given yourself."

With that, the old lady walked away, talking about finding Raymond at the slots and making him take her to see Celine Dion in concert.

The silence hung between us, as the rest of the restaurant goers lived their life unbothered by the turmoil we felt.

"Do you think she's right?" Sloane asked in her silky voice, sipping her orange juice, finally looking across the table at me.

"Do I think the feral post office lady that chased a naked Dane through a cornfield is right about anything? No." I joked and then toyed with my fork absently. "Which part are you talking about?"

"That this could be an opportunity. That maybe it could work."

In the time I had known Sloane, not once had I seen her uncertain of herself. Not once had I seen hesitation and question in those golden eyes, and it made something in my chest ache a little knowing I caused part of that change.

"I do." My reply, I hoped, would give her some needed confidence. "I meant what I said last night."

She snorted gently and widened her eyes, "You said you don't remember anything."

"I didn't. But I do now."

"You do?" She leaned forward, intrigued. "All of it?"

"All of it." I held her stare. "I remember telling you I love you." Her chest rose quickly, remembering the same moment after dinner. "I remember watching you interact with the feral geriatric cougars all night and thinking that I hoped you were just like them when you were in your golden years, and how I want to be around when that happens."

"Tamen." She whispered, searching my eyes for something.

"I remember you nudging me when Dolly and Handyman Hank said *I Do* and whispering how it all made you almost want to have a midnight Vegas elopement too."

"I did?"

"And I remember kissing you right there in front of the Elvis wannabe after he said you were mine, *my wife*."

"Jesus." She sighed, falling into her seat.

"Far from it, Rainbow." I lifted her hand into mine where it sat on the table and gave her a gentle squeeze, rejoicing in her return one. "But for you, I'll try to be as good as I can be."

"And if I don't want that?" She asked hesitantly, and my chest ached at her rejection. How could I grieve something I didn't even know I had until moments ago? Her fingers fell from mine as I sat back in surprise.

"Then we'll annul it."

She rose to her feet and walked around the table in a flash, sitting down onto my lap sideways, uncaring of the other guests in the restaurant. "That's not what I mean."

My hands fell to her waist, holding her tight as she laid her lips against mine in a chaste kiss, "I mean I don't want you to be good for me." Pulling back, she stared at me, "I don't want you to be anything but the crass butthole you always are with me. I want the moody and broody man who groans every time I walk into the room in a ridiculous outfit picked specifically to drive you nuts. I want the overprotective jerk who thinks he has a say in who or what I spend my time doing."

I grunted in response, countering the fact that she believed I only *thought* I had a say in that. We both knew her days of letting other men touch her were done.

"I want the dark man with scars on his body that only I get to touch." She pressed on, drawing our conversation back to a serious note. "I want you Tamen. Just the way you are. Because I think the crazy old lady is right, I think our souls knew long before we did that we were meant to give this a try. I think it's why we've been so drawn together, even though most days we can't stand our own damn selves, let alone each other."

"You want this?" I lifted her left hand, twisting the pathetic ring with my thumb. "Figuratively, because this ring is pitiful, and I'll upgrade it immediately. But it was all they had there."

"I want this. Even though I don't think anyone will ever actually love me. I don't think anyone can. But I'm willing to let you try."

She smiled brightly, kissing me again. "Under one condition." She hesitated, "Two actually."

"There it is," I grumped, jokingly and then nodded for her to lay down her rules.

"Condition number one," She wrapped both arms around my neck and sat up straight. "This is a probation period marriage. You're on a tight leash, and if you fuck it up, I get to make your life hell."

Snorting derisively, I rolled my eyes, muttering, "As if that would ever change, no matter how long we're married. But sure. And the second?"

She took a deep breath and brought her hand with the tiny ring up between us again, "My second condition is that we have to keep this ring somehow, maybe have it melted down into a wedding band or something to go with a new ring." Her amber eyes misted over slightly as she stared at me. "Even though it's not either of our styles, it's still the one you slid on my finger the night we got married. I think that makes it special, somehow."

"Deal." I replied instantly, loving the idea of using it as part of the new ring. "Whatever you want."

"Whatever?" She smirked, "Because there's something I've been wanting again for a while now."

"Blimey."

"Remember that night at Prism, right after we opened? The night where you gave over full control to me and pretended to be such a good boy for a short while. I want that. All of that."

"You bloody would." I groaned, already bricking up at the mere mention of another night as Sloane's toy. "Deal."

"Mmh, good boy." She hummed, kissing me again. "My perfect bad boy, who's only good for me."

Chapter 33 - Sloane

Turned out, the crazy old lady was right.

Honeymoon sex was freaking hot. I had been thoroughly fucked on every surface of our suite, as well as in two separate cabs and countless bathrooms across the Vegas strip. And there wasn't a single part of me that was ashamed or embarrassed by how deeply I ached for Tamen.

My husband.

Jesus, what a weird change of events our trip took.

Actually, my whole life since he walked into it a few months ago and derailed every plan I had with his cocky, snide, self-righteous attitude.

And now he was my husband. Imagine that.

I was loving the little bubble of honeymoon bliss we had encapsulated ourselves in, but tomorrow morning we were going back to Boston and Prism, where reality would either find a new norm, or pop our bubble completely.

Which was why I had something special planned tonight for him. And he was going to hate every second of it.

The dinging of the private elevator in the foyer announced its arrival with my delivery and Tamen looked up from his spot opposite of me at the table where we just finished our room service dinner. "Expecting something, Wife?"

Damn if I didn't shudder every time he said that.

"I am, actually." I rose, wiping my mouth on the napkin and kissing him on the temple as I walked past him to the foyer. He gave chase, following me out to the private entrance as if someone was going to nab me from the marble floor if he wasn't near, but I didn't mind. His protectiveness always excited me, because I knew he could back up that ominous, dark threat he used. "Ah, perfect." I greeted the four different employees that came off the elevator with a cart ladened down with supplies. "Please take that all right into the primary bathroom. Thank you so much."

"Yes, Ma'am." One employee said with a nod before they all scurried off to set up the things I ordered. I could only imagine what they were thinking, though if they were long-time employees of the hotel, I was sure they'd seen their fair share of weird.

My purchase wasn't weird, but it was bold.

"What did you do?" Tamen asked, sliding his hands around my waist to crowd me into the wall of the foyer.

"I ordered you a long night of sexual stimulation." I smirked, gliding my hands up his chest with a naughty wink.

From the bedroom, the loud sound of the air pump started up and Tamen leaned around the wall to chase the sound visually in confusion. "What the hell is that?"

"Them inflating your blow-up doll." I rolled my eyes, "Duh."

He leaned back over to me and glared. "I don't know whether to allow myself to get excited or fear for my life right now. I thought we agreed to a relaxed evening tonight after all the crazy shenanigans we've gotten ourselves into over the last week."

"Oh baby," I purred seductively, sliding my body up and down against his, "I promise you're going to be *so* relaxed when I'm done with you. That's the whole premise of tonight."

He opened his mouth to reply but stopped when the employees came back out of the bedroom pushing their empty cart. "You're all set, Mrs. Bryce. Have a wonderful evening."

I froze at the title, but Tamen slid in and acknowledged him. "Will do, thank you." When they were all in the elevator on their way back down to the lobby, he stared back down at me. "Everything okay, *Mrs. Bryce*?"

Elbowing me in the ribs with a glare, I shook my head. "It caught me off guard, that's all." I mentally brushed off the slip and slid back into excitement for the night. "Mr. Bryce, your room is almost ready for the evening. Give me ten minutes and then come in."

"Very well." He stepped back, letting me have the evening I planned, even though I knew he wanted nothing more than to derail it for the fun of it.

He was going to love the plans I had for him. I couldn't wait to see the look on his face when he saw what we were doing.

THE LINE WALKERS

Ten minutes later on the dot, he called out from the other side of the bedroom door.

"Oh, Mrs. Bryce." His deep voice tickled my senses, "I hope you're ready for me."

"Come in, Mr. Duke." I sang out seductively, taking my place in the middle of the bedroom in my tiny silk robe. When he cleared the doorway, he looked around like he was expecting to find something telling in the bedroom. "Thank you for choosing me to spend your evening with, you may call me Ember during our time together."

He smirked knowingly, sliding into the roleplay scene I was trying to create for him.

"Very well." He cocked his head to the side dominantly and put one hand in his pants pocket. "What do you have planned for me this evening?"

"Come with me." I waved for him to follow me and I opened the double doors into the bathroom suite, stepping to the side so I could see his face when he saw the layout of my plans. "Welcome to your Nuru massage, Mr. Duke."

He groaned deep in his chest as his eyes roamed from the inflated air mattress on the floor and the large bowl of special oil sat atop of a warming bed of hot stones to keep it the perfect temperature. From there, he looked over at the large glass shower with an array of soaps and scrubs along the ledge and then to the hundreds of candles lit, casting the entire room in a sensual glow.

He turned just his head to look over at me as he worked his jaw back and forth silently before stating, "I paid extra for the happy ending. I hope you're prepared to make it worth my while."

My body hummed with excitement at how well he was playing along with my game as I walked over to the shower and turned it on, steaming up the space. When I turned back to him, I pulled at the sash on my robe, slowly and seductively removing it, letting it flutter to the floor, revealing myself to him. It didn't matter that we had sex a million and a half times already, every time I stripped myself bare, Tamen stared at me like it was the very first time all over again.

It was such a rush and a sexual high.

"I'm going to make all of your fantasies come true tonight, Mr. Duke." Sauntering back to him, I purred and pulled his shirt free of his waistband. "I know you came to me tonight because you have needs you aren't getting fulfilled at home." A shudder ran through me as he groaned, the sound a low thrum against my skin, and from under my lashes, I watched him, licking my lips. "I'm so good at being a dirty little secret, Mr. Duke." I pulled the button on his pants free and slowly, so painfully slowly, I lowered his zipper. "Can I be your dirty little secret, baby?"

"Show me how good you can be for me." He instructed, holding his hands out at his side, giving me permission to strip his body free of his clothing. Pulling his shirt off over his head, I then slowly pulled his pants and boxers down, lowering myself into a squat as I did, holding his stare until I was at his feet with his hard dick dripping right in front of my face.

He stepped free of his clothes until he was bare, just like me, and I took his hand, pulling him with me to the shower, silently sliding my body against his as he stood under the hot spray. "There won't be a single inch of your body that doesn't know my touch by the time you go back home to her tonight." I hummed, rubbing my breasts against his back as I took the expensive soap off the shelf. "I promise you've never been as satisfied as I'll make you feel."

"Show me." He demanded, glancing over his shoulder as I started rubbing the soap over his skin, starting at the nape of his neck and working down his back. Reaching around his body to rub my hands over his chest and abs, his head lolled to the side as I slid my soapy hands down to the massive prize between his thighs.

"You're so big Mr. Duke." I purred, rubbing my body against him as I circled him and came around to his front. "I don't know if you'll fit in my mouth completely."

He grinned his mischievous smirk and raised one brow at me. "Most can't. Maybe you should try it."

"I'm an overachiever by nature." I lowered myself down onto my knees, stroking his cock with my soapy hands and then letting the water rinse his skin. "And very determined."

"Show me how determined you can be." The depth of his voice sent shivers through my body as I forgot it was all a game and got aroused by the entire scene.

I stuck my tongue out and swirled it around the head, chasing my hands down the shaft until I got to his groin and then reversed the motions. Over and over again, I teased him, swirling and licking, but never gave him what he really wanted.

Not until he was nearly demanding it, with hands in fists at his side and his body tight and tense from the teasing. That's when I finally hollowed out my cheeks and sucked him deep into my mouth.

A few inches in, I gagged, but I didn't let it stop me. I had learned long ago how to overcome the urge to quit and push on. Staring up into his cobalt blue eyes, I rocked my jaw back and forth until my nose hit his pubic bone, and my lips met the base of his cock.

"Good girl." He growled, staring down at me as I came up off his cock and did it again, smoother this time thanks to the practice. "You're doing such a good job, Ember."

I groaned, letting the vibrations wash across the sensitive head of his cock before taking the soap and lathering my hands up and down his thighs as I licked my lips for him. "I'm so glad you're enjoying yourself so far, Mr. Duke." Washing the rest of his body and then stepping back so the water could rinse the suds from his skin, I then took his hand, sliding it around my waist and led him from the shower stall. "Tell me something, do you seek sexual pleasures outside of your home very often?"

Turning me to face him he towered over me and pulled my body flush to his, naked and bare from nose to toes, we stood in the center of the bathroom with just droplets of water between us. "Why do you care so much about my pleasures?"

He had deepened his British accent, playing a role in the scene just like I was, and my body heated even more.

"Call it intuition. Something tells me your sexual appetite is very big, and not easily sated. It makes the giver in me want to send you to the stars of ecstasy so many times that you can't even walk out of my room tonight."

"Do it then." He leaned down, wrapping his hand around my throat and bending me backward over the counter until his cock was pinned against my lower stomach, pushing toward my wet lips like it was seeking its own pleasure. "Because you're right, I'm always hungry for more and I ache to be fulfilled."

"Lie down, Mr. Duke." I spread my thighs, letting the bulbous head of his dick rub through my wetness, once, and then twice as his hips flexed. He growled as his eyelids fluttered closed and a tempted smirk teased his lips. "Let me make you feel so good."

Begrudgingly, he laid down in the center of the blown up bed, adjusting himself so that his dick was aimed down between his thighs. "Show me what you've got."

I dipped my hand into the bowl of warm oil, scooping up a large amount before pouring it down the front of my body, rubbing it in.

Taking another handful, I straddled Tamen's thighs and poured the liquid over his back and ass. Instead of using my hands to rub it in, I leaned forward, gliding my body across his back to coat his skin.

I loved touching Tamen's body even long before that moment, but the sensuality of the entire night made my body hum with need. "How does that feel, Sir?" I whispered into his ear on a slide up and he moaned in response.

"Wonderful, Ember."

"Good." I licked the shell of his ear and slid back down before sitting up on his ass, rocking my aching center over the swell of his ass for my own pleasure. I dug into his back with my palms, massaging the muscles with skills long ago learned. "How about that?" I purred, massaging down his back to his ass and then lower to his thighs.

"Even better."

I continued on, rubbing him down with my body until every inch of his back had been thoroughly massaged. "Roll over for me, please." Leaning to one side, I stayed hovered over him as he adjusted himself onto his back. When he was settled, his hands found my hips and pulled me down until my pussy laid directly against his hard dick laying on his stomach. "Mr. Duke." I gasped theatrically. "How very presumptuous of you." I shook my finger at him and he grinned, "For a married man, nonetheless."

"I'm ready for a different kind of rub down, Ember." He growled, flexing his hips and lifting me until the thick head of his dick was nudged right against my opening. "Something a little more tight, and hot."

"Oh, is that so?" I hummed, laying my hands on his defined chest to lean forward, granting him the access he didn't need but would take either way if he wanted to. "Show me what you need, baby. And I'll make sure you get it."

"This." He pushed forward, pushing the head into me and then thrusting forward, giving me every thick inch of him. "Mmh, yes. That kind of rub down." He groaned, pulling out and pushing back into me. "Hot and tight."

"I'm so glad you're enjoying my services tonight." I teased, and then took over the motions, raising my hips up and choosing a tempo to ride him. "I'm so glad I'm able to pleasure you tonight, Mr. Duke."

"Be careful Ember, if you spoil me too much, I might be tempted to make you the next Mrs. Duke."

I chuckled, shaking my head at how our scene went rogue and just embraced the pleasure he was giving me. "God, you feel so good Tamen."

"That's it." He growled, palming my oily breasts and playing with them. "You know exactly who's fucking you tonight, don't you?"

"Mmh," I moaned, knowing exactly where he was going with it.

He wrapped one hand around the front of my throat and pulled me back down against his body, leisurely thrusting up into me and grinding my clit against his pubic bone. "Tell me who's fucking you right now, Love."

"Tamen." I replied in a whimper, toying with my monster.

"Hmm, try again."

"I'm going to come." I cried as I neared bliss at his expert hands. "Oh god, you feel so good."

"Who's dick is making you feel so good, Rainbow? Who's deep inside of you, making you come?"

"You!" I cried out, digging my nails into his peck as he spanked my ass, spurring me on. "My husband."

"That's it, baby." He praised, slowing his thrusts as I shot off into an orgasm. "Take your husband's cock, Wife. Take it like no one else ever has."

"Fuck!" I clenched my teeth and then relaxed against his body as I came off the high. "Fuck me," I demanded, knowing he didn't come with me. "Cover me with it, baby."

He chuckled and then rolled us so I was underneath him, which was no easy feat considering the oil coated every inch of the bed and his skin. "Oh, I plan to. But it will have to wait a few more minutes."

"Why?" I asked, and then squealed as he rolled me onto my stomach aggressively and straddled my thighs with his strong ones.

"Because I want to get a little payback."

"Payback?" I asked and moaned when he poured a generous amount of oil onto my back and ass. "That sounds ominous. I think you mean repay the favor."

His big warm hands started massaging the oil into my skin and I crossed my arms under my head, resting my cheek on my arm as I enjoyed his massage. "Yeah," He hummed, rubbing his hands down over my ass and playing with my cheeks. "Something like that."

I moaned when he started kneading them down to my upper thighs. However, I should have paid better attention to his words instead of the feelings he was giving me. Seconds later, his oily fingers spread my cheeks and both of his thumbs pushed in against my asshole, making me buck from the surprise. "Jesus, Tamen."

His dark, evil chuckle answered as he pushed one thumb directly in without warning. "I told you there's nothing heavenly about me, Rainbow. I'm so evil, even your sage couldn't burn away my demons."

"Fuck." I moaned, biting my arm when he switched out two oiled fingers for his thumb, penetrating me and scissoring them. "Tamen!"

I wasn't new to anal, but damn, warm a girl up to it first. We never got to play the other night after our impromptu wedding, which was probably a good idea because we were obviously too drunk to play safely.

I mean hell; we were too drunk to get married too, but still.

More oil spilled over my ass, and I braced for what I knew was retribution for that night at Prism. It felt like a lifetime ago when we spent the evening pushing boundaries and playing games, compared to now, locked away in a suite in Vegas, newlywed, and terrified of what life was going to be like when we went back to the East Coast.

"I want to hear your screams tonight, Rainbow." He growled above me as he slapped his dick against my asshole and pushed against it. "Tonight, you were my dirty little secret, and I'm going to be your Bully. Just how you like me."

"God, yes." I hissed with the burn as his other hand slid between me and the bed to rub my clit. "Don't ever be anything but that."

"Never, Wife. This is who I am. Like it or not."

"I love it." I hummed, tensing when he went deeper before relaxing and letting him in. "The same way I love that I hate you."

He chuckled and pulled out, before thrusting back in deep. "Just how I hate that I love you, Rainbow."

"We're a match made in depraved Heaven."

Chapter 34 - Tamen

THE LINE WALKERS

"I need to borrow your kid." I said through the phone, and Olivia's snarky reply came back so fast it was almost like she was expecting it.

"I thought you weren't a trafficker."

Rolling my eyes, I stopped pacing around my office, trying to come up with the courage to even make the call to Peyton's sister. "Liv."

She sighed dramatically, "What for?"

"It's personal." I countered, offended that she'd even think I'd share.

"It's my kid, Tamen." She argued. "You don't get to just take her somewhere without giving me the details."

"Liv!" I groaned.

"Goodbye, Tamen."

"Bloody hell, wait!" I snapped, scrubbing my hand down my face, trying to figure out what to tell the evil woman without giving her too much info so she could ruin my plans. "It's for Sloane."

"Sloane?" She asked, "Well, why didn't you just say so. Fine, when?"

"Seriously?" I stammered. I knew I should be offended, but I was too relieved to chance it.

"Yeah. We love Sloane. As long as you're using Rory to make Sloane happy, which I'm guessing you are or Rory will no doubt make you cry worse than I could, then I'm good with it."

"Good." I shut my loose jaw, choosing to just get what I wanted instead of arguing with her. God knew Liv and I could argue for days just for the fun of it. "I'll pick her up tomorrow. Say noon."

"Cool. I'll have her ready."

"Thanks."

"Yep, no problem."

I stared at the phone, a cold apprehension settling in my stomach as I tried to put the bizarre conversation behind me and concentrate on the rest of my day's plans after she hung up. "Bloody wacko."

I didn't have a choice though—I had to call in the big guns to pull off my plan. And Rory had the only thing that no one could say no to; dimples.

How else was I going to convince Sloane to stay married to me? As soon as her friends got word of our drunken nuptials, I knew they were going to do everything in their power to convince her to annul it. Sunday Brunch was in the morning, and I knew she'd leave there either ready to leave me, or upset with her so-called friend's reactions.

And I couldn't let that happen—because for the last few months with Sloane in my life, the evil in my soul finally didn't feel like a curse. It felt like a personality trait I could choose to let come out to play when I wanted or not.

It didn't feel like it controlled me any longer, but if I lost Sloane, evil would hold me captive for good. So, I was going to prove to her I could be a good husband, all while being the bad guy and the good boy she loved in equal parts.

CHAPTER 35 - SLOANE

THE LINE WALKERS

"Oh my god, I just about pulled my ass cheeks that night. I ran so fast from that man!" Lola cackled, slapping her hands over her face as our group laughed loudly, drawing stares from other tables.

The mimosas were bottomless at Sunday brunch, surely they expected bad behavior.

"So," Raven drew everyone's attention to her, but she was staring across the table at me. "Tell us about your trip."

Tamen and I had returned to Boston on Tuesday and I had actively avoided any in-depth conversations with any of the girls since then, simply because I knew I'd cave and tell them our secret as soon as they started prying.

It wasn't a secret, necessarily, Tamen didn't want to keep it a secret, but it felt like he was far more interested in moving forward with our marriage than I was. Wait, that wasn't true, I wasn't opposed to staying married to him. I was just scared.

I was a loner. Completely self-sufficient; I had managed everything myself for years.

The idea of letting someone else have a hand in being responsible for my happiness—terrified me. Like to the point I wanted to shit my pants every time I contemplated what the future looked like with him.

Yet at the same time, the idea of going back to that same solitude I had enjoyed before meeting him scared me more.

I was so confused. Was he my biggest weakness in some way? He said I thought I couldn't love anyone, which was right, but I'd already proven myself wrong about that. Waking up the morning after our wedding, I knew that I was in love with him. Could he truly love me in return? And all of my weird antics? Or would I drive him insane until I drove him away?

"Hello! Earth to Sloane!" Trixie snapped her fingers with a giggle, "Are you drunk already?"

"No." I shook it off, brushing my hair over my shoulder and taking another sip of my water to prove my point. "I was just thinking about Vegas."

"Vegas?" Valentina cried. "You went to Vegas and didn't take me with you? Ugh! It's my favorite place on earth. It's a hooker's Disney, and you left us behind. How rude!"

I chuckled and gave her a pointed glare. "You went to Miami two months ago without taking any of us."

"Ooh, true." Lola added, "But Miami is like the cheap knock off Six Flags edition of Disney."

"True." I grinned. "I had little heads up before we left, to be honest. I didn't even know how long we were staying when we got there."

"How does it feel being God's chosen one?" Mya questioned with a smile. "You have an incredible job, an amazing apartment, a fearless confidence I'd literally shank a bitch for, *and* you seem to have landed a good guy that spoils you with luxurious vacations. I mean, you're literally glowing like the baby Madonna put a hand on your forehead and blessed you."

I rolled my eyes, grabbing for my mimosa instead of water as the conversation got thicker. Val cut in with a dose of reality before I could respond.

"Well, I don't know that I'd call Tamen Bryce a good guy necessarily."

"You wouldn't?" Trixie challenged, "Rich, dominant and spoils her. Oh, and did I mention maybe the sexiest man I've ever seen?"

The girls chuckled and agreed. But Val wouldn't let it go.

"Yeah, and he was active with half a dozen different girls at the club the day he met her. That hardly makes him a knight in shining armor."

I opened my mouth to shut it down, but Raven cut in. "It also doesn't make you a virgin. Considering it was your throat he was in that first night after all." The girls all froze and looked between me and Val, since we've always been friends, like they were afraid I didn't know about it.

"Okay stop." I held my hands up, looking from Raven, who was always down for a fight, over to Val, who was particularly prickly for a Sunday brunch date. "Tamen Bryce is far from a golden boy, I know that. But let's give him a little credit here, we're all hookers for fuck's sake, we're no better selling sex than he is for buying it. We're all consenting adults, that's all that should matter." Val deflated a bit and Raven nodded in full agreement. "I don't want the perfect boy next door, I'm actually pretty fond of Tamen's sharp edges and everything that comes with it. So don't worry about me, I'm doing just fine."

Mya grinned like a cheshire cat and leaned forward on the table. "What exactly happened in Vegas?"

The other girls looked over at her, and then at me, confused.

"What do you mean?" I asked, self-consciously.

"Well, I can tell you got some sun," she nodded to my chest over the top of my strapless top, "You have a tan line."

Waving her off, I relaxed, my thoughts drifting back to the private balcony attached to our suite as I deciphered the direction of the conversation. "I sunbathe in the nude, toots. No tan lines here."

"It's not clothes I was talking about." With a smirk, she lifted her hand, pointed at her ring finger, and then nodded toward mine, which was wrapped around my glass. "Looks like you were wearing something else while you were sunbathing."

"Oh, my god!" Trixie gasped, grabbing my hand and staring at the faintly lighter strip around my left ring finger. "You got married!"

"What!" Val cried, and Raven gave me a broad grin from her side of the table.

"Damn girl. Congrats."

"It's not—" I stammered, ripping my hand back from Trixie and glancing around at everyone. "I didn't—." Then I stopped, because denying it, even though I'd tucked the wedding ring Tamen bought me in the chapel that night away in my jewelry box the minute we returned to Boston, it didn't feel right. Shame, heavy and suffocating, settled on me as I contemplated hiding Tamen and what he meant to me. "Actually, I did." I sat up taller in my chair, accepting the shocked glares from the girls. "We got married in a drunken midnight chapel surrounded by crazy nursing home patients and other boozed up couples, looking to declare their love or lust or whatever else they were feeling at two am in Vegas." I paused, smiling as I thought back to the way Tamen told me everything he remembered from that night, spurring my own memories to return. The way I felt that night, in Tamen's arms, at the altar, was indescribable, yet the only thing that came close to capturing the emotions behind it was peace. Tamen gave me peace. "And I don't care if you agree or not. Because I'm happy."

"Wait, wait, wait," Val rubbed her forehead, pushing her alcohol away. "Seriously? You hardly know each other. And he's a player and sketchy."

"So what?" I blinked at her, "You've just described half of the men in America currently."

"We've all done things with him!" She cried, drawing a few glances from the other tables again. "Doesn't that bother you? That should bother you!"

I sighed, knowing there was going to be no more productive conversations on the topic at the moment, and pulled some money out of my purse before rising to my feet. "And I've done stuff with most of you at one point or another, for fun and for work. Does that make me a bad person?"

"No!" Trixie called in her sweet innocent way, shaking her head, "No, it doesn't. And I don't think he's a bad guy either."

"I agree." Mya nodded firmly, "I think this is great, Sloane. I'm excited for you. Congratulations."

"Thank you." I replied softly as I walked behind her chair, facing Val. "I know you aren't trying to be bitter or mean right now, Val. But that's what is happening. So, to save our longstanding friendship, I'm going to walk away, and we can come back to this after the shock wears off."

"Don't go." Lola tried, "We're sorry, we were just surprised."

"It's okay." I smiled, feeling braver and more at peace, having it out there and no longer treating it like a dirty little secret. "I have somewhere else to be, anyway."

Walking away from the table, I took a deep breath as I waited for my car at the curb outside the restaurant.

I was married to Tamen Bryce.

My boss.

My bully.

And the only man, in all of history, to ever make my heart soar, accepting me exactly as I was.

I also had a date with him. Or at least I thought it was a date.

The address he sent me an hour ago to meet him at was in Hollowbrook, the sleepy little town that both Peyton and Olivia lived in with their men outside of the city. I didn't know what he could possibly want to show me there, but I was going to find out.

As I got in the back of the car, the driver smiled at me, introducing herself and making small talk as we turned to leave the city. "Do you have any fun plans for the rest of today?" She asked.

I grinned to myself, feeling a blush crawl up my cheeks as I replied to the total stranger. "I'm meeting my husband. He's always making some sort of fun for us."

My husband.

Mine.

Chapter 36 - Tamen

THE LINE WALKERS

"She's here." I called out, walking through the room to the spot I marked out. "You know what to do right? You remember your lines? You can't mess this up. If you mess this up for me, I'm going to delete your profile on my Netflix account. Got it, kid? If this goes wrong, those pony shows get canned."

Rory rolled her eyes at me and walked away like I hadn't just spoken the ultimate warning to her in toddler talk. "Rainbow!"

"Uh—" Sloane's voice called from the front door where she had her head peeked in. When she saw Rory and me standing in the empty space, she tentatively walked in, closing the door behind her. "Where are we?" She wore a navy-blue wrap dress and sandals, straight from brunch with the girls, and her rainbow hair cascaded down her back in the soft curls I loved to run my hands through. And pull.

"The future." I said, smiling at her breathtaking beauty as she scowled at me briefly before leaning down to pick up Rory, who stood on her feet, begging to be held.

"I don't understand." She looked around the empty living space of the house and then at Rory. "Where is Liv?"

"I recruited Rory for a special mission. It's just the two of us here." I took Rory from her arms, letting her back down to tot around and find mischief. "I wanted to ask you something."

"Uh oh." She widened her eyes at me, "What did you do?"

"Bought us a house." I replied, and her lips parted as she stared at me. If there were ever a picture worthy of a buffering circle to be stickered onto it, she was it. "Hello?" I waved my hand in front of her face, and she swatted me away. "Oh good, you're still here."

"What do you mean, you bought a house?"

"I bought *us* a house." I held my hands out at my side. "This house, actually."

She looked around us at the modern craftsman style house we were standing in with exposed brick along one wall and rough timber beams in the ceiling. "I don't understand. We live in Boston. We work in the city."

"I know." I stopped her, "But I thought maybe we could have a place to go to when the city gets to be too much. Someplace to escape to, like our suite in Vegas, where only our happiness matters and everything else can kind of disappear, for just a small amount of time. Someplace we can build something together."

"Tamen." She whispered as her golden eyes misted up. "You bought a house."

"A home." I corrected her. "I'm hoping maybe you'll give me a chance to make it *our home*. Together, as husband and wife." Anxious and uncertain, I rushed on, blurting, "I know you wanted time to think, but I really want this, Rainbow." Unable to resist the urge anymore, I ran my hand around the back of her head through her locks and pulled her close to me, clinging to her for dear life. "I want you.

I want us." Her shoulders trembled with emotion, tears tracing paths down her cheeks as my forehead touched hers. "I want forever with you, Rainbow. And I want to start living for it. You make me feel like I'm not broken anymore, you make me feel loveable, even the dark and scarred parts of me. I didn't think it was possible, or that I would ever want this, but dammit, I do. I love you, Rainbow. And I don't even hate it. Not even a little. I just love you. Even if you think you aren't loveable, you are. And I love you."

"God." She cried, wrapping her arms around my waist and smiling up at me as I kissed her. "You have me! I want this too. I'm scared, don't get me wrong. But I want it, and I'm not going to hide it anymore. I love you Tamen, and I don't even hate it. Not even a little."

I kissed her again, deepening it, and she clung to me as I did her. I was going to lie her down on the center of the hardwood floor and show her exactly how much I meant those words when a little voice interrupted us.

"Fire!" Rory called out with a chuckle and we both whipped our heads to the side and found the little girl standing in front of the massive fireplace with her hands above her head, staring at the newly lit fireplace in glee.

"Jesus fuck." I tore off after her, pulling her back from the toddler incinerator, and flicked the switch off the wall. "Who puts a fireplace switch that bloody low on the wall?" I cursed, carrying the giggling girl over to my sappy one. "Do you want to show Rainbow your shirt, Rory?" I asked and my niece eagerly wiggled to get down, before ceremoniously ripping her jacket off to reveal the messy, handmade shirt I made for her underneath.

Sloane covered her mouth as more happy tears fell from her eyes, nodding her head yes, as Rory cheered and danced around.

Her shirt read, *Will you be my Auntie Rainbow?*

As Sloane cried, I sank to one knee in front of her and pulled out the puny little ring we got that night in Vegas together that she hid in her jewelry box. "I swore I'd have more time to get a real one made for you, but this will have to do for one more day, at least." I shrugged in embarrassment but trudged on, "Sloane Ivy Archer, will you marry me and build a life together with me here?"

"Yes!" She cheered, throwing herself at me and tackling me to the floor in excitement, "Yes, ten times over!"

"Yay!" Rory yelled, dog piling on top of us until we all laid sprawled out across the hardwood floor of our new getaway home.

I had a wife.

And a home.

And while it was dysfunctional and blended in weird ways, I had a family, too. Which was the first thing I could ever remember wanting as a child. It was all because Sloane taught me that I was loveable, just as I was.

Broken, scarred, and most days a jackass.

I was enough.

And she was so much more.

Epilogue - Sloane

"Thanks for inviting us tonight." Peyton said, as we walked down the hall from my office toward the stage room. "I feel like we're breaking the rules by being here."

I snorted, "Tamen really has to get off that kick of not allowing you guys to come here. There's so much to learn!"

"Like pole dancing." Liv chuckled, "I'll be honest, I never in a million years imagined my big ass on a stripper pole, but hey, I hear it's a great workout."

"And a great aphrodisiac." Peyton snickered, nudging her sister. "If I like it, I'm making Dane put a pole up in the bedroom."

I gave her a high-five and Liv shook her head aggressively. "Not me. I told Maddox I was taking a painting class tonight with you two. He doesn't get to know the truth."

"Um, why not?" I asked, opening the door to the stage room for them where there were two dozen temporary poles set up for the class. The club was closed for the evening and the class was open to the public for signups, which filled up within a day of announcing.

It turns out the public wanted in on the sexual fun at Prism, even without wanting to hire services for the evening.

"Maddox has a breeding kink." Liv answered plainly, "And he wants a third baby. If he knew I was here, he would impregnate me just with the look he gave me when I got home." She shuddered, "No thank you."

Peyton and I cackled at her plight, but I had no advice to give to her on the topic. I was enjoying the easy-going marital bliss of the first year of marriage with Tamen, even if it was nearing our anniversary. We talked about kids, and we know we both wanted them someday, but for now, we *loved* our lifestyle, working at the club four days a week, living in my apartment together, and then living in Hollowbrook in the home Tamen bought us for the other three days.

It wasn't the forever plan, but it worked lovely for us currently.

Someday we'd embrace family life in Hollowbrook, with Tamen's family around us. That day wasn't today, though.

Liv and Peyton picked two spots near the stage as other class members started filling in from the main entrance.

I greeted guests, learning their names and pointing them in the direction of different places to choose from, but it was nearing the time for class to start, and we were still missing three guests. Tamen ran the sign-up sheet, but assured me it was full. The women signed up were all between twenty and forty and most wore athletic clothes and sneakers, as was recommended on the sign-up information. We didn't need anyone breaking an ankle on night one in a pair of stripper heels.

"Okay everyone." I called out, taking my place up on stage, ready to start in the absence of the others. "We're going to get started and if the missing guests come in, they can join where we are. My name is Sloane, I'm one of the owners of Prism and I'm going to be your instructor for this class. I want to start off by welcoming you all to Prism and expressing to you all how excited I am to have you here for this fun class. We're going to learn a lot over the next six weeks of class and we're going to make fools of ourselves along the way, so let's get the nerves out of the way and just enjoy our time together, what do you say?"

"Wait!" A voice called out from the back as the double doors to the front lobby banged open, "Dammit Janice, I told you not to make a Bloody Mary for the road, we didn't have time. Now we're late."

"Oh god." Peyton uttered, facing the stage with wide eyes as the late comers got all the way in the room.

"Oh god, is right." Liv added with a cackle. "Tonight, just got far more interesting."

"Ladies." I put my hands on my hips as the three geriatric cougars from my wedding night black out stood looking slightly guilty, and very tipsy. Oh, and indecently dressed in skimpy clothes suited for someone far younger than their retirement community would allow if they could see them now. "You're disrupting my class."

Dolly grimaced, "We're sorry, Disco-ball. We'll be perfect little ballerinas, just let us stay. Please? Big Ben himself said we were invited as special guests!"

"Yeah," Janice added, "Besides, Dolly promised Ray a lap dance for their anniversary in a few weeks and believe me when I say," She tilted her head dramatically, "her routine needs help. She looks like a starfish stuck on a fish tank wall."

I rolled my eyes so far and waved them over to three poles coincidentally empty all near each other and the stage. "Take your places, but I'm the boss tonight. I don't want to hear any lip from you, got it?" I stared at each of them in turn to prove my point.

"Got it." Martha said with a salute.

Janice hiccupped and nodded with a wink, "Yes, Domme Mommy."

Dolly stood at her pole and started stretching like an Olympic athlete, "You got it, Disco-ball. We'll be perfect angels all night long."

I snorted and Liv cheered them on, "I somehow doubt that." I added, before sliding back into my role as instructor.

"Ooh," Dolly stage whispered, leaning around Liv. "Hi there Peyton! I haven't seen you around town lately. You know what," She walked around Liv, not even trying to hide the fact that she was chatting and not getting ready for class at all. "I'm on the planning board for the haunted Halloween festival this year and we're doing it at the old corn maze right outside of town. You should join us at our next meeting. I bet you and that hunky husband of yours could help spice up the event." She nodded to Liv, "Oh you too! That lumber snack husband of yours would be so helpful to have on hand setting up the rides!"

Peyton paled and gave some sort of wave off without making eye contact with Dolly as she stared up at me and mouthed, *help me*.

Liv held her hand out for a handshake with the woman and said with a wink, "I'm always down for a good, haunted ride from time to time. Count us three girlies in."

"Perfect!" Dolly cheered and then cringed, hightailing it back to her spot as I glared at her good heartedly. "Sorry, this is your show, Disco-ball. Dolly will be a good girl and let you teach us your wicked ways."

The End.

AUDIOBOOKS

THE LINE WALKERS

Did you know that the entire Line Walker Series is getting Audiobooks? EEK!!! I know, I'm so excited too!

Make sure to check out website- www.ammccoybooks.com, social media – Twisted After Dark: A.M. McCoy's Reader Group – on Facebook, and Audible for more details!

Also, did you know that my Beauty In The Ink Series got their very own audiobooks as well? Find those on Audible too!

Other Books

THE LINE WALKERS

Did you know Ally writes across so many other types of tropes and themes?

Check out some of her other books here.

Looking for Series and Duets?

The Line Walkers Series:
https://a.co/d/bx376wq
Beauty In the Ink Series:
https://a.co/d/6tc8M7M
Bailey Dunn & Co Duet:
https://a.co/d/i9gwqL2
Shadeport Crew Series:

https://a.co/d/dVzGcyo
Kings of Hawthorn Series:
https://a.co/d/h1AITKM

How about some spicy standalones?

Sinister Vows:
https://a.co/d/gbe35fF
Guilty For You:
https://a.co/d/1ef3UPU
Secrets Within Us:
https://a.co/d/cTZ04XQ

Stalk Me!

THE LINE WALKERS

Want to stay up to date with all of my shenanigans and upcoming news? Pretty Please?

Check out my website: www.ammccoybooks.com

How about TikTok, are you there? https://www.tiktok.com/@ammccoy_author?is_from_webapp=1&sender_device=pc

Facebook? I've got a readers group there! Twisted After Dark: A.M. McCoy's Reader Group is mostly unhinged and full of exclusive news! https://www.facebook.com/share/g/b41rkBMkSurWz43i/

IG? https://www.instagram.com/ammccoy_author/

Amazon?
https://www.amazon.com/stores/A.-M.-McCoy/author/B07QNRJ

MLB?ref=ap_rdr&isDramIntegrated=true&shoppingPortalEnabled=true

I think that's all for now!

Made in the USA
Coppell, TX
01 May 2025